NEIGHBOURHOOD HOUSES

NEIGHBOURHOOD HOUSES

Building Community
in Vancouver

Edited by Miu Chung Yan
and Sean Lauer

UBCPress · Vancouver · Toronto

30 29 28 27 26 25 24 23 22 21   5 4 3 2 1

Printed in Canada on FSC-certified ancient-forest-free paper
(100% post-consumer recycled) that is processed chlorine- and acid-free.

Library and Archives Canada Cataloguing in Publication

Title: Neighbourhood houses : building community in Vancouver /
   edited by Miu Chung Yan and Sean Lauer.
Names: Yan, Miu Chung, editor. | Lauer, Sean, editor.
Description: Includes bibliographical references and index.
Identifiers: Canadiana (print) 20200370502 | Canadiana (ebook) 20200370596 |
   ISBN 9780774865814 (hardcover) | ISBN 9780774865821 (softcover) |
   ISBN 9780774865838 (PDF) | ISBN 9780774865845 (EPUB)
Subjects: LCSH: Community organization – British Columbia – Vancouver. |
   LCSH: Community life – British Columbia – Vancouver. | LCSH: Social action –
   British Columbia – Vancouver. | LCSH: Social participation – British Columbia –
   Vancouver. | LCSH: Neighborhoods – British Columbia – Vancouver.
Classification: LCC HN110.V3 N45 2021 | DDC 361.809711/33 – dc23

Canadä

UBC Press gratefully acknowledges the financial support for our publishing program of the Government of Canada (through the Canada Book Fund), the Canada Council for the Arts, and the British Columbia Arts Council.

This book has been published with the help of a grant from the Canadian Federation for the Humanities and Social Sciences, through the Awards to Scholarly Publications Program, using funds provided by the Social Sciences and Humanities Research Council of Canada, and with the help of the University of British Columbia through the K.D. Srivastava Fund.

Printed and bound in Canada by Friesens
Set in Segoe and Warnock by Artegraphica Design Co. Ltd.
Copy editor: Frank Chow
Proofreader: Amy Haagsma
Indexer: Noeline Bridge
Cover designer: Will Brown

UBC Press
The University of British Columbia
2029 West Mall
Vancouver, BC V6T 1Z2
www.ubcpress.ca

We would like to dedicate this book to all the people who participate in the settlement and neighbourhood house movement in Canada and other countries. ▪ Meanwhile, Miu dedicates this book to Florence Lee and his siblings for their love and support. ▪ For her inspiration and support, Sean dedicates this book to Carrie Yodanis.

Contents

Figures and Tables

Tables

Foreword

Affluent societies have always been socially and spatially divided by income and wealth disparities, which have become much greater over recent decades. We have become increasingly polarized socially and spatially due to the steady loss of the once numerically dominant and growing middle-income group.

Although economic inequality is not solely an urban problem, it is most evident in cities, where wealth and poverty tend to be concentrated. Researchers have thoroughly documented the social and economic polarization of metropolitan areas, using terms such as "divided cities," "dual cities," "polarized cities," "fragmented cities," "partitioned cities," or "unfairly restructured cities."

Decades of post-industrial economic restructuring have eliminated jobs in primary and secondary sectors and created a polarized labour market. Over the last three decades, political, economic, and social policy has reflected the philosophy of neoliberalism, facilitating the operation of market forces, principles, and practices. The retreat from the welfare-state philosophy of the mid-twentieth century produced major policy shifts that have redistributed poverty and affluence across the urban fabric. This increased inequality and polarization is the result of public policy choices – the way we have chosen to allocate societal resources and regulate economic activity. There is nothing natural or accidental about the outcomes.

In metropolitan areas, wealth and poverty are increasingly concentrated in disparate neighbourhoods that have unequal access to the benefits of urban life. Researchers and policy makers agree that neighbourhoods are important in people's lives. Neighbourhoods help shape the routines of daily life, affect access to services, and can contribute to well-being in many ways. Living in a poor neighbourhood can reduce the opportunities for education and employment. The pattern of concentrated urban advantage and disadvantage – producing multiple types of urban disconnection – affects the life chances of urban residents in terms of health, education, housing, and employment. Strengthened socio-spatial divisions within cities with increased inequality and sharper lines of division undermine social cohesion, economic productivity, and political stability.

Neighbourhoods are part of the solution. Neighbourhoods have always been at the fault line of social isolation and spatial separation. There is a long history of both support for, and neglect of, the neighbourhood level.

This book, *Neighbourhood Houses: Building Community in Vancouver*, is a detailed look at the neighbourhood house model of building welcoming and supportive communities using Vancouver's fifteen neighbourhood houses as case studies. It provides an insightful analysis of the way in which neighbourhood houses carry on the early-twentieth-century settlement house "machinery of connection" tradition, as place-making mechanisms within the context of contemporary urban conditions. Settlement houses have a 135-year history internationally. They are today a global movement represented by the International Federation of Settlements and Neighbourhood Centers, an umbrella organization established in 1922 with more than 10,000 members from thirty countries. Neighbourhood houses in Vancouver are a continuation of the social settlement movement that began with Toynbee Hall in 1884.

Neighbourhood houses are place-based community service organizations with a mandate to serve and advocate for the well-being of residents sharing the same geographical area. They provide services for the local community while being a constitutive part of this same community. They are locally governed by elected members mainly drawn from the local community. They are multi-service organizations serving as a community service hub for all age groups. The services and programs that they offer can facilitate meaningful interaction and engagement among diverse residents.

Neighbourhood houses are a unique form of social infrastructure due to their place-based and multi-service approach to serving the neighbourhood. Single-purpose agencies do not have this community development potential for significant individual-level relationship-building outcomes as well as community capacity-building outcomes. When a metropolitan area has many neighbourhood houses, as Vancouver does, they can also become an integral part of a city's governance structure. They can play a significant role in identifying problems in the neighbourhood and setting the agenda for new policies and programs, and they help bring government and civil society actors together.

In addition to providing a history and assessment of Vancouver's neighbourhood houses that contributes to a better understanding of their potential, this book is an important contribution to the literature on the "community problem" of modern urban life. The community problem is generally considered to comprise the following problems of connection and engagement: the avoidance and superficial level of interaction, the living together at high densities as strangers, and the feeling of isolation while surrounded by others. This can lead to alienation and a social disconnection from the social world around us. As a form of social infrastructure focused on the development of relationships and social capacity, neighbourhood houses have the potential to contribute to the ideal of creating welcoming communities in cities and societies that are often less than welcoming and supportive for marginalized, racialized, and disadvantaged groups.

The growth of income inequality is widely acknowledged to be the defining social challenge of our time. Neighbourhood income inequality and polarization continue to grow. As income inequality rises, access to opportunity decreases. Middle-income neighbourhoods continue to disappear, and most are replaced by low-income neighbourhoods. Canada needs more place-based programs as part of an inclusive neighbourhood strategy at the community level to support the macro social and economic change that is required to reverse this trend, a trend greatly exacerbated by COVID-19. Neighbourhood houses can play a vital role as part of this process, as this book demonstrates.

Neighbourhood houses face many challenges, with short-term and precarious funding at the top of the list. They must be well managed, have open democratic governance, and seek to provide services and supports in a way that fosters community development. The work of community-building is not easy. We should not be over-optimistic about its potential impact. But community-based organizations working in the tradition of the settlement-house movement are important neighbourhood institutions. Not all community organizations have a place-based focus. As this book points out, neighbourhood houses have a proven record as essential community players in a place-based governance approach. As such, they not only provide important supports and services but can also be the glue that holds together diverse and disadvantaged communities by fostering collective capacity and social inclusion. They can be places for meaningful social, family, and civic engagement, and serve as hubs for social and economic development and for self-development. They are, in short, places full of potential.

John David Hulchanski
University of Toronto
July 2020

Acknowledgments

As we finish this book, Canada and the world are responding to the COVID-19 pandemic. To contain the spread of this novel virus, people all over the world are being asked to socially isolate and distance themselves from each other. This moment is an ironic one for us, as these safety requirements are at odds with many of the arguments we have made in this book concerning the success of the neighbourhood-house (NH) model in building social connection in urban communities. To combat COVID-19 through social isolation and social distancing, all NHs in Metro Vancouver have reluctantly closed down their physical sites. These are the exact sites, as we demonstrate in the chapters of this book, where people feel a sense of home and are safe to connect and be connected with friends, neighbours, and strangers.

We believe our book shows that NHs have successfully inherited the early settlement-house mission of connecting local residents and bridging them to different organizational stakeholders in the wider community. Facing the challenge of COVID-19, NHs have not forgotten their mission and tradition in this challenging moment of social isolation. They are mobilizing their staff and volunteers to find alternative ways to connect with, and provide supports to, members of the community, particularly the most vulnerable groups, such as seniors who live alone.

A dedication to serving the well-being of local residents in Metro Vancouver and building connections in a seemingly fragmented urban context was what first brought us to initiate a systematic investigation of NHs.

Although the history of NHs in Canada can be traced back over a hundred years, our study is the first systematic empirical study of a total network of NHs operating in an urban region. This project emerged from the need expressed by some of our NH colleagues to empirically demonstrate the operation of the NH model as a place-based community organization. Together we formulated a proposal for a four-year multi-disciplinary and multi-method study of all NHs in Metro Vancouver. That proposal was successfully funded by the Social Sciences and Humanities Research Council of Canada' Insight Grants program (grant number 435-2012-1276), and we could not have completed the project without this financial support.

We owe our greatest appreciation to the numerous staff, volunteers, service users, and community partners of NHs who lent us their time and assistance. We could not have done this work without them. While working with our colleagues at NHs, we developed both trust and friendship. We particularly would like to thank Karen Lacombe (former executive director of South Vancouver NH), Joel Bronstein (ED of Little Mountain NH), Antonia Beck (ED of Burnaby NH), and Mami Hutt-Temoana and Debra Bryant (both former CEOs of the Association of Neighbourhood Houses of BC), who initiated the conversation for this project idea. They served in our advisory group, which met regularly over five years to provide valuable advice on every step of the study until the project ended. We still have their voices in our heads as we finish this book. We are also in debt to a group of colleagues that includes Jennifer Gray-Grant (ED of Collingwood NH), Donna Chang (ED of Cedar Cottage NH), Allan Smith (ED of Kitsilano NH), Carol White (ED of Downtown Eastside NH), Jocelyne Hamel (ED of Mount Pleasant NH), Diane Wilmann (Frog Hollow NH), Diana Hooper (Association of Neighbourhood Houses of BC), and David Phu (a consultant) who worked together to develop a communication strategy that translated our findings into clear and practical messages for policy makers, staff, participants, and the general public. That work allowed our findings to have their greatest impact. The Alexandra Foundation generously provided the financial support to this communication work, as it has been generously supporting the neighbourhood-house movement in British Columbia for over thirty years.

We are also grateful to the following group of dedicated students who tirelessly helped us to collect and analyze the data: Molly Ancel, Jenny Francis, Nicky Grunfeld, Alexander Gunn, Jennifer He, Benjamin Kearney, Gojjam Limenih, Erika Ono, Vicky Li, Maya Reisz, Rory Sutherland, and

Tsering Watermeyer. Their curiosity and creativity helped us overcome more than a few obstacles in the research process and inspired the data analysis. Meanwhile, as shown in the resource maps of different neighbourhood houses in each chapter, Vicky Li's talent has also added an artistic value to our findings. We must also thank Professor John David Hulchanski for his encouraging Foreword. David's famous studies of poverty and inequality in urban communities certainly provide an important context for readers, allowing them to appreciate the roles and functions of NHs as problem-solving community organizations. We would also like to thank the two anonymous reviewers for their valuable feedback. Finally, we are grateful to James MacNevin, Megan Brand, Carmen Tiampo, and other colleagues of UBC Press for their support and valuable editorial advice leading to the publication of this book.

NEIGHBOURHOOD HOUSES

Introduction

SEAN LAUER, MIU CHUNG YAN

What would it be like to live in a welcoming community? Perhaps residents of a welcoming community would share rich sets of social ties that span the community and form a dense network of relationships with friends, family, and neighbours. Through these ties, the community would work together to achieve shared goals and tackle issues that arise. The dense relationships and the sense of efficacy that develop from successfully working together would, in turn, encourage a positive sense of community.

Of course, given its name, the community would make welcoming new-comers to the social life of the community a priority and include an openness that invites differences and change. In the contemporary world, where residential mobility is high, neighbours often leave their communities for new destinations, and new neighbours arrive in the community from all walks of life. The welcoming community would demonstrate its uniqueness with its approach to welcoming diversity – immigrants and refugees who are new to Canada and others who bring unique differences to the community.[1]

To succeed, a welcoming community would rely on support from local municipalities and a social infrastructure made up of formal and informal organizations and groups that help to develop and nurture these aspects of the community. Neighbourhood houses in Vancouver, Canada, provide one model for what these organizations might look like. Neighbourhood houses are long-standing place-based multi-service community organizations that developed from the legacy of the settlement house movement. They serve the local residents of urban communities in Canada as they have for over a hundred years. Their work is guided by a community-building mission, so that neighbourhood houses not only provide services to residents but also build their social capacity to fully participate in the community and the greater society.

Our goal for this volume is to provide a detailed look at the neighbour-hood house model in Vancouver and consider how it contributes to building welcoming communities. This goal did not originate in the offices, corridors, and meeting rooms of a university. Rather, it developed as a collaborative research project including three universities and the fifteen neighbourhood houses operating in Metro Vancouver. The idea for and focus of the research emerged from conversations between academics and the staff of local neighbourhood houses, and the research process was guided by an advisory committee that included four neighbourhood house leaders. All together, over a thousand board members, staff, volunteers, users, and community stakeholders participated in individual interviews, focus group meetings, or a survey conducted through eleven data collection activities that took place from 2012 to 2014 (see Appendix 1).

This volume is also the result of an interdisciplinary collaboration among a group of academics representing the disciplines of anthropology, geography, history, political science, social work, and sociology. Some of us already had experience working with neighbourhood houses. Prior to his academic career, Miu Chung Yan worked at neighbourhood houses in Hong Kong and Toronto in a variety of roles. Since moving to academia, he has published and advocated for the community work done by neighbourhood houses as essential to the social work discipline. Miu introduced Sean Lauer to neighbourhood houses through work on an earlier research project. Sean got more involved in the operational work of neighbourhood houses by sitting on the board of the largest neighbourhood house organization in Vancouver for seven years. The work of all of the academic contributors to this volume already explored themes involving community-building and non-profit organizations. It was this shared interest that brought us academics together, and over the course of this project, we all became even more engaged with the work of neighbourhood houses.

The Community Problem in Vancouver

At the outset of the project, a public discussion dominated local non-profit and government circles concerning the community problem in Metro Vancouver. The conversation was spurred by the release in 2012 of the Vancouver Foundation's first *Connections and Engagement* report.[2] For many in the region, the findings were startling. The report found that connections – the strength of relationships Vancouverites hold with others – are hard to make; they are cordial but weak. Concerning engagement – commitments to community and willingness to take steps toward improving community – the report found that residents were retreating from community. People were not participating in clubs or local activities, not volunteering, and in many cases not voting. In short, the report determined that Metro Vancouver had a community problem.

It would be difficult to overstate the reaction to the report's findings. The *Vancouver Sun* ran a four-part series on the report that addressed issues of social isolation, relationships with neighbours, ethnic divisions, and difficulties for newcomers to feel at home. Simon Fraser University organized its first community summit inspired by the report. "Alone Together: Connection in the City" was a week-long summit that attracted thousands of participants to events such as panel discussions with urban planners, social scientists, and artists, and a mayors' roundtable that brought together seventeen representatives from local governments in the region. Vancouver mayor Gregor Robertson initiated the Engaged City Task Force to address the problems raised by the report. Once the community problem was recognized, there was enthusiasm for overcoming it.

Within the social sciences, the community problem in urban areas has been a long-standing topic of discussion (Simmel 1950; Wirth 1938; Wellman 1979). Interestingly, the themes and findings described in the Vancouver Foundation report are a common part of these academic discussions. The problems of connections and engagement are often attributed to the larger processes of urbanization, technological development, growing insecurity, and rampant individualism. Today we might include pressures from globalization, financialization, and growing inequality that are sometimes grouped under the term "neoliberalism." The influence of these processes on community life was first addressed by the Chicago School of Sociology, and have continued to draw the attention of scholars interested in urban areas. One outcome of these processes comprises the superficial interactions and avoidance of interaction attributed to urban life. The sheer number of people with whom urban residents come into contact on a day-to-day basis is one factor contributing to the problem of community. Louis Wirth (1938) recognized that in large metropolitan areas it is impossible to interact in a meaningful way with everyone with whom we come into contact. Consider trying to say hello to everyone when walking down a busy street, or waving to every car that you pass while driving. Urbanites stop trying, and the majority of their interactions with others are superficial, and in many cases, such as walking through a busy street or taking public transportation, they avoid social interaction altogether. A man interviewed by the *Vancouver Sun* about the community problem in Vancouver described with dismay his experience of running along a popular route on the Vancouver seawall. In his experience running in other places, runners typically greet each other in some way, such as with a nod. In Vancouver, those who passed him carefully avoided social interaction as he passed, even ignoring him when he said hello: "If you simply wave ... they almost move away from you" (Carman 2012a). For another new resident of Vancouver, "it got to the point where I was contemplating printing up a T-shirt: 'Would it kill you to just say hello?'" (Carman 2012b).

This avoidance and superficial level of interaction often extend to the neighbours who reside in close proximity to one another. Today, urban residents live in large apartment buildings or dense neighbourhoods, surrounded by many fellow residents but simultaneously not knowing most of their neighbours very well. In many cases, neighbours do not know each other at all. The *Connections and Engagement* report found that 60 percent of respondents do not talk to their immediate neighbours living in the four households closest to them more than two or three times a month, and 15 percent talk with them only once a year or never. A woman interviewed by the *Vancouver Sun* captured this well when she described living in her apartment building: "To give up more [privacy] and get to know my neighbours ... feels a little too invasive for me. I never have sugar and I don't want them coming over and asking for sugar" (Carman 2012c). This desire for a superficial relationship with neighbours, or the outright avoidance of them, captures the community problem well. Georg Simmel (1950) first described this as the paradox of living together as strangers – living in close proximity to many others but being socially distant from them. For some, there is even a paradoxical experience of feeling isolated while surrounded by others. This quality, Simmel suggests, is an underlying aspect of modern urban life that leads to feelings of isolation and alienation from the social world around us.

Along with large numbers of people living in dense contexts, urbanization also brings people from diverse backgrounds and experiences into contact. Cities and metropolitan areas are typically diverse places, and the implications of that diversity for social life is a common and sometimes controversial topic in discussions of urban life. Vancouver is traditionally one of the top immigrant-receiving locations in Canada, and over 40 percent of the metro area residents are immigrants to Canada (Statistics Canada 2017). One of the key findings of the *Connections and Engagement* report suggests that diversity limits opportunities to make meaningful connections. Few respondents reported close friends outside of their ethnic group, and many expressed a belief that people prefer to be with others of the same ethnicity. This finding may not be that surprising given the well-known *homophily principle*, which is often described with the aphorism "birds of a feather flock together" (Lazersfeld and Merton, 1954; McPherson, Smith-Lovin, and Cook 2001; Marsden 1987). Interpersonal attraction is a driver of homophily, as similarity influences attraction and signals ease of communication and shared interests (McPherson, Smith-Lovin, and Cook 2001, 435). Evidence that relationships between similar people occur at higher rates than between dissimilar people has accumulated in research on co-workers, romantic partners, and friends (McPherson, Smith-Lovin, and Cook 2001, 416).

There are good reasons to expect close friends and affiliations to be co-ethnic when we consider ethnic and immigrant communities. There are simple advantages that come with co-ethnic affiliation, including language and cultural similarities and shared experiences. Alejandro Portes's theory of immigrant and ethnic enclaves proposes that there are clear advantages for newcomers to affiliate with those like themselves in language, culture, and national origin. Along with his colleagues, Portes has shown that similarity breeds trust, and for newcomers with particular needs, these ties can lend support in their new circumstances (Portes and Sensenbrenner 1993; Wilson and Portes 1980; Portes and Rumbaut 2001, 2006; see also Breton 1964). Living in large metropolitan areas allows for the possibility of ethnic enclaves to form, given the critical mass of co-ethnic populations. As the co-ethnic population grows, the possibility of ethnically homogeneous communities that are institutionally complete increases.

The formation of ethnic enclaves suggests a fragmented community, including strong connections among co-ethnics with boundaries between these groups. Robert Putnam (2007) has advanced the more dismal proposition that growth in diversity within communities threatens social cohesion overall. Rather than allowing for strong co-ethnic connections, diversity leads to a lack of connections between, but also *within*, ethnic groups. In an invited lecture at Uppsala University in Sweden, Putnam presented findings suggesting that, when faced with diversity, all community members tend to "hunker down – that is, to pull in like a turtle" (Putnam 2007, 149).[3] These findings have been challenged empirically, and a review of sixty-five studies from around the world finds only limited support for the proposition – and this support comes primarily from the United States (van der Meer and Tolsma 2014). In Canada, research does not appear to support the hypothesis of diversity leading to a decline of social cohesion (Aizlewood and Pendakur 2005; Phan 2008). Diverse neighbourhoods and trust are not associated with declining social trust, but Feng Hou and Zheng Wu (2009) find a slightly more complex dynamic where minority concentrations in neighbourhoods are associated with declines in social trust among white residents.

Questioning the Community Problem

The community problem as described in the *Connections and Engagement* report reflects a general retreat from local social life among Vancouver residents, and these findings echo long-standing academic discussion of community in large metropolitan areas. But there are those who challenge the argument of community decline. For some, the question is whether local, place-based communities remain important today. Others question the assumptions of an ideal community that is presumably being lost through the pressures of modern society.

It is possible to see the retreat from community as described above as a mistaken empirical observation that is based on an assumed quality of previous community life that never actually existed. Conceptions of the loss of community often owe their origin to Ferdinand Tönnies's (2001) well-known description of a *Gesellschaft*-like modern world characterized by individualized, rationally motivated relationships, which he famously contrasted with *Gemeinschaft*-like natural social bonds between family, friends, and neighbours that reflect his conception of community. But whether a natural, *Gemeinschaft*-like community ever existed or is a conception based on nostalgia remains a question. As Stephen Brint (2001) has noted, community studies have consistently found that small communities are rife with power, self-interest, stratification, and privilege.

Perhaps more importantly, as Patricia Hill Collins (2010) has suggested, the rhetorical use of an ideal community includes moral and political implications that are characterized as seemingly natural but actually do make political claims. In this sense, harking back to an ideal community often assumes a geographic specificity, cultural homogeneity, and inherently apolitical entity that is in fact a political ideal. Alejandro Portes and Erik Vickstrom (2011) make a similar criticism of Robert Putnam's communitarian ideal of community in their critique of diversity and community decline. Our image of a welcoming community at the beginning of this chapter is explicitly constructing an ideal set of relationships with moral and political implications. In doing this, we are not suggesting that a welcoming community existed in the past, or is even an obtainable goal in the current social and political landscape. It is aspirational, however. In this sense, we are following Hill Collins's (2010, 25) suggestion that the construct of community enables people to imagine new forms of community, and to participate in building toward that ideal.

Another line of questioning the community problem raises is whether the retreat from community and social life is as a sign of changing forms of social connection and community rather than a community problem. For some scholars, the relevance of the local, residential community of place is questionable. Residential mobility today includes moving from neighbourhood to neighbourhood within cities, across the country, or from country to country. And technological developments allow us to maintain meaningful connections over long distances. This idea was first described by Barry Wellman as *community liberated* in an influential paper published in the 1970s that described the social life of residents of the Yorkville neighbourhood of Toronto. The argument suggests that urban residents are liberated from the confines of their local neighbourhoods by a confluence of factors, including high rates of residential mobility and cheap, effective means of transportation and communication (Wellman 1979, 1206).[4] As a result, ties to family and close friends are still important, but the assumption that local community is important to organizing these relationships is abandoned. Today, with the advent of social networking technologies, Lee Rainie and Barry Wellman (2012, 12) argue that we have entered a period of *networked individualism* where people act as free-floating, connected individuals rather than as embedded group members (see also Benkler 2006).

Whether or not the local, residential neighbourhood remains relevant has been one of the more enduring debates among the social scientists who study urban life. Despite the arguments for the declining importance of local neighbourhoods, many scholars still believe that where we live has an important influence on the quantity and quality of our social interactions. Robert Sampson, among the most compelling urban scholars who argue that place matters, rejects the notion that technology, dispersed social networks, state policy, and the accoutrements of (post)modernity explain away neighbourhood differences (Sampson 2012, 21).[5] He focuses instead on the enduring differences across neighbourhoods, often differences that reflect persistent inequalities, arguing that a durable spatial logic organizes or mediates much of social life. We agree with the continuing importance of communities of place, and discuss it in more detail below.

Place and Place-Based Practice

What is a place? This question has been persistently debated in the literature.[6] Very often, as Arif Dirlik (1999) observes, the theorization of place is inevitably appropriated by the priority of an academic discourse. Despite the disciplinary differences, different theoretical articulations of place may at least agree that a place is a geographical space, often including its architectural components. Some may argue (e.g., Liu and Freestone 2016) that as a concept, place does not have a discernible geographic or spatial scale. For neighbourhood houses (NH), however, the local community that they serve is always relatively small and within a certain geographic proximity, or, self-evidently, the neighbourhood, which as John Friedmann (2010) argues, has existed in the urban history for over 5,000 years.

It is not easy to delineate the boundary of a neighbourhood, however. From an urban planning perspective, Friedmann (2010) suggests that in terms of size, a place should be small enough in geography, possibly within walking distance, for the residents to be able to functionally engage in meaningful social interaction through daily activities. For everyday people, their neighbourhood is the physical locale where their everyday life takes place. Their understanding of the boundaries of their neighbourhood may be more fluid, experiential, and functional. For instance, the City of Vancouver has administratively divided the city into twenty-two distinct neighbourhoods. The boundaries of these twenty-two neighbourhoods are arbitrary, mainly for the purposes of "delivering services and resources and [to] identify the distinct culture and character of different areas of [its] diverse population" (City of Vancouver 2020). One of the co-authors of this chapter, Miu, resides on the west side of Alma Street, which is a boundary between the neighbourhoods of West Point Grey and Kitsilano. While he routinely takes leisurely walks along the beaches in West Point Grey, in which his residential address is located, most of his daily shopping activities take place in Kitsilano. To him, the boundaries of his neighbourhood are a mix of the two officially defined neighbourhoods.

What Is a Place?
Why is the concept of place important? A place is not just an inhabitable space where people reside. As some phenomenological geographers suggest, human existence is experientially inseparable from place. In his canonical text, *Place and Placelessness*, human geographer Edward Relph (1976, 1) contends that "to be human is to have and to know your place." While human activities are one of the key elements in defining a place, people need a place that defines them. In other words, place and its residents dialectically shape each other (e.g., Dirlik 1999; Escobar 2001). Residing together in the same neighbourhood, for instance, people shape "its character, its daily and seasonal rituals, and the recurrent socio-spatial patterns"; in return, people are also shaped by the place by "imprint[ing] themselves on its memory" (Friedmann 2010, 154). Sharing the memory, residents engage *intersubjectively* with and make sense of each other in their everyday interaction.

A place is where people's "here and now" social interaction with others takes place and where they co-create the material and cultural conditions of and within a close geographical locale (Escobar 2001, 152). As Doreen

Massey (1994) suggests, social interrelations are critical to a place. A place is meaningful to its residents not only as a physical locale but, more importantly, for networks of social relations and understandings. Similarly, Arturo Escobar (2001) argues that the notion of a place is derived from a mixture of influences of social relations found together there. In other words, a place is not only about a physical locale. People's sense of a place is more than just a static physical setting and the human activities taking place within this setting. It is also an "organized set of practices for dealing with oneself, other people, and things that produces a relatively self-contained web of meanings" (Escobar 2001, 17). The existence of a place is therefore rooted in the shared meanings among residents who reside in this setting and engage in these activities.

Meanwhile, people's sense of a place also gives meaning to who they are. Yi-Fu Tuan (1977) argues that through the shared meanings of a place, people organize their identities and sense of belonging. The physical setting and objects, human activities, social relations, and shared meanings are all "raw materials of the identity of places, and the dialectical links between them are the elementary structural relations of that identity" (Relph 1976, 48). People's identity of a place is a manifestation of the integration with and socialization of knowledge to each other. From the place that they identify, people can have a secure point to look out on the world.

Sense of Insideness

By sharing a web of meanings, residents also foster a sense of "insideness," which implies the unconscious connection of residents to their neighbourhood (Relph 1976). Some people equate "insideness" with a sense of place, a sense of attachment, or a sense of belonging (Liu and Freestone 2016). Underneath all these different kinds of sense is the notion that people cherish the place in which they spend most parts of their everyday, i.e., the neighbourhood (Friedmann 2010). To Relph (1976), "insideness" is also an authentic attitude toward a place – a direct and genuine experience of the entire complex of the identity of the place. Graham Rowles (1983) has articulated three types of insideness of place that insiders share and treasure: 1) physical insideness is a sense of familiarity and mastery of the physical space and architectures; 2) social insideness is the sense of knowing and being known through everyday social exchanges and relationships; and 3) autobiographical insideness is a sense of self-identification generated by memories embedded and connected to the place.

This insider authentic attitude subjectively demarcates the boundaries of a neighbourhood that distinguish the "insiders" from the "outsiders." To insiders, a place is a pause – relatively stable and permanent (Tuan 1977). To an outsider, such as a tourist visiting Jericho Beach in West Point Grey, the neighbourhood is just a space of movement (Tuan 1977). To the tourist, Jericho Beach is just a beach like many other beaches that "offer the same bland possibilities for experience" (Relph 1976, 20). The tourist has no awareness of the deep and symbolic significances of places and no appreciation of the identities that the "insiders" share.

Place and Placelessness in a Globalized World

Tuan's notion of permanency is under siege in today's increasingly globalized world. A place can no longer be defined only within the local geographical boundaries. The rapid advancement in communication technology enables people to extend their social relations from afar. The everyday life of many people, such as shopping, and personal emotional connection, is no longer confined to a fixed locale. In a global era, the distinction between place and placelessness is also fading as a result of cultural globalization. As Relph (2016b, 30) observes: "Everywhere has become, to some degree, a microcosm of everywhere else. It doesn't matter if somebody has stayed in one locality and avoided a multi-centered life; the rest of the world has slipped into their place anyway."

The growing diversity among the residents due to global migration has also prompted radical human geographers to question the politics of place. As Tim Cresswell (2004, 29) summarizes: "Place was not simply an outcome of social processes though it was, once established, a tool in the creation, maintenance and transformation of relations of domination, oppression and exploitation." Indeed, by making places, we create social identities and boundaries that include some but exclude others.

However, David Harvey argues that Tuan's optimism regarding the seeming permanency of place may still give people the sense of a secured haven in the unpredictable, globalized world (quoted in Cresswell 2004). As Escobar (2001, 147) observes, despite the high mobility within blurring boundaries, people still functionally and existentially "construct some sort of boundaries around their places, however, permeable and to be grounded in local socio-natural practices, no matter how changing and hybridized those grounds and practices might turn out to be." People still hold on to the place where their everyday life takes place.

Escobar's observation also indicates an important notion that place making is a conscious effort. In the era of globalization, this conscious effort of making a place is a re-embedding process through which like-minded people from diverse backgrounds collaboratively select a place to live and to invest themselves (Relph 2016b). As Ash Amin (2002) suggests, to build a sense of togetherness among the socially diverse population of a place, we need to go beyond the mere proximity of physical coexistence. In a highly mobile world, to make place among diverse groups of residents requires not only their concerted effort but also "both informal and formal political processes that can facilitate re-embedding and inclusion for those who come from elsewhere" (Relph 2016a, 271).

Place-Based Policy

Recently, place has been increasingly discussed in public policy (Bradford 2005). Place is indeed also a nexus where power relations are produced, enacted, reproduced, or transformed. Similar to the radical human geographical articulation, in public policy place is articulated as a dynamic locale – with its own diversity and power relations – where the larger forces and flows that structure daily life are contested and given meaning. In place-based policy, neighbourhood as a place is an open system aligned "with larger areas such as metros and regions and the geography is embedded in market forces and public policies" (Ferris and Hopkins 2015, 100). Thus, proponents of place-based policy are critical for the state in mobilizing concerted efforts to address challenges confronting local communities (Shugart and Townsend 2010). They see that a place, like a neighbourhood, is seen not only as where people live but also where social problems are manifested and policy should take effect. A place is also rich in local knowledge and resources that make innovation possible in resolving social problems. The shared identity of a place is a source of social capital – social cohesion and reciprocity – that can be used to supplement limited public resources.

A place-based approach advocates for enhancing opportunities for participation of local people to work with policy elites and professionals, support local initiatives, and create local innovation. To do so, we need some effective mechanisms of place making to generate various opportunities that facilitate social interactions among local residents and foster social inclusion of the diverse populations in the neighbourhood (Friedmann 2010). Community gardens, religious gathering places, and libraries are some examples of place-making mechanisms that provide a safe space for residents to meet, gather, and interact with others. Indeed, the idea and practice of place-based local mechanisms of connection are not new. Settlement houses have historically proven to be successful place-based community organizations connecting people in many urban communities (Ferris and Hopkins, 2015).

Neighbourhood Houses as Place-Based Community Organizations

One key finding of the *Connections and Engagement* report is respondents' lack of engagement in their communities. Most Vancouver respondents did not participate in neighbourhood or community activities, with many explaining their lack of engagement as a result of their not feeling they had much to offer. In academic discussions, a primary concern following from the observation of guardedness in personal relationships is that it will translate to an inability of neighbourhoods to act together to improve where they live or tackle problems that confront society as a whole. Perhaps Alexis de Tocqueville ([1840] 2003, 587) first expressed this concern when he described the embracing of a calm and considered feeling that persuades a person to withdraw into small groups of family and friends and leave society to fend for itself. Here again, Robert Putnam (2000) has successfully started an international discussion about the decline of community and engagement in contemporary life. Putnam has warned of declines in trust in others, personal connections, and face-to-face interactions, and documents a parallel trend of retreat from participation in large voluntary organizations over time and declines in informal gatherings such as neighbourhood picnics and inviting friends to homes for dinner.

While de Tocqueville feared the retreat of individuals from society, he maintained a sincere optimism for local associations to bring people together to participate collectively in their communities. He believed that the pleasure gained in coming together enabled participants to recognize the value of collective life. Others have suggested that participating in local, community organizations forms an essential infrastructure for building local communities. Such organizations bring together people who share a residential location in common but often come from a wide variety of other social positions. New, diverse connections are formed, different experiences are shared, and new ideas and worldviews are confronted. This sounds a lot like the proposal of Amin (2002), who envisions community organizations generating opportunities for intercultural understanding and fostering social inclusion in socially diverse local communities. Amin recognizes the intense social diversity of contemporary urban communities as the foremost challenge to engagement, and close physical proximity of a diverse population alone can lead to retreat from society or conflict. Effective mechanisms of community-building are needed to achieve a functioning community life.

The term "community organization" refers to a loose social category comprising social service organizations that are established and operated by civil society. Very often, community organizations are also labelled as voluntary organizations, NGOs and/or non-profit organizations, or third sector social organizations. Not all community organizations have a place-based focus, however. Many are mandated to serve and advocate for a group of people who have similar psychological and social needs and predicaments due to personal characteristics such as ethnicity, disability, gender, or life-cycle stages such as aging and youth. Service users of these organizations do not necessarily share physical proximity. In contrast, place-based organizations define community as a locally bounded place within which users reside and share. It is also the place that facilitates and limits the everyday life of local residents and the place with which the residents identify themselves. Community organizations not only serve the needs of local residents but also help them build a sense of belonging and togetherness as residents sharing a place.

Questioning the Effective Solution

There are those who see problems with proposing community organizations as a solution to the community problem in contemporary society. A common analytical tool for examining community organizations is to contrast the role of these organizations with that of the governmental and for-profit sectors (Hansmann 1987). Using this framework suggests that community-building is non-sustainable as a for-profit endeavour, and falls outside of the mandate of local governments. As a result, when it continues to be recognized as a public good, the work of community-building falls to community organizations (Williams 2003). This working division between sectors assumes that community organizations maintain some autonomy from the political sector and remain locations where participant identities and interests are formed independently (Clemens 2006, 207); in this case, they are building local identities and collective interests around community.

Perhaps this image of a division of responsibilities among government, for-profit, and community organizations, and community organization as an effective solution to the community problem, is unrealistic? John Shields and Mitchell Evans find that community organizations not only do the work of community-building but also provide essential services to local residents that have previously been the responsibility of local government (Evans and Shields 2010; Shields and Evans 1998). As the governmental sector retreats from service provision, these responsibilities have been devolved to local community organizations, which rely more and more on government funding. As local governments move these services outside their mandate, such funding becomes piecemeal, short-term, and unstable. Community organizations are asked to do more with less, while also being required to work under extensive accountability and oversight measures (Evans, Richmond, and Shields 2005; Yan et al. 2017). Evans and Shields (2010) express concern that these processes move community organizations away from their mission, commercialize their operations, and compromise their autonomy. Given these challenges, we might question the view of community organizations as effective solutions to the community problem in contemporary society.

Similar concerns have been expressed with regard to the settlement houses. Judith Trolander (1987) documented the trend toward professionalization within settlement houses. For her, this trend challenged the settlement houses' ability to maintain focus on their core mission. Michael Fabricant and Robert Fisher (2002) have documented the commercialization of operations and the compromised autonomy of settlement houses in New York City. Miu Chung Yan (2004) is aware of these challenges to the settlement house movement, but despite them, he remains optimistic about the potential of local community-based organizations, seeing the legacy of the settlement house movement as a model for community-building for place-based organizations such as neighbourhood houses. Noting that the movement has lost some momentum in the West, Yan points out that the community-building approach of settlement houses has spread around the world to countries and regions including India, Hong Kong, Eastern Europe, and Japan (Kaul 1988; Chow 1980; Yan 2002). Today, Yan suggests, neighbourhood houses, as community-based organizations working in the tradition of the settlement house movement, are important neighbourhood institutions that both provide services and build community among local residents.

The Settlement House Tradition
What is the tradition of the settlement house movement? The first settlement house, known as Toynbee Hall, was established in London's East End in 1884 in response to growing urbanization, industrialization, and

immigrant concentrations in neighbourhoods in London. The goal was to overcome these destructive forces and maintain face-to-face friendship in a society becoming increasingly impersonal and anonymous (Meacham 1987). The settlements earned the name from the educated, middle-class residents of the houses who moved to neighbourhoods deemed particularly in need. The presence of these relocated residents alone was thought to be important, but the settlement houses also developed a multifocal, reformist approach to programs and activities. There were services addressing direct needs in the community, programs geared toward building community in the neighbourhood, and activities that promoted individual development, such as learning to play musical instruments.

While Toynbee Hall was the first settlement, perhaps Hull House in Chicago went on to more notoriety, along with its founder, Jane Addams.[7] Addams's inspiration to start Hull House followed from a visit to Toynbee Hall and her witnessing of the work being done there. After sharing her experience with her friend Ellen Gates Starr, they opened the Hull House settlement together. Addams received the Nobel Peace Prize in 1931 after her work at Hull House became well known due to her advocacy work and her writings. In her written works, Addams developed many of the principles of the settlement house tradition that are useful for understanding their continued importance for neighbourhood houses today.

Addams introduced the concept of perplexity as the organizing concept of her first book, *Democracy and Social Ethics*. The concept of perplexity arises from her interest in pragmatism and her recognition of the limitations stemming from pre-reflective, habitual, non-thinking behaviour (Schneiderhan 2011). For Addams, perplexity describes those moments when situations no longer accommodate non-thinking, habitual behaviour. We feel perplexed when we get out of our comfort zones and are forced to challenge our assumptions about how to be a good person in the world.[8] Hull House embodied the perplexities of its times, according to Addams. Entering the house and engaging with other participants through activities posed a challenge to preconceived ideas about the problems of the day and the people who inhabited the neighbourhoods and city. Neighbourhood houses today continue to provide these opportunities for interacting with people from different walks of life that lead participants to have moments of perplexity that can challenge assumptions as well as develop new abilities for working with others (Yan and Lauer 2008; Lauer and Yan 2013; Lauer and Yan, forthcoming).

A second important aspect of Addams's conception of a settlement house addresses the reciprocal relationship of Hull House to the community. Eric Schneiderhan (2011) develops this in his examination of Addams's pragmatism in both ideas and practice. In *Twenty Years at Hull House,* Addams describes the aim of Hull House: "To develop whatever of the social life of its neighbourhood may afford, to focus and give form to that life and to bring to bear upon the results of cultivation and training." Schneiderhan describes how the many early activities undertaken at Hull House developed gradually through regular interaction with residents in the surrounding area, and responded to the needs that followed from these interactions. Addams herself said that they had no definitive theories as they started their work at Hull House, but their approach reflected the interactions with local neighbours. In Schneiderhan's analysis, Addams's approach was reciprocal between residents of Hull House and residents of the surrounding neighbourhood. He quotes Dorothea Moore, writing in the *American Journal of Sociology* in 1897, who emphasized that "the exchange [was] the vital thing," and Addams's emphasis that the work was a two-way exchange between Hull House residents and the community. This idea of a two-way, reciprocal exchange between neighbourhood houses and the local community remains today. This localized exchange results in each neighbourhood house developing its own character, which reflects the uniqueness of the neighbourhoods where they operate (Yan, Lauer, and Sin 2009).

Nina Eliasoph (2011, 2013) sees Jane Addams's work as being about more than building reciprocal relationships with the local community to solve problems, and more than providing opportunities for perplexity. She describes Addams as a community builder who saw a direct link with that work to political activism. We can see this in Addams's own writing, where perplexity, for instance, provides opportunities for new connections and shared experiences among diverse others, but also translates into a broader social ethic. In *Democracy and Social Ethics,* she says: "We are learning that a standard of social ethics is not attained by travelling a sequestered byway, but by mixing on the throng and common road where all must turn out for one another, and at least see the size of one another's burdens." Addams thought that these experiences would lead to an adoption of a social ethic that recognized our interdependence and the need for collective solutions. For her, that experience is fundamental to a successful democratic system.

Eliasoph (2013, 30) sees a similar link in the way Addams practised reciprocity in the work of Hull House. Drawing on an example from *Twenty*

Years at Hull House in which a local slaughterhouse was disposing of dead animal carcasses in the streets of a local ghetto, with local children getting sick as a result, Eliasoph describes the multiple responses to the problem. On the one hand, an individualistic approach warned parents and encouraged children to avoid the area. A second, collective response led to local residents assisting in building a small incinerator to deal with the waste. But Eliasoph is particularly interested in Addams's third, political response, in which Hull House put pressure on the city to pave the streets and establish regular garbage pickup. For her, this is an illustrative example of how Addams's community-building focus translates to political action.

Drawing on the legacy of Jane Addams and Hull House provides a framework for understanding the contributions of neighbourhood houses, as local, community-based organizations, in addressing the problems of community. In this book, we provide evidence of how neighbourhood houses, which inherit the "machinery of connection" mandate and tradition of early settlement houses, persist as place-making mechanisms in contemporary urban communities.

Organization of the Book

We organized this book into seven chapters that are interrelated and intersect at the themes discussed above. We make many key connections across the chapters clear, and encourage readers to find their own connections in order to fully appreciate the nature of neighbourhood houses (NH) as a long-standing place-based organization that meets local service needs while connecting and organizing local residents.[9]

Neighbourhood houses are a continuation of the early social settlement movement. However, this history of how settlement houses are transformed into today's neighbourhood houses in Vancouver is neither linear nor smooth. In Chapter 1, Sean Lauer, Miu Chung Yan, and Eleanor Stebner briefly capture the unique historical background of the formation of the first settlement house, Toynbee Hall, which was part of the social movements aiming to correct the social ills caused by the rapid industrialization and urbanization in the Victoria era. The social reform orientation and success of Toynbee Hall quickly appealed to the rising new middle class in the United States, where the urban centres also experienced similar social problems. With the support of churches, the new middle class, comprising mostly women, enthusiastically copied this model from across the Atlantic and spread it throughout the country. Experiencing relatively slow economic development, Canada was a latecomer to the social settlement movement.

Due to social and physical proximity, early Canadian settlement houses were significantly influenced by the American pioneers. When the movement arrived in Vancouver in the 1930s, many traditions of early settlement houses were lost. Unlike their predecessors elsewhere, they were all started as secular and professionally run place-based and community-based organizations. The church, the new middle class, and the university played a minimal role in the development of NHs in Vancouver, where almost all NHs were formed by the concerted effort of local residents and/or as an outcome of professional intervention of social planners and community developers.

The involvement of social planners in the development of early neighbourhood houses in Vancouver indicated a close relationship between NHs and the state. For NHs in Vancouver, this relationship has become closer over time. As with many social service organizations in Canada and elsewhere, government has become a major source of funding of NHs. However, the prevalent neoliberal influence on government expenditure has significant impacts on the operation of NHs and their perceived place-based mandate. In Chapter 2, Oliver Schmidtke focuses on the role of NHs in governing the local community from a place-based perspective, considering their dual role as service providers and community advocates. What are the political ambitions of NHs in terms of working with and on behalf of the community as an independent, grassroots civil society organization? How do NHs in Metro Vancouver contribute to governing the community and stimulating democratic practices? Addressing these questions, the chapter explores how NHs in Metro Vancouver have provided institutional capacity for the empowerment of marginalized social groups, bottom-up governance, and effective policy initiatives. The analysis draws on semi-structured interviews conducted with NH executive directors and representatives of the city, as well as on surveys and focus groups conducted at various NHs. Based on the analysis, Schmidtke elaborates on two central aspects of NHs as agents of civic engagement and political change. First, NHs are critical in facilitating the development of social capital by connecting citizens, helping them to overcome their social isolation, and providing them with the tools to become involved in communal affairs. Second, NHs provide a significant forum for place-based governance operating at a complex intersection between community members and different levels of government.

In Chapter 3, Miu Chung Yan offers an analysis of NHs both as a mechanism to generate community assets among local residents and as an organizational asset that is accessible to local residents. As place-based organizations, NHs are not only physically close to local residents who can access multiple services and help within walking distance, they are also psychologically close to local residents who find them a safe and welcoming place, like home. The homey feeling is reflected in the strong sense of ownership and volunteerism among their service users, which have converted service users from passive receivers to active participants. As reflected in the results of the service users survey, respondents agreed that NHs are a community asset that solves community problems by successfully nurturing resources. Most often these resources are from other community organizations and public institutions that are fragmented and that often operate in isolation. NHs have enabled an institutional accessibility that bridges the gap between the needs of local residents and the public resources hidden in the hard-to-navigate service network. Their proximity to local residents has made them a local place-based hub of the web of multiple service networks.

In Chapter 4, Sean Lauer examines the concept of social infrastructure more closely. He considers social infrastructure the physical places and organizations that shape the interactions of people in a community, and he uses this definition to show that neighbourhood houses are a unique form of social infrastructure. The place-based focus of NHs discourages focus on a narrow set of programs and activities and encourages attraction of a diverse set of participants from varied backgrounds and from across the life course. These characteristics of neighbourhood houses enable participants to engage in a variety of different activities and to come into contact with the demographic variability of participants at the NH. These unique aspects of NHs provide opportunities for community-building through the maintenance and development of relationships and the development of social capacity. The chapter demonstrates these outcomes through an analysis of survey data collected from neighbourhood house participants.

Based largely on life history data, in Chapter 5, Pilar Riaño-Alcalá and Erika Ono examine how structural challenges such as racism and poverty, and everyday obstacles related to lack of inclusion, discrimination, and other social attitudes of dominant members of society toward new immigrants and refugees, have historically impacted immigrants' economic, social, and political incorporation. This chapter considers neighbourhood houses as place-based organizations that have played a unique role in immigrants' pathways toward incorporation in the economic and social life of the city. Based on life history interviews, it traces two complementary dynamics and functions of the NHs: as places for meaningful social, family, and civic engagement and as hubs for exchange, career path, and self-development. Applying holistic place-based approaches to the understanding of civic engagement and to Arjun Appadurai's notion (2004) of individual and collective aspirations as a navigational capacity, the authors find that in the context of a settler colonial country such as Canada, immigrants have played a central role in the envisioning and maintenance of NHs as places of social and racial inclusion, place-based learning, and leadership. They also interrogate this dynamic of inclusion and engagement from the lens of a racialized architecture of power where racially minoritized staff and volunteers have scant presence in the decision-making roles and systems of the NHs.

Neighbourhood houses exist to serve local residents, making the lived experiences of NH participants central to their story. In Chapter 6, Jenny Francis summarizes the stories of twelve immigrants to Canada whose lives have been transformed through connection with their local neighbourhood house. The people who shared their stories initially struggled to find employment, navigate new systems, make friends, and develop a sense of belonging in their new home. Social isolation, non-recognition of foreign experience and credentials, and low incomes left them feeling out of place, lonely, and "worthless." In these contexts, their narratives underscore the role of neighbourhood houses as critical sites of empowerment and belonging that helped them develop both a sense of place and a feeling of trust in Canadian institutions. Through volunteer and paid work opportunities, neighbourhood houses foster the connections that enable immigrants who once felt like useless outsiders to develop a feeling of "insideness" and become contributing members of society. In other words, neighbourhood houses empower immigrants to help others, which is in turn empowering! The stories reveal the means by which the networks that evolve around the neighbourhood house transform disconnected urban residents into a community, creating the "ripple effect" of care and belonging that makes a neighbourhood home.

Finally, we are cautious that this book not be over-optimistic about the roles and functions of neighbourhood houses as place-based organizations. In Chapter 7, we highlight three major challenges for NHs. Financial constraints are neither new nor unique to NHs. Under the neoliberal funding model, the community service sector experiences ongoing challenges driven by financial shortages and precarious employment conditions. De-professionalization has led to questions about service quality. However, NHs uniquely experience a place-based paradox: being successful in their local community but invisible in the greater society. Coupled with growing competitiveness in public funding, this paradox erodes collaboration among NHs and further hinders the NH movement from raising funds from government and donations. Despite these challenges and limitations, we contend that NHs are vital place-based community organizations in contemporary urban communities.

Notes

1 This description of a welcoming community is inspired in part by that of Lars Meier (2017). In Canada, welcoming community initiatives at the municipal level have inspired a small literature on welcoming communities and integration of immigrants and refugees at the community level (Guo and Guo 2016; Brown 2017). Esses and colleagues (2010) have suggested seventeen characteristics of a welcoming community for new immigrants that include both aspects of a welcoming community and characteristics of communities that facilitate these welcoming aspects. See Power and Bartlett 2018 for a discussion of non-immigration-focused welcoming communities in Britain and Canada.
2 It released a follow-up report in 2017.
3 The notably folksy description came to be known as the constrict proposition.
4 Wellman actually develops a total of five factors that contribute to this outcome. His own view is that only some aspects of the liberated view have empirical support.
5 Sampson has made a career out of documenting what he calls neighbourhood effects that has culminated in the publication of *Great American City* (2012).
6 For further discussion of the idea of place, place attachment, and place identity, please refer to Chapter 5.
7 There are numerous good introductions to Jane Addams, including Knight 2010, Elshtain 2002, and Stebner 1997. Of course, Addams's own *Twenty Years at Hull House* ([1910] 1960) and *Democracy and Social Ethics* (2002) are also excellent introductions.
8 This is a paraphrase of Nina Eliasoph's (2013, 26) use of the concept. I also rely on Schneiderhan 2011 and Seigfried 2004 in my discussion of perplexity.
9 Readers will note that although the majority (77 percent) of our respondents are women, gender does not provide an analytical focus in the chapters that follow. We intend to pursue this important avenue of inquiry fully in subsequent publications, which we invite readers to explore.

References

Addams, Jane. (1910) 1960. *Twenty Years at Hull House.* New York: Signet.
—. 2002. *Democracy and Social Ethics.* Urbana, IL: University of Illinois Press.
Aizlewood, Amanda, and Ravi Pendakur. 2005. "Ethnicity and Social Capital in Canada." *Canadian Ethnic Studies* 37 (2): 77–102.
Amin, Ash. 2002. "Ethnicity and the Multicultural City: Living with Diversity." *Environment and Planning* 34 (6): 959–80.

Appadurai, Arjun. 2004. "The Capacity to Aspire: Culture and the Terms of Recognition." In *Culture and Public Action,* edited by Vijayendra Rao and Michael Walton, 59–84. Palo Alto, CA: Stanford University Press.

Benkler, Yochai. 2006. *The Wealth of Networks.* New Haven, CT: Yale University Press.

Bradford, Neil. 2005. *Place-Based Public Policy: Towards a New Urban and Community Agenda for Canada.* Ottawa: Canadian Policy Research Networks.

Breton, Raymond. 1964. "Institutional Completeness of Ethnic Communities and the Personal Relations of Immigrants." *American Journal of Sociology* 70 (2): 193–205.

Brint, Steven. 2001. "*Gemeinschaft* revisited: A Critique and Reconstruction of the Community Concept." *Sociological Theory* 19 (1): 1–23.

Brown, Natalya R. 2017. "Housing Experiences of Recent Immigrants to Canada's Small Cities: The Case of North Bay, Ontario." *Journal of International Migration and Integration* 18 (3): 719–47.

Carman, Tara. 2012a. "Part One: Social Isolation Has Far-Reaching Effects on Us and Neighbours, Survey Finds." *Vancouver Sun,* June 19.

–. 2012b. "Part Two: Vancouver a Difficult Social Atmosphere for Many Newcomers." *Vancouver Sun,* June 19.

–. 2012c. "Part Three: Relationships with Neighbours Polite but Indifferent, Survey Finds." *Vancouver Sun,* June 20.

Chow, Nelson. 1980. *Social Welfare in Hong Kong: Development and Policies* [in Chinese]. Hong Kong: Hong Kong University Press.

City of Vancouver. 2020. *Areas of the city.* Accessed August 21, 2020. https://vancouver.ca/news-calendar/areas-of-the-city.aspx.

Clemens, Elisabeth. 2006. "The Constitution of Citizens: Political Theories of Nonprofit Organizations." In *The Nonprofit Sector,* 2nd ed., edited by Walter Powell and Richard Steinberg, 207–20. New Haven, CT: Yale University Press.

Cresswell, Tim. 2004. *Place: A Short Introduction.* Malden, MA: Blackwell.

de Tocqueville, Alexis. (1840) 2003. *Democracy in America.* New York: Doubleday.

Dirlik, Arif. 1999. "Place-Based Imagination: Globalism and the Politics of Place." *Review (Fernand Braudel Center)* 20 (2): 151–87.

Eliasoph, Nina. 2011. *Making Volunteers: Civic Life after Welfare's End.* Princeton, NJ: Princeton University Press.

–. 2013. *The Politics of Volunteering.* Cambridge, UK: Polity Press.

Elshtain, Jean Bethke. 2002. *Jane Addams and the Dream of American Democracy.* New York: Basic Books.

Escobar, Arturo. 2001. "Culture Sits in Places: Reflection on Globalism and Subaltern Strategies of Localization." *Political Geography* 20 (2): 139–74.

Esses, Victoria M., Leah K. Hamilton, Caroline Bennett-AbuAyyash, and Meyer Burstein. 2010. "Characteristics of a Welcoming Community." Welcoming Communities Initiative. Ottawa: Citizenship and Immigration Canada. http://p2pcanada.ca/wp-content/uploads/2011/09/Characteristics-of-a-Welcoming-Community-11.pdf.

Evans, Bryan Mitchell, and John Shields. 2010. "The Third Sector and the Provision of Public Good: Partnerships, Contracting, and the Neo-Liberal State." In *The*

Handbook of Canadian Public Administration, edited by Christopher Dunn, 305–18. Toronto: Oxford University Press.

Evans, Bryan, Ted Richmond, and John Shields. 2005. "Structuring Neoliberal Governance: The Nonprofit Sector, Emerging New Modes of Control and the Marketisation of Service Delivery." *Policy and Society* 24 (1): 73–97.

Fabricant, Michael B., and Robert Fisher. 2002. *Settlement Houses under Siege: The Struggle to Sustain Community Organization in New York City.* New York: Columbia University Press.

Ferris, James M., and Elwood Hopkins. 2015. "Place-Based Initiatives: Lessons from Five Decades of Experimentation and Experience." *Foundation Review* 7 (4): article 10. https://doi.org/10.9707/1944-5660.1269.

Friedmann, John. 2010. "Place and Place-Making in Cities: A Global Perspective." *Planning Theory and Practice* 11 (2): 149–65.

Guo, Shibao. and Yan Guo. 2016. "Immigration, Integration, and Welcoming Communities: Neighbourhood-Based Initiative to Facilitate the Integration of Newcomers to Canada." *Canadian Ethnic Studies* 48 (3): 45–67.

Hansmann, Henry. 1987. "Economic Theories of Nonprofit Organizations." In *The Nonprofit Sector,* 2nd ed., edited by Walter Powell and Richard Steinberg, 277–309. New Haven, CT: Yale University Press.

Hill Collins, Patricia. 2010. "The New Politics of Community." *American Sociological Review* 75 (1): 7–30.

Hou, Feng, and Zheng Wu. 2009. "Racial Diversity, Minority Concentration, and Trust in Canadian Urban Neighbourhoods." *Social Science Research* 38 (3): 693–716.

Kaul, Mohan L. 1988. "Developing Neighbourhood Organizations as Social Structures for Peace." *International Social Work* 31 (1): 45–52.

Knight, Louise W. 2010. *Jane Addams: Spirit in Action.* New York: W.W. Norton.

Lauer, Sean, and Miu Chung Yan. Forthcoming. "Social Infrastructure and Social Capacity Development among Newcomers to Canada: The Role of Neighbourhood Houses in Vancouver."

–. 2013. "Voluntary Association Involvement and Immigrant Network Diversity." *International Migration* 51 (3): 133–50.

Lazersfeld, Paul F., and Robert K. Merton. 1954. "Friendship as Social Process: A Substantive and Methodological Analysis." In *Freedom and Control in Modern Society,* edited by M. Berger, T. Abel, and C.H. Page, 18–66. New York: Octagon Books.

Liu, Edgar, and Robert Freestone. 2016. "Revisiting Place and Placelessness." In *Revisiting Place and Placelessness,* edited by Robert Freestone and Edgar Liu, 1–19. New York: Routledge.

Marsden, Peter V. 1987. "Core Discussion Networks of Americans." *American Sociological Review* 52 (1): 122–31.

Massey, Doreen S. 1994. *Space, Place and Gender.* Minneapolis: University of Minnesota Press.

McPherson, Miller, Lynn Smith-Lovin, and James M. Cook. 2001. "Birds of a Feather: Homophily in Social Networks." *Annual Review of Sociology* 27 (1): 415–44.

Meacham, Standish. 1987. *Toynbee Hall and Social Reform 1880–1914: The Search for Community.* New Haven, CT: Yale University Press.

Meier, Lars. 2017. "Three Types of Neighbourhood Reactions to Local Immigration and New Refugee Settlement." *City and Community* 16 (3): 252–56.

Phan, Mai. 2008. "We're All in This Together: Context, Contacts, and Social Trust." *Analyses of Social Issues and Public Policy* 8 (1): 23–51.

Portes, Alejandro, and Erik Vickstrom. 2011. "Diversity, Social Capital, and Cohesion." *Annual Review of Sociology* 37 (1): 461–79.

Portes, Alejandro, and Julia Sensenbrenner. 1993. "Embeddedness and Immigration: Notes on the Social Determinants of Economic Action." *American Journal of Sociology* 98 (6): 1320–50.

Portes, Alejandro, and Ruben Rumbaut. 2001. *Legacies: The Story of the Immigrant Second Generation.* Berkeley, CA: University of California Press.

–. 2006. *Immigrant America: A Portrait.* Berkeley, CA: University of California Press.

Power, Andrew, and Ruth L. Bartlett. 2018. "Self-Building Safe Havens in a Post-Service Landscape: How Adults with Learning Disabilities Are Reclaiming the Welcoming Communities Agenda." *Social and Cultural Geography* 19 (3): 336–56.

Putnam, Robert D. 2000. *Bowling Alone: The Collapse and Revival of American Community.* New York: Simon and Schuster.

–. 2007. "E Pluribus Unum: Diversity and Community in the Twenty-first Century." *Scandinavian Political Studies* 30 (2): 137–74.

Rainie, Lee, and Barry Wellman. 2012. *Networked: The New Social Operating System.* Cambridge, MA: MIT Press.

Relph, Edward. 1976. *Place and Placelessness.* London: Pion.

–. 2016a. "Afterword." In *Revisiting Place and Placelessness,* edited by Robert Freestone and Edgar Liu, 269–71. New York: Routledge.

–. 2016b. "The Paradox of Place and the Evolution of Placelessness." In *Revisiting Place and Placelessness,* edited by Robert Freestone and Edgar Liu, 20–34. New York: Routledge.

Rowles, Graham D. 1983. "Place and Personal Identity in Old Age: Observations from Appalachia." *Journal of Environmental Psychology* 3 (4): 299–313.

Sampson, R. 2012. *Great American City: Chicago and the Enduring Neighborhood Effect.* Chicago: University of Chicago Press.

Schneiderhan, Erik. 2011. "Pragmatism and Empirical Sociology: The Case of Jane Addams and Hull House, 1889–1895." *Theory and Society* 40 (4): 589–617.

Seigfried, Charlene H. 2004. "Jane Addams, 1860–1935." In *The Blackwell Guide to American Philosophy,* edited by A.T. Marsobian and J. Ryder, 186–98. Cambridge, MA: Blackwell.

Shields, John, and Mitchell B. Evans. 1998. *Shrinking the State: Globalization and Public Administration "Reform."* Halifa, NS: Fernwood.

Shugart, Ian, and Thomas Townsend. 2010. "Bringing 'Place' in: Exploring the Role of the Federal Government." *Horizons (Sustainable Places)* 10 (4): 4–6.

Simmel, G. 1950. *The Sociology of Georg Simmel,* translated by Kurt H. Wolff. New York: Free Press.

Statistics Canada. 2017. "Census Profile, 2016 Census." Updated June 18, 2019. https://www12.statcan.gc.ca/census-recensement/2016/dp-pd/prof/index.cfm?Lang=E.

Stebner, Eleanor. 1997. *The Women of Hull House: A Study in Spirituality, Vocation, and Friendship*. Albany, NY: SUNY Press.

Tönnies, Ferdinand. 2001. *Tönnies: Community and Civil Society*, edited by Jose Harris. Cambridge, UK: Cambridge University Press.

Trolander, Judith. 1987. *Professionalism and Social Change: From the Settlement House Movement to Neighborhood Centers, 1886 to the Present*. New York: Columbia University Press.

Tuan, Yi-Fu. 1977. *Space and Place*. Minneapolis: University of Minnesota Press.

van der Meer, Tom, and Jochem Tolsma. 2014. "Ethnic Diversity and Its Effects on Social Cohesion." *Annual Review of Sociology* 40 (1): 459–78.

Vancouver Foundation. 2012. *Connections and Engagement: A Survey of Metro Vancouver*. Vancouver: Vancouver Foundation. https://www.vancouverfoundation.ca/about-us/publications/connections-and-engagement-reports/connections-engagement-report-2012.

Wellman, Barry. 1979. "The Community Question: The Intimate Networks of East Yorkers." *American Journal of Sociology* 84 (5): 1201–31.

Williams, Colin C. 2003. "Developing Community Participation in Deprived Neighbourhoods: A Critical Evaluation of Third-Sector Approach." *Space and Polity* 7 (1): 65–73.

Wilson, Kenneth L., and Alejandro Portes. 1980. "Immigrant Enclaves: An Analysis of the Labor Market Experiences of Cubans in Miami." *American Journal of Sociology* 86 (2): 295–319.

Wirth, Louis. 1938. "Urbanism as a Way of Life." *American Journal of Sociology* 44 (1): 1–24.

Yan, Miu Chung. 2002. "Recapturing the History of Settlement House Movement: Its Philosophy, Service Model and Implications in China's Development of Community-Based Centre Services." *Asia Pacific Journal of Social Work and Development* 12 (1): 21–40.

–. 2004. "Bridging the Fragmented Community: Revitalizing Settlement Houses in the Global Era." *Journal of Community Practice* 12 (1/2): 51–69.

Yan, Miu Chung, Chun-Sing Johnson Cheung, Ming-Sum Tsui, and Chi Keung Chu. 2017. "Examining the Neoliberal Discourse of Accountability: The Case of Hong Kong's Social Service Sector." *International Social Work* 60 (4): 976–89.

Yan, Miu Chung, and Sean Lauer. 2008. "Social Capital and Ethno-Cultural Diverse Immigrants: A Canadian Study on Settlement House and Social Integration." *Journal of Ethnic and Cultural Diversity in Social Work* 17 (3): 229–50.

Yan, Miu Chung, Sean Lauer, and Rick Sin. 2009. "Issues in Community (Re)building: The Tasks of Settlement Houses in Two Cities." *Social Development Issues* 31 (1): 39–54.

1

History of Vancouver
Neighbourhood Houses and Beyond

SEAN LAUER, MIU CHUNG YAN, and ELEANOR STEBNER

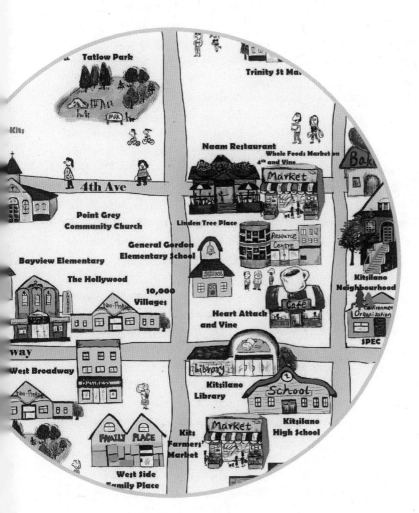

With over 135 years of history, the settlement house (SH) movement is a global movement. Today the International Federation of Settlements and Neighborhood Centers (IFS), the umbrella organization of the movement established in 1922 (Matthews and Kimmis 2001), has more than 10,000 members from over thirty countries across the five continents (IFS, n.d.). The whole movement originated in the late Victorian era, during the heyday of the Industrial Revolution, which generated tremendous wealth but also widened the gulf between classes. A group of socially conscious members of the new middle class, particularly those with a religious calling, experimented with a new approach to bridging the gap between the rich and the poor by "settling" themselves in economically deprived urban communities. The first settlement house was established in 1884 by the Reverend Samuel A. Barnett and his wife, Henrietta, in Whitechapel, a notoriously deprived working-class community in East London at the time. Known as Toynbee Hall, it turned previous settlement experiments into an institutional success and inspired like-minded individuals from many other countries to join the movement. Toynbee Hall still stands today as a testament to the persistence of the social settlement movement.

Despite sharing many similarities, as a social institution, settlement houses in different countries were unique in many ways. In this chapter, we first summarize briefly the social context that gave rise to Toynbee Hall. Inspired by the success of Toynbee Hall, SHs in the United States evolved into a women-led movement. The expansion of SHs in the United States in the early 1900s was so massive that it is beyond what we can cover in this chapter. Instead, we focus on a few unique dimensions of American SHs in the early days. The American settlement movement also spilled over into Canada, with Toronto as its early stronghold. After briefly describing the early history of settlement houses in Toronto, we return to Vancouver, the focus of this book. We examine the history of the movement in that city, where the first SH was established in 1938. As a latecomer to the movement, Vancouver took a different turn. Not only was the name "neighbourhood house" (NH) adopted instead of "settlement house," but its religious connection was much more remote than that of its predecessor in the early movement. The history of NHs in Vancouver combines resident engagement through community development with a planning approach toward social infrastructure creation in a growing and changing metropolitan area.

Toynbee Hall and the Social Settlement Movement

After spending six months in Toynbee Hall, Robert A. Woods (1891), who was sent to London to learn about the settlement movement by Andover Theological Seminary in Newton, Massachusetts, provided a detailed report on social movements in England. These movements were progressive social responses to the economic inequality and depression, social ills, and class division and tensions caused by rapid industrialization and urbanization driven by unfettered capitalism. On the labour front, the New Unionism movement began to organize the many low-wage workers who used to be excluded from the trade skills. Besides organizing them for strikes, the movement formed new workingmen's clubs to provide a physical and social venue to enrich the social life of the labourers. According to Woods, there were 200 workingmen's clubs in London at the time of his visit.

The New Unionism movement was tied closely to the Socialist movement, which, as Woods observed, was led by a few major organizations, such as the Socialist League and later the Fabian Society, formed and supported by a group of "literary proletariat" (or a new middle class) who were the "result of increase of education and the entrance of women into the professions" (Woods 1891, 61). Socialist ideas were attractive to a group of young ministers who sympathized greatly with labourers living under appalling socio-economic conditions. As Woods (1891) documented, a group of forty young clergymen from London formed a Christian Socialist Society and met once every two weeks in a winter to discuss the stand of the church in specific labour problems. Its manifesto stated: "The Christian Socialist Society believes that by the changes which it advocates in the industrial system men [sic] will be enabled, under the altered conditions of modern life, to put into practice the principles taught by Christ in all their dealings with one another as fellow-men and fellow-citizens" (quoted in Woods 1891, 63). Christian Socialism spread all over England. Sharing a similar focus on social policy, the proponents of socialism and New Unionism worked together on many occasions to try to change the country's labour laws.

Parallel to this radical unionism and socialism, the Charity Organization Society (COS) movement was at the forefront of philanthropic endeavours, the focus of which was not on the social causes of poverty but on immediate relief to the individual deserving poor (Hunter 1902). The COS was first established in London in 1869 (Fraser 1984). By 1890, in London alone there was a central council and forty branch committees that served as the organizing body for distributing voluntary charities from churches and other charitable organizations in their local district (Woods 1891). The early COS leaders believed that the purpose of charity transcended materialist relief of the deserving poor; it was for their moral improvement as well. Measures therefore had to be taken to guard against "fraudulent applicants." A scientific method was needed to systematically investigate each applicant through personal contact (Fraser 1984). Indeed, the idea of scientific spirit adopted by the COS also influenced many social reformers who initiated the social settlement movement (White 1911).

Inspired by Christian Socialism, the settlement movement distinguished itself from the COS movement by focusing on the social causes of poverty. Unlike the radical socialists and New Unionists, who advocated for a fundamental structural change of capitalism, the SH pioneers were largely social reformers. Their goal was "to reconcile classes not to eliminate class lines, and in that sense its intention was conservative" (Reinders 1982, 47). The purpose of SHs, as articulated by Toynbee Hall founder Samuel Barnett, was clearly that "a university settlement ... be viewed as an alternative to 'revolutionary schemes' which 'turn the world upside down'" (Abel 1979, 607).

The idea of settlement was not new. Decades before the establishment of Toynbee Hall, Thomas Hill Green, a philosopher from Oxford University, and John Ruskin, the first professor of fine arts at Oxford, had been exploring the idea and possibility that "men might hire a house, where they could come for short or long periods, and, living in an industrial quarter, learn to 'sup sorrow with the poor'" (Barnett, quoted in White 1911, 47). Edward Denison, a bishop's son, who resided in the slum district of Stepney, and Arnold Toynbee, an Oxford-educated economist who settled at Whitechapel, were two prominent pioneers who experimented with this idea (Meacham 1987; Scheuer 1985). They inspired Barnett, who later successfully institutionalized the idea.

Barnett was appointed vicar of St. Jude Church in the Whitechapel area in 1873. Since moving into the area, he and his wife, Henrietta, had tried to fill the local leadership gaps by serving as poor-law guardians, establishing COS branches and the Sanitary Aid Commission (Abel 1979). However, they noticed that the Whitechapel area was demoralized not only by poverty and crime but also by social tension due to the influx of Jewish immigrants, with whom the local churches were unable to connect. In 1884, when a group of friends of Toynbee, who had died at the age of thirty-two, decided to build a lecture hall in Whitechapel in his memory, the Barnetts took the opportunity to turn the lecture hall idea into the first settlement house, named after Toynbee (Meacham 1987). Through their connection with Oxford and Cambridge universities, they recruited a group of young educated elites to settle in Toynbee Hall, the first of 102 settlers over the period 1884 to 1900, most of them Oxbridge undergraduates (Meacham 1987).

To the Barnetts, Toynbee Hall was a "machinery of connection" to bridge the well-off educated elites and the poor as a community in the deprived neighbourhood (Meacham 1987). The connection was mutually beneficial: educating members of the upper class about the local conditions of life from their personal observation and mobilizing them to help where help was needed (Matthews-Jones 2017, 35). The young settlers were supposed to be "friends" and "neighbours" to the working poor. They helped organize and support a variety of activities for local residents. Despite his religious background, Barnett decided to keep Toynbee Hall away from Christian missionary work. His intention was to make it an inclusive place to reach residents who were from different Christian denominations or who had a different faith, such as the Jewish immigrants in the neighbourhood (Meacham 1987). As Woods (1891) noted, learning from the New Unionist movement, Toynbee Hall organized many clubs for different groups of people as a means of developing sociability. It also served a strong educational purpose by providing free or inexpensive courses in different grades taken up in college, public lectures, a library, outings, and night school classes. Settlers also actively participated in local organizations such as COS branches and labour unions. Later, influenced by Charles Booth's poverty survey, Toynbee Hall also actively engaged in social inquiry and investigations (Meacham 1987).

Toynbee Hall was not without criticisms. Perhaps the major criticism had to do with its architectural design, which was largely a replica of an Oxbridge college. As Woods (1891) noted, the building and its interior design served to keep fresh the reminiscences while providing working people with a taste of the classic university atmosphere. It gave a sense of "home away from home" to the settlers (Matthews-Jones 2017). Toynbee Hall was seen as "an oasis in the midst of the brutal and ugly slum" and settlers were more or less living in isolation and hardly integrated into the community outside the premises (Abel 1979, 611). Barnett believed that the educated well-off settlers were there to uplift and regenerate moral character through their own example (Abel 1979). As this could not be done effectively in a large group, he encouraged settlers to connect with local residents one-on-one or in small groups so that they would know better "each other's characters, thoughts and beliefs" (Meacham 1987). Settlers could invite individual local residents to their dormitory or the drawing room for parties, tea, food, and conversation. While the classic architectural and interior design and the upper-middle-class social etiquette were meant to inspire the poor with a necessary material condition for proper living, they might have unintentionally alienated the local people and reminded them of the class differences (Matthews-Jones 2017; Abel 1979).

Despite these criticisms, Toynbee Hall had great success with this place-based approach toward tackling the social tensions between classes and the social ills caused by capitalism in deprived working-poor neighbourhoods. Its success inspired many like-minded people in the United Kingdom. By 1911, there were forty-nine settlement houses in Britain (Abel 1979). More importantly, the success of Toynbee Hall also attracted as visitors many social reformers from different parts of the world, who then replicated the approach in their home countries. Many visitors were from the United States, where urban communities were troubled by similar social tensions and social ills, and by 1910, there were more than 400 in that country (Abel 1979). The sheer number of SHs in the United States also signified the shift of the centre of the movement from Toynbee Hall to North America.

Early Social Settlement Movement in the United States

From 1877 to the First World War, American society experienced deep economic, social, and political crises (Ehrenreich 1985). As a rapidly emerging industrial economy, the United States experienced similar class tensions and social ills as the United Kingdom. A report on the social conditions of South Philadelphia provides a vivid description of the late-nineteenth-century American urban slum: "Though these conditions had existed since colonial times, immigration, class antagonisms, political corruption, and labor militancy promised even wider disturbances to the social order of the late 19th-century city" (Juliani 2007, 22). In this context, the Progressive Movement arose as the response of the well-off classes to the chaotic industrial and social orders. Benefiting from the industrial system, the "new" middle class, who largely occupied professional-managerial positions, saw the imminent threats of social instability caused by the unjust conditions of the poor. Similar to British social reformers, they intended to restore justice and morality to the chaotic and morally degraded society. Their goal was to modify, but not abolish, the capitalist system (Ehrenreich 1985). The success of Toynbee Hall inspired many members of the new middle class to replicate the settlement house in the United States.

In 1887, Neighbourhood Guild, the first US settlement house, was set up in New York City by Stanton Coit, a resident of Toynbee Hall. In 1892, it became University Settlement, the first warden of which was James B. Reynolds, who had also studied at Toynbee Hall. Perhaps the country's most famous settlement house was Hull House in Chicago, established in 1889 by Jane Addams, who had visited Toynbee Hall three times from 1887 to 1889. Hull House was seen as the nurturing ground of many settlement house leaders in North America. As a Nobel Laureate, Addams has been considered the leader of the settlement movement by many historians (Carson 2001). Her success was in multi-faceted areas, such as advocating for world peace, leading the feminist movement, and formulating American pragmatism. All these could be tied to her experience and success at Hull House. One of Addams's major contributions to the settlement movement was her articulation of the movement's philosophical framework as "the solidarity of human race." She also articulated the three motives behind the movement: to extend democracy to the social domain, to foster a full progression of the human race, and to actualize the humanitarianism of Christianity (Addams 1999, 95). This framework provided a normative common ground for the movement.

Industrialization in the United States attracted a massive influx of immigrants from Europe that made ethnic divisions a major social concern. As Addams (1961) noted, Hull House was located in a neighbourhood of immigrants, including Southern Italians, Germans, Russians, Jews, Poles, and others. Facing diverse ethnic groups in the neighbourhood, what American settlement houses needed to bridge was not just class differences but also cultural diversity. In South Philadelphia, Richard Juliani (2007) found that SH workers tended to customize their services by learning from the response of the immigrants of their needs and culture. For instance, one SH hired Italian-speaking doctors and workers to serve the Italian immigrants in its neighbourhood. Unlike Toynbee Hall's focus on adults, American SHs focused on children, particularly from immigrant families (Carson 2001). The immigrant reality that American SHs experienced has also left an unfinished debate over whether American SHs were an exemplary experiment in pluralism and democracy or a palatable alternative of assimilation to the harsher strategies of Americanization (Lissak 1989).

As with the British movement, religious ideas and feelings also played a significant role in the early phase of the settlement movement in the United States (Carson 2001). Indeed, like Addams, the founders of many American settlement houses were Christian social reformers who were attracted to the ideas of the Social Gospel movement, the basic tenet of which was that Christianity required the pursuit of not only personal redemption but also a better temporal life for less fortunate human beings (Juliani 2007). As Juliani (2007) notes, at least in South Philadelphia in the early 1900s, SHs operated under the auspices of Baptist, Presbyterian, Quaker, Roman Catholic, Methodist, Episcopalian, and many other Christian churches as well as Jewish groups. As Gaylord White (1911) reported, a study called "Religious Work in the Settlements of the Borough of Manhattan" covered twenty-seven SHs, eleven of which maintained some form of religious work. However, many SH proponents in the United States openly advocated for a secular path (White 1911).

Unlike Toynbee Hall, which mainly recruited men as settlers, women played a significant role in the American settlement movement. John Rousmaniere (1970) found that between 1889 and 1914, three-fifths of all settlement residents were women, and among them, almost nine-tenths had been to college. Besides Addams, Vida Scudder, an instructor at Wellesley College, was a notable leader in the American settlement movement. In 1890, she and her friends and colleagues founded the College Settlement Association (CSA), which later opened three houses in New York, Boston, and Philadelphia (Nicols 1898). From 1889 to 1914, over half of the houses' residents were from Wellesley College, Vassar College, and Smith College (Rousmaniere 1970). In the Progressive Era, women had more opportunities to pursue education, but employment opportunities were limited and largely confined to charity work and teaching. For those who were adventurous and had a moral calling, the settlement house was a "home" where they could help and be helped, according to Jean Fine, the paid head resident of the CSA's New York settlement house (Rousmaniere 1970, 64). Echoing sentiments expressed by residents at Toynbee Hall, many women found the settlement house to be a semi-protected environment in a hostile world where they could have an ideological and social sense of home, where "the camaraderie among the residents provided an alternative to family life" (Trolander 1975, 13). It was also a middle-class outpost where they could actualize the social ideals and sense of superiority that their education conferred (Rousmaniere 1970).

Due to the Reverend Barnett's strong personal connections, Toynbee Hall was abundant in resources, and residents, who were mostly from wealthy families, were able to pay a resident fee. However, this was not the case in American settlement houses, which mostly "started humbly; often they were no more than a tenement, or a large home of faded gentility lost in a slum" (Reinders 1982, 46). Many actively raised funds from churches and local philanthropies or worked with other organizations. As Robert Reinders (1982) suggested, not long after SHs were established in America, a policy of stipends for residents, particularly the head resident, was adopted. Most American SHs did not have a ready supply of college students from local universities, so paid residents became an inevitable option. Another possible reason why paid staff were introduced to American SHs was due to the movement's aspiration to scientific charity (Rousmaniere 1970). The scientific charity spirit was a driving force of professionalization in the COS and SH movements, which were the two legacies of the social work profession.

Evolution of Canadian Settlement Houses

Canada was a latecomer to the settlement movement, lagging in industrialization and urbanization, two root causes of the class tensions and social ills that gave rise to the movement. In 1884, when Toynbee Hall was established, the population of Toronto, one of the largest cities in Canada, was just over 100,000. According to Allan Irving, Harriet Parsons, and Donald Bellamy (1995), the socio-economic conditions of Toronto deteriorated in the early 1900s. The population grew 82 percent from 1901 to 1911. Meanwhile, in the early 1900s, the federal government aimed to develop Western Canada by aggressively recruiting immigrants, mainly from Europe. In 1913 alone, more than 400,000 immigrants arrived in the country (Boyd and Vickers 2000). Many were from outside Britain and the United States, such as Doukhobors and Jewish refugees from Russia, Hungarians, Mormons from the United States, Italians, and Ukrainians. The arrival of many non-English-speaking immigrants who also had different faiths triggered ethnic and religious anxieties and prejudices in many urban centres, including Toronto (Harold 2013). Exploitation, poverty, and unemployment were prevalent. Trade unions were weak. With 244 churches and fifty-five charitable organizations in 1909, Toronto was not short of charitable services (Irving, Parsons, and Bellamy 1995), but what was needed was a social institution that could address the social tensions and ills that most urban centres in Britain and the United States also faced.

In Toronto, churches were instrumental in providing services to the poor and initiated the settlement ideas in Canada. In 1889, a Presbyterian minister and journalist, the Reverend J.A. Macdonald, visited Toynbee Hall and introduced the idea to Torontonians. Instead of replicating the entire model, however, he chose to support only the establishment of the Dorset Mission, which focused on adult education for the working poor (Irving, Parsons, and Bellamy 1995). Canadians James Joseph Kelso, who was later recognized as the pioneer of Canada's child welfare service, and William Lyon Mackenzie King, who later became prime minister of Canada, visited Hull House in 1893 and 1896, respectively. Despite being impressed and inspired by Addams and her work at Hull House, they did not feel that Canada was ready for the settlement movement in the late 1890s. Instead, it was an American who broke ground for the Canadian settlement movement. Sara Libby Carson, who had established the Christodora House in New York City in 1897, came to Toronto in 1902. With her friend from Montreal, Mary Lawson, she established Evangelia House, the first settlement house in Canada, with support from Toronto YWCA and the Dominion YWCA. She secured the support of the Toronto Local Council of Women and the University Women's Club, and attracted many female students from the University of Toronto and other colleges to volunteer (James 2001). She also helped the Presbyterian Church of Canada to establish St. Christopher House in 1912. Carson has been called the "Jane Addams of Canada" because she also went on to establish – while working for the Presbyterian Church – neighbourhood houses in Montreal (Chalmers and St. Columba), Toronto (St. Christopher), and Winnipeg (Robertson Memorial) (Irving, Parsons, and Bellamy 1995; Jennison 1969).

Given the diversity of faiths among the mixed population, secularization of settlement houses in Toronto was natural. In 1912, the Memorial Institute was created by the Walmer Road Baptist Church, which started the Institute intentionally to provide settlement-like services to local residents regardless of their class, race, or religion (Irving, Parsons, and Bellamy 1995). In 1913, Carson's successor, Edith Elwood, helped establish the Riverdale Settlement (James 2001). Since Toynbee Hall, universities had always played a significant role in the secularization of the settlement movement. In 1907, after establishing himself and his family in Toronto, James Kelso returned to his interest in settlement houses. He convinced Robert A. Falcon, the newly appointed president of the University of Toronto, who had also been familiar with the Scottish settlement movement in Edinburgh when he was a student, to consider establishing a university settlement. With the support of the University Young Men's Christian Association, University Settlement opened its door in 1910. A year later, with the support of University Settlement, a group of concerned local residents established the Central Neighbourhood House (CNH), with Kelso as its first chair of the board.

CNH vowed to provide secular services to the mixed population of the neighbourhood it served. It was criticized by many for its secular stance. It was said that Sara Libby Carson "disapproved of it" and considered it a "heathen place" with a "Greenwich Village atmosphere" (Irving, Parsons, and Bellamy 1995, 117). Elizabeth B. Neufeld, the first head resident of CNH, was a Jewish woman from Baltimore. Responding to complaints from Anglo-Saxon Protestant Torontonians that the house was engaged in promoting Judaism, she said: "We don't talk religion at all. We leave that to the ministers and the rabbis. Citizenship is our gospel. Jane Addams is our John the Baptist and our Bible is the daily press when it knows enough to speak" (Heyworth, Palmer, and Philpott 1986, 18). Allying with CNH, University Settlement also took a strong secular stand by hiring a trained social worker as its second resident director. Milton B. Hunt came from Chicago and had previously worked at Hull House (Irving, Parsons, and Bellamy 1995). Indeed, unlike Toynbee Hall, settlement houses in Toronto did not have many university residents. Instead, college students who took part in the settlement houses contributed only a few hours of their time each week during the academic year (James 2001). Professionalization of settlement houses in Canada started almost right at the beginning.

The success of settlement houses in Toronto was well noted by G. Tower Ferguson (1926, 131), who made the following remarks in a radio talk: "So the Settlement aims to bring about a richer, fuller life for all – realization of individual, family and district possibilities, larger interests, greater sympathies, a spirit of mutual helpfulness, a wider horizon – a more abundant life for all." Toronto's success inspired other cities. By 1920, three SHs were established in Montreal and one each in Hamilton, Winnipeg, Ottawa, and Vancouver. The expansion of SHs in Canada was credited to the churches' effort. In Halifax, for example, what is now the Veith House Community Centre grew out of an orphanage first opened in 1857 under the leadership of an Anglican rector, Robert F. Uniacke. In Montreal, the Iverley Settlement House – later called the Negro Community Centre – was founded in 1929 but had its roots in a Methodist congregation; also in Montreal, a neighbourhood house for Jewish children was established in 1926 but with roots dating to 1891, when a free school and home for immigrants and children was opened as the Baron de Hirsch Institute. In 1907, the All People's Mission in Winnipeg, a Methodist Sunday School for immigrant children created by Dolly Maguire in 1886, was converted to a famous "settlement" in 1907 under the leadership of Methodist and social gospel leader J.S. Woodsworth.

In Vancouver, the name "neighbourhood house" was adopted almost right from the beginning. The first settlement house in Vancouver was established by Carson, who, along with Ethel Dodds, a recent graduate of the University of Toronto and worker at St. Christopher House, visited the city in 1915 to establish a settlement in the downtown core – the Vancouver Community House. It was short-lived and closed in 1931; it never took off as a settlement house although it did offer community recreational programs (Morrow 1948).[1] It was not until 1938 that the first neighbourhood house opened its doors in Vancouver.

Metro Vancouver Neighbourhood Houses: A Historical Overview

Metro Vancouver today encompasses nearly 3,000 square kilometres and is home to almost 2.5 million people of diverse cultures and languages, with English as the dominant public language. Its numerous and distinct communities exhibit a mixture of residential, industrial, entrepreneurial, governmental, and public spaces. It has an intricate system of roadways, bridges, sidewalks, and bicycle paths that are often packed with people, cars, buses, and trucks, as well as a light rapid transit system, SkyTrain (parts of which run underground). While many people, including tourists, rave about the natural beauty of this area, its numerous problems include exorbitant housing costs, homelessness, poverty, and human isolation and loneliness (Vancouver Foundation 2012). Boasting the third-largest metropolitan population area in Canada, it is regularly ranked number one in cost of living (Jones 2019).

What a contrast the early twenty-first century is to the late nineteenth century, when colonial settlers began arriving where Aboriginal people – the Coast Salish peoples – had lived for thousands of years! Vancouver itself was named after British naval captain George Vancouver, who charted the coastal areas of this northwest side of the continent toward the end of the eighteenth century. Exploration by sea was followed by exploration from the east, with a land route through the Rocky Mountains discovered by explorer Simon Fraser in the early nineteenth century. Both Vancouver and Fraser claimed the land for Great Britain.

The 1858 Fraser Canyon Gold Rush temporarily attracted some 20,000 British and American men (and a few women) into this region, and led Britain, under Queen Victoria, to establish the Colony of British Columbia that same year. In the wake of American expansionist desires, the colony was persuaded to join the nascent Dominion of Canada as its sixth province in

1871. In return, the federal government promised to build an intercontinental railway to connect Montreal with the west coast. In order to accomplish this task without going bankrupt, it imported Asian workers to do much of the treacherous and backbreaking work. The City of Vancouver itself was incorporated in 1886 when it became clear that transcontinental trains would soon reach their western terminus.

Vancouver was a small settlement in 1886, with a population of approximately 1,000 settlers who were mostly from Europe. Forest, water, mud, and mountains dominated the topography. Lumber provided the city's first economic base. And with the end of the Gold Rushes, the discovery of "black gold" – coal – became important. Pulp and paper mills, fisheries, and canneries developed. Shipping and the railway came to dominate the city. One scholar has said that in its early years, Vancouver was nothing more than an "overblown company town," and that company was the Canadian Pacific Railway (CPR). The CPR was awarded extensive tracts of land in what is now the metropolitan area, and its executives oversaw "clearing the land, grading the streets, and selling the lots" – and made a lot of money (Gutstein 1975, 11–13). Indian reserves existed where the neighbourhood of Kitsilano and Stanley Park (named after Lord Stanley, then the British colonial secretary and today perhaps best known for his namesake, the Stanley Cup hockey trophy) now sit, but within two decades the reserves and their Aboriginal inhabitants had been dispossessed of their ancestral lands (Barman 2007).

From 1891 to 1901, Vancouver's population mushroomed from 13,000 to 27,000 (Vancouver School Board 2017). Many new settlers arrived, most of them from other provinces, the rest from Great Britain and Ireland, China, Japan, India, as well as the United States and Europe (MacDonald 1977). As with other places in the world, rapid urbanization and industrialization resulted in some people becoming very wealthy while the majority – working for the CPR and associated industries, and in domestic and retail services – struggled to subsist. Distinct economic, racial, and ethnic neighbourhoods developed. Huge tracts of land were devoted to industry while other areas were set aside for housing, some specifically for labourers, others reserved for the well-off.

The Origins of Neighbourhood Houses in Vancouver

In 1891 the province passed its Benevolent Societies Act. The act provided for the possibility of individuals to "unite themselves into a society or corporation" in order to engage in charitable or moral reform undertakings, and social, intellectual, and recreational activities, through the formation of clubs and organizations. It also called for the establishment of hospitals and "refuge homes" for women and children, and for citizens to address "vice and cruelty to children" as well as the "prevention of cruelty to animals" (Government of British Columbia 1891). The Masons, the YMCA (followed by the YWCA), and Christian churches (overwhelmingly Protestant in an area that very much wanted to claim its British colonial roots), and numerous other associations sprang into being.

The origins of Vancouver neighbourhood houses can be traced back to this context. People, many of them recent migrants – and especially women and children – needed attention and care. The Alexandra Women's and Children's Hospital opened in 1891, and a year later the Alexandra Non-Sectarian Orphanage and Home for Children opened at the corner of Seventh Avenue and Pine Street in Vancouver (Purvey 1991). Incorporated as the Alexandra Non-Sectarian Children's Home in 1894, the orphanage opened a fresh air camp at Crescent Beach in 1918, some fifty kilometres south of downtown Vancouver, to meet the recreational and community needs of urban children and mothers. (Such camps, sometimes called "health" or "open air" camps, originated in England and the United States in the 1890s and were intended to temporarily get working people and children out of the cramped and unsanitary industrial centres [Tennant 2005].)

The home was named after Her Royal Highness Alexandra, Princess of Wales, wife of Prince Albert Edward, who became King Edward VII in 1901. Princess Alexandra was popular with the public and was admired for her beauty and fashion and, because she wielded little direct political power, for her charity work. Members of the Woman's Christian Temperance Union (WCTU), many of whom had connections to leading city magnates (such as Sarah Salsbury, the mother of the first CPR treasurer, and Annie E. Webster, the wife of the first manager of the Union Steamship Company) were central in recognizing the need for an orphanage and providing leadership for it, but other, less prominent women were also significant.

A member of the first orphanage board and an early matron at the orphanage, for example, was Sarah Bowes. Bowes did not have upper-crust or money connections. Born in what is now Ontario, she taught school in her younger adulthood and then cared for her aging parents. Very active in her Methodist church, Bowes joined the WCTU in Ontario, but in 1886, after the death of her parents while she was in her fifties, she joined the westward surge and moved to Vancouver to work as a city missionary and lay preacher for a Methodist congregation. She dedicated her twenty-plus years in British

Columbia to advocating for better laws to protect both women and children (Johnston, n.d.).

The staff and activities of the Alexandra orphanage and home were overseen by a board of prominent community leaders. The home was financially supported through private individual donations, like all social service organizations during this period. With various groups vying for limited resources, and with crooks who often solicited people's money for themselves, it was necessary to establish a centralized system to collect donations and distribute them to legitimate groups. In 1929, the agencies invited John Howard Toynbee Falk, who was then in Montreal, to Vancouver to conduct a survey of the metro area's charitable organizations. Falk was then invited to establish and direct the Community Chest and Councils in 1930. The Chest (later known as the United Way of the Lower Mainland) consistently supported the Alexandra Orphanage and Fresh Air Camp and the neighbourhood houses that followed. Falk was born in Liverpool and was the first cousin of Arnold Toynbee. While a student at Oxford, he volunteered at Toynbee Hall and was influenced by some of the great English social reformers, including Samuel and Henrietta Barnett, Octavia Hill, and Beatrice and Sidney Webb (Shepherd 1957).

The orphanage played an important role in the early decades of Metro Vancouver, but over time it became apparent that orphanages were not the best solution to the problems associated with parentless children, or children whose parents could not financially or emotionally support them. The board decided to close it and open a neighbourhood house in its place. It studied neighbourhood houses in other cities, such as Toronto and Chicago, and invited to Vancouver American social settlement leaders Helen Hall, then director of the Henry Street Settlement in New York City, and her husband, Paul Kellogg, editor of the *Survey Midmonthly* journal, to help organize what became Alexandra Neighbourhood House in 1938.

Two other neighbourhood houses were initiated during the Second World War, North Shore Neighbourhood House and Gordon Neighbourhood House. Their institutional roots are very different. North Shore started informally in 1939 when a couple, Hugh and Rose (née Smith) Beattie, opened their house to children in order to provide a much-needed social and gathering space in their community. During the Second World War, their community also very much needed a kindergarten for the children of men and women employed in the shipbuilding yards on the north side of Burrard Inlet, directly across from downtown Vancouver. Hugh Beattie was a janitor at the local elementary school while Rose was a housewife and took care of their six children. When their attic became too small for the children gathering there, Rose discussed the children's needs with several neighbours. They approached city council and received the use of an old building for $1 per year.

Gordon Neighbourhood House started in 1942 and was initially linked to Alexandra Neighbourhood House. Gordon was located in Vancouver's West End, an area overcrowded with people and beset by poor rooming houses. One of its early heads was Kathleen "Kay" Gorrie, who had been a concert soprano soloist in her youth before studying social work at the University of Toronto, graduating in 1924. As head of Gordon Neighbourhood House, she established summer playschools and day camps, and organized programs for seniors and cooking classes for young adults (Gorrie 1946).

Whereas the orphanage and the early Vancouver neighbourhood houses relied on the leadership and commitment of talented and concerned community leaders, they came to be heavily influenced by the emerging field of social work. The University of British Columbia started its program in 1929, fifteen years after the University of Toronto started the first social work training program in Canada. The new program was initiated by S.E. Beckett and implemented by C.W. Topping, both of whom began their professional careers as Protestant ministers influenced by the late-nineteenth- and early-twentieth-century Social Gospel movement, a collective effort to transform the economic and social structures of society as a way to build "God's kingdom on earth." It was not unusual for such men to replace a religious calling with a secular one, and both Beckett and Topping appear to have done so.

Many women social settlement leaders worked as instructors in university programs, but as the profession became more established, men were usually hired for regular academic appointments. This was not the case at UBC, as the first full-time social work instructor was Marjorie J. Smith. Professor Smith had received her bachelor's degree from the University of Minnesota and her master's degree from the University of Chicago. By the time of her 1943 appointment at UBC, she had already taught at Washington State College School of Social Work and Smith College in Massachusetts, and had worked in both the United States and Europe (Bliss 1954). She oversaw field placements of UBC students, many of them at the Gordon Neighbourhood House. Vancouver also received more than its fair share of early social workers – and neighbourhood house leaders – from Eastern Canada as well as the United States.

Laura Holland, for example, was the first professionally trained social worker in Vancouver. Dubbed one of "wise women from the East," she was invited to Vancouver to reorganize the child welfare system. She arrived in 1927 and revolutionized the Children's Aid Society (Hill 2005). She also lectured weekly in the UBC social work program, influencing many students, who often did their field placements at Alexandra and Gordon Neighbourhood Houses. Born in Toronto, Holland initially trained as a nurse and served overseas in the Canadian Army Medical Corps before returning to North America to study social work at Simmons College in Boston. She exemplified both the eastern Canadian and American influences on early neighbourhood houses in Vancouver.

Kathleen Gorrie provides another example. Gorrie was the executive director of Gordon Neighbourhood House in the mid-1940s. A 1926 graduate of the University of Toronto social work program, she served as the executive secretary of the Toronto Welfare Council, and was also a sessional faculty member in the University of Toronto social work program for almost a decade. During her tenure at Gordon, she emphasized not only work with children and their mothers – which was typical of early neighbourhood houses in Vancouver – but also work with older people. In an article in *Survey Midmonthly: Journal of Social Work* (Gorrie 1946), she described the number of people aged threescore or older who were a vital part of the house through their participation in drop-in programs, in various social clubs, and in Saturday evening jive and dance sessions – as well as in imparting some of their skills by teaching dance or giving cooking lessons to children and young adults. Gorrie left Gordon in 1949 to become head of the university settlement in Toronto. After she retired and returned to the west coast, she did some short-term work at North Shore Neighbourhood House.

Although initially focusing on women and children, the early neighbourhood houses in Vancouver quickly developed programs comparable to those of other houses in Canada, the United Kingdom, the United States, Australia, and other places throughout the world: organizing nurseries and clubs, pushing civic government to establish parks and gymnasiums, housing a public library, advocating for adequate and affordable housing, and so on. The specific programs have changed through the years in response to the needs of the local communities.

Postwar Development
As in many metropolitan areas in Canada, the postwar period in Vancouver was a time of growth and change that initiated trajectories that still influence us today. Many of these changes involved redevelopment, including that of Vancouver's downtown core, the West End (Punter 2003). Metro

Vancouver was racially and ethnically homogeneous before the Second World War and into the 1950s and 1960s. The 1931 Census of Canada, for example, lists 77.1 percent of its inhabitants as British, 13.7 percent as European, 5.3 percent as Chinese, 3.8 percent as Japanese, and 0.1 percent as Black. (It is worth noting that according to this census, Aboriginal people seem to have neither existed nor been counted.) In the 1991 census, 42 percent of the population was listed as British, 28 percent European, 19 percent Asian, 4 percent Aboriginal, 4 percent French, 3 percent Canadian, and 1 percent "Other." These demographic changes were largely due to the postwar modification of national policies regarding the acceptance of refugees and to major changes in the immigration regulations in 1962 and in the Immigration Act in 1976. Such revisions in racist attitudes toward non-Europeans made it possible for an array of immigrants and refugees from Asia, South America, India, Africa, Europe, the Middle East, and other parts of the world to settle in Vancouver.

In the 1960s, the delivery of social services became a contested issue in Vancouver. On the surface, it was a question of how to deliver services to families, children, and the poor. Maintaining the status quo would include supporting a number of existing organizations already engaged in service provision. Those advocating change supported integration of services by looking at individuals and families as a whole. Existing service provision broke families apart and required separate agencies or programs serving parents and children from the same family, for instance. Individuals themselves could also receive fragmented support from different agencies. The moderate proposal was to integrate services so as to avoid redundancy and fragmentation. The more ambitious argument against the status quo viewed individuals and families as part of local communities. This suggested not only integration of services but decentralization of service delivery to the local level, and encouraged participation of local residents in decisions about service provision in their neighbourhoods. This more ambitious program of decentralization and resident participation evolved during the 1960s and '70s in Vancouver. These were tumultuous times, and their legacy can still be seen today.

The neighbourhood house movement had an important influence on the direction and implementation of these ideas in Vancouver, and its involvement in the changing provision of social services had important consequences for the local neighbourhood house movement itself. This can be seen most clearly in the dramatic growth in the number of neighbourhood houses. After Gordon Neighbourhood House opened in 1942, twenty years passed without any new neighbourhood houses in the city. Between 1962 and 1978, however, seven new neighbourhood houses opened in Vancouver, starting with Cedar Cottage in 1963, Kiwassa in 1967, and Kitsilano in 1972. The wave of growth crested in the mid-1970s with South Vancouver opening in 1975, Mount Pleasant in 1976, Frog Hollow in 1977, and Little Mountain in 1978. Less immediately visible is the influence on the kinds of services provided by neighbourhood houses. This is partly reflected in the decision to change the name of the Alexandra Community Activities Society to the Neighbourhood Services Association (NSA) in 1966. The activities promoted as part of the move toward integration, decentralization, and local resident participation can still be seen in the programming of neighbourhood houses today.

Ascent of the Local Neighbourhood

Political Reorganization of Social Service Provision in Vancouver

The 1960s and 1970s were a period of tremendous experimentation and change in the political organization of Vancouver. One place this can be seen is in the changes to the provision of social services that took place at this time. The seeds of these changes grew from a strategy initiated by a group of local social service professionals and reformers in the mid-sixties who came to be known as the Action Slate (Mitchell 2008, 69; Clague 1984, 22). The group implemented a strategy of nominating themselves for election to the boards of local charities and non-profits. Their aim was to shake up the existing approach to social service provision by directing work toward integration, decentralization, and citizen engagement. The work of the Action Slate suggests a kind of challenger strategy that can lead to change in institutionalized settings, and future developments bear this out. One of its members, Norm Levi, became minister of human resources in the 1970s and ushered in a dramatic reorganization of social service provision along reformist lines. He established Community Resource Boards (CRBs) made up of citizens elected from their neighbourhoods, which took control of the administration of social services. Looking back today, this period of reorganization is one of the most interesting in Vancouver's history, particularly with regard to the provision of social services.[2]

At the city level, two important developments took place in the mid-1960s. First, in 1966, the city established the first Social Planning Department in Vancouver's history. The new department was created in cooperation with the United Community Services (UCS) (previously the Community

Chest and Councils and precursor to the United Way), which operated its own social planning department. Together, these social planners demarcated local areas that set the blueprints for the neighbourhoods in Vancouver we take for granted today. Second, a Social Development Committee of the city council made up of elected representatives of all the major social service agencies and a Joint Technical Committee made up senior staff of social service agencies were convened.

Along with these developments at the city level, an effort to coordinate services at the neighbourhood level was initiated by the UCS. The UCS adopted reformers' concerns over the fragmented nature of service provision, and addressed these with a program called the Local Area Approach (LAA). UCS social planner Ernie Hill divided the city into twenty-two local areas with the intention of coordinating local services within these areas through community engagement (Mitchell 2008). According to a 1965 Community Chest press release, the LAA would combine "health, social welfare, education and recreation services in a concerted attack on the social problems in selected areas of Vancouver ... Emphasis will be on coordinated and integrated services in place of fragmented, unilateral services ... Local community planning and self-help will be stressed" (quoted in Clague 1984, 22).

The idea of coordinating services locally can sound ideal, but perhaps a bit abstract as well. Fortunately, Michael Clague (1988, 5–6) has provided a detailed description of what the LAA meant in practice for one area, the Grandview-Woodland neighbourhood. First, the UCS organized a local area council made up of community service workers and local residents with the mandate of improving local social services. This one council soon split into two different councils, one made up of residents and the other of service providers. A community development worker was hired to work with the councils to help them achieve the goals of coordinating services locally and helping the local community guide service provision decisions and goals. A social planner from the newly formed city Social Planning Department coordinated the area service team. Clague's (1988) description captures the commitment to making a change and the significant amount of organizing involved in implementing the ideas of the LAA. It also captures the close collaboration between the new Social Planning Department and the UCS. Together, they set up councils like the one in Grandview-Woodland in each of the twenty-two city neighbourhoods outlined by Ernie Hill. The LAA moved ahead as intended in the late 1960s.

In 1972, these early initiatives toward local control were realized politically across the province after the election of a left-leaning, labour-oriented

New Democratic Party (NDP) government. This was the first new government in fifty years, and the first-ever NDP government in British Columbia. The new government paid particular attention to revamping the provision of social services under the leadership of Norm Levi, former Action Slate member and the new minister of human resources. Levi's most profound accomplishment was the creation of CRBs across the province. These boards set community priorities for non-statutory social services and made recommendations to the minister about the allocation of funds to community organizations for these services. Each CRB had its own locally elected board of directors and management staff. The Vancouver Resource Board (VRB) also handled statutory services, took over children's aid and the city Welfare Department, and provided grants to community organizations to fund locally developed services. The VRB was made up of representatives from the neighbourhood CRBs and appointed members from the city, the school board, and the ministry (Clague 1997, 96–97).

The establishment of the CRBs represented a radical devolution of control and authority from the province to the local level. Michael Clague recognized this: "In so many ways the community resource boards ... represented the full realization of the pioneering ideas and experiments of the 1960s: decentralizing services to the local community; coordinating, integrating, and rationalizing them; and creating a local political accountability for human care services to the whole community where none had existed before (or since)" (Clague 1997, 98). The election of the conservative Social Credit provincial government in 1975 brought with it the demise of the CRBs. Their legacy persisted, however, in the establishment of local community-based organizations. Clague (1997) has discussed this legacy in the creation of community resource societies that emerged from the non-metropolitan CRBs that formed multi-service agencies in their communities that still operate today. In Vancouver, the LAA combined with the creation of the CRBs and the community development movement led to the emergence of new neighbourhood houses across the city.

Community Development and Neighbourhood Houses in Vancouver

In 1956, Margaret Mitchell, a young social worker employed at Alexandra Neighbourhood House, took a leave to join a six-month Canadian Red Cross mission to Austria. Her work there included community development among Hungarian refugees crossing the border into Austria. This experience had a profound influence on Mitchell. In her 2008 memoir, she describes returning to work in Vancouver:

I began to assess my social work career. I had always enjoyed working with people, but I realize much of it involved superficial activities. I now wanted to become more involved in social change ... I thought about the community development work I had done with refugees in Vienna, and wondered how I could use my experience there to help people in Vancouver. (Mitchell 2008, 69)

Mitchell devoted herself to community development work in Vancouver through the 1960s and '70s. Her work began with demonstration projects associated with the LAA, which led to a position as community development coordinator for Vancouver, responsible for leading a team of community development workers across the city.[3] A large part of Mitchell's community development work was done as an employee of the NSA, which oversaw operations at Alexandra and Gordon Neighbourhood Houses. Her community development work had an important influence on the neighbourhood house movement in Vancouver because of this affiliation with the association.

Mitchell's affiliation with neighbourhood houses in Vancouver is notable because the relationship between community organizing and neighbourhood houses was rocky in many parts of North America. Saul Alinsky was perhaps the most famous community organizer of this period. In the United States, he contributed to the difficult, sometimes conflict-ridden, relationship between the community development movement and neighbourhood houses. A number of well-known confrontations between Alinsky and neighbourhood houses have been documented by Judith Trolander (1982). Alinsky's work and ideas were well known among community workers in Vancouver. Despite this, and perhaps because of Mitchell's role as a neighbourhood house employee, the community development and neighbourhood house movements in Vancouver were intimately intertwined. This is not to suggest that differences in approach to community work did not exist. These differences were debated within the neighbourhood house movement rather than criticisms coming from outside the movement. As a result, the community development approach merged with the neighbourhood house approach. This merger can be seen by looking at Mitchell's community development work, beginning with the Area Development Project (ADP).

In 1964, the UCS initiated a three-year ADP with the goal of exploring new approaches to the provision of social services. As described in the Red Door Report (Mitchell 1968, 2), an objective of the project was "the social development of the neighbourhood, that is development concerned with human resources and with social institutions established to meet human needs ... They were also charged with developing demonstration services to meet assessed needs and operating a neighbourhood service centre, which later became known as the 'Red Door.'" Mitchell, an employee of the NSA, was seconded to the project and led the ADP team, which included two social workers, social work students, a nursery school teacher, and administrative and clerical support.

The Red Door demonstration project was conducted in the Riley Park area, close to the first social housing project in Vancouver, known as Little Mountain. One thing that comes through in the demonstration project report is the neighbourhood houses' contribution of a community development approach that emphasized the role of residents in the planning and management of services in their local area. The UCS placed emphasis on decentralization in order to develop inter-agency structures for coordination of services in the local areas. UCS social planners hoped that local residents would eventually become engaged in planning, but did not incorporate a community development approach into the project. It was Mitchell's influence that introduced a resident engagement component. This is summed up by Mitchell (1968, 22) in the Red Door Report:

> There is a continuing tendency for organizations, institutions, and political groups to make decisions for populations or constituent groups rather than with these groups. There is still little provision within institutions to permit clientele to share in making decisions, taking action towards and participating in a variety of roles to create specialized programs to satisfy their needs and help them cope with difficulties in their lives.

Mitchell rectified this problem by combining the top-down approach of the UCS with her community development ideas. This can also be seen in the major tasks of the project outlined in the Red Door Report (Mitchell 1968, 15): 1) to assist in bringing neighbours together around common interests and concerns; 2) to assist them in determining neighbourhood characteristics, needs, and problems; 3) to encourage local citizens in planning and development of appropriate programs and services; 4) to collaborate with existing organizations within the neighbourhood; 5) to facilitate the establishment of neighbourhood councils or action groups where there are none in existence; and 6) to bring together professionals working at the neighbourhood level in order to coordinate existing services.

The core of the UCS agenda is included in points four through six, while the first three points clearly reflect local resident engagement from the community development approach advocated by Mitchell. The importance of empowering residents as citizens can be seen throughout the Red Door Report. Alinsky and other community development thinkers are quoted at length. Important to our discussion here, the move to engage local residents through community development was due to the influence of the neighbourhood house movement in Vancouver.

Neighbourhood houses were undergoing a transformation in their vision at the time of the ADP. Central to that transformation was the leadership of Elmer Helm, a social worker committed to the neighbourhood house movement who was first hired as assistant executive director and then became the executive director of Gordon Neighbourhood House from 1953 to 1966 (Elmer Helm, personal communication, 2012). Helm earned his Master of Social Work degree at UBC in 1952, writing a thesis that examined the role and function of Alexandra Neighbourhood House in the neighbourhood. The thesis starts from the point of view of the neighbourhood house, emphasizing the need for the institution to adapt to the changing needs of the neighbourhood. To this, Helm adds that for the institution to successfully adapt, local residents must take a leadership role in the activities of the neighbourhood house (Helm 1952).

While Mitchell's approach started from the ground-level aspects of community development and resident engagement, Helm focused his attention on building the institutional and physical infrastructure of the neighbourhood house movement in Vancouver. In 1966, three neighbourhood houses were operating in the city: Alexandra, Gordon, and the new Cedar Cottage Neighbourhood House, which opened in 1962. These three houses were all part of the Alexandra Community Activities Society, but operated more or less independently. Helm spearheaded the move to integrate the three separate organizations into a single entity and to rename the society as the NSA. He took over as the association's executive director.

It is important to note that, while envisioning the growth of the new association, Helm recognized Mitchell's community development work and integrated it into the association. This is clear in his first director's report (Helm 1967), where he recognizes the ascent of the local neighbourhood:

The spotlight today is on neighbourhoods. The neighbourhood services of the Area Development Project have shown the effectiveness of an area approach and Mrs. Mitchell, on loan from this society, has played a leading role in this project ... Our recent reorganization makes it possible for us to be more effective than ever in extending services into local areas.

Helm goes on to discuss the importance of resident engagement in all the work of neighbourhood houses: "Our conviction of the importance of involving citizens and of developing local community responsibility is reflected in all our services." And the combined experience of Mitchell in the ADP and the commitment to engaging citizens became a founding mission of the association:

> In the reorganization of the NSA "Community Development" was set out as one of our primary functions. Last fall, a joint meeting with the United Community Services were held and a new service definition called "Citizen Development" came into being. At these meetings it was clarified that coordination and planning were the functions of the UCS and citizen development was the role of NSA.

By 1968, when the Red Door Report was written, it was clear that Mitchell's role in both the community development and neighbourhood house movement had led to a mutual influence in Vancouver:

> The philosophy and practices of Vancouver neighbourhood houses had an influence on neighbourhood approaches that were added to the ADP. Neighbourhood teamwork and multi-family services which were developed in the Joint Family Services Project were familiar to both the director of ADP and the Director of Neighbourhood Services (Mitchell). The Director of Neighbourhood Services had been an active leader in the formation of both the Vancouver Association of Neighbourhood Services and a similar Canadian association. In both these voluntary organizations, she urged that the major priority be given to community development and out-reach services. (Mitchell 1968, 8–9)

This captures the intertwined working of the community development and neighbourhood house movements in Vancouver.

The collaboration between Mitchell and her community development work with Helm and the neighbourhood house movement continued with an intensified community development project from 1968 to 1974. After the end of the ADP, the NSA brought Mitchell back as the director of community development. The work included leading a team of three community development workers and assessing needs for more community development work. Community development workers were also hired by the city's Social Planning Department and the UCS. Seeking greater efficiency, in 1969 all three parties agreed to have the NSA take sole responsibility for community development. To do this, the NSA established a new Community Development Department that operated from 1969 to 1974. The new department had from nine to seventeen individuals at any one time working in neighbourhoods across Vancouver. The department's work has been documented in the report *Do Not Rest in Peace!*, written by Mitchell and published by the NSA in 1975.

New Neighbourhood Houses in Vancouver

The dual influence of Elmer Helm's interest in growing the social infrastructure of neighbourhoods through the development of new neighbourhood houses and Margaret Mitchell's keen focus on community-led initiatives can be seen in the opening of seven new houses in Vancouver in the 1960s and '70s.

The opening of the Frog Hollow Neighbourhood House in 1977 is a good example of how Margaret Mitchell's community development work contributed to the local initiative to open a neighbourhood house.[4] From 1966 to 1974, four community development workers contributed to local resident engagement in the neighbourhood, beginning in the Skeena Terrace Housing Project, a new affordable housing project. Tensions had developed between homeowners and tenants, and the first community workers sought to improve relations by bringing members of the two groups together to discuss neighbourhood improvement. This initial group soon became the Frog Hollow Committee, and began operating the Frog Hollow Information Centre temporarily from a vacant space at the local school. The space became known as the Frog Hollow House, and included a decentralized team of volunteers, youth workers, and welfare workers.

The group struggled initially to find a permanent location, even operating out of a member's basement for a time. In 1973, it secured a storefront location, hired a coordinator, and continued to develop local services while also operating as a casual people place staffed by volunteers. Throughout this time, the new coordinator of the Frog Hollow Information Centre worked closely with Mitchell to involve residents in activities, while also securing a Local Initiative Program project for seniors and establishing a local newspaper. Four years later, in 1977, Frog Hollow became an official neighbourhood house and joined the NSA. This step included moving to a new location owned by the association, at East Broadway, close to Frog Hollow's first location at the local school.

The origin of the Frog Hollow Neighbourhood House provides an example of a community development–supported and local resident–led initiative leading to the opening of a new neighbourhood house. Most of the seven new neighbourhood houses established in this period developed in a similar way, though each reflected the unique aspects of its neighbourhood. Little Mountain Neighbourhood House emerged from the same neighbourhood where Mitchell's Red Door ADP was operating. In South Vancouver, local residents were engaged through the LAA and the election of the CRB. After the demise of the CRBs, they formed a storefront information centre that quickly joined the NSA as South Vancouver Neighbourhood House in 1975. Kiwassa Neighbourhood House grew out of the Kiwanis wives' clubs, who were concerned with the recreational needs of young girls.[5] The group started in 1949 and grew into a social service organization for girls over time. In the 1960s, the organization followed the local area turn, and directed its attention to the local neighbourhood in north Grandview-Woodland. With mentorship from North Vancouver Neighbourhood House, it adopted the neighbourhood house model in 1967.

In all these cases, the community development approach spearheaded by Mitchell resulted in the desire of local residents to formalize the work with the establishment of a neighbourhood house serving the local area. In this way, local resident motivations drove the establishment of these new houses. The origins of Kitsilano Neighbourhood House provide a contrast, showing that the turn to LAAs was not always the result of community development work.[6] As early as 1968, a survey of Kitsilano residents showed a desire for a neighbourhood house in the western part of the neighbourhood around Yew and Vine streets. The neighbourhood had seen a lot of changes at that time, including an influx of young adults, over 3,000 of whom moved into the neighbourhood in the late 1960s.

The desire in the area for services that neighbourhood houses typically provide was becoming clear. Elmer Helm was aware of this and drew attention to the need for a new Kitsilano Neighbourhood House to combat youth alienation, family breakdown, and anti-social behaviour resulting from poverty and urban life. The provincial government, concerned about seniors living in the area, supported the establishment of a neighbourhood house that would also serve as a recreation centre for seniors in the area.

In 1968, the NSA purchased a yellow heritage home at 2325 West Seventh Avenue known as the Hay House. In those early years, the Hay House operated as a western satellite location for Alexandra Neighbourhood House. Its immediate neighbour was St. George's Greek Orthodox Church, located at the corner of Seventh and Vine. The church had been the centre of the Greek community in Kitsilano since its erection in 1930. In 1971, St. George's planned to relocate and offered to sell the building to the NSA. The expansion of services associated with the purchase of the church building initiated the development of Kitsilano Neighbourhood House. The area including Hay House and St. George's Church was rezoned for the neighbourhood house in 1971. After some remodelling, it opened its doors in 1972 and formally began operating as Kitsilano Neighbourhood House in 1974.

The development of a new neighbourhood house in the western part of Kitsilano was not without critics, chief among them the Kitsilano Ratepayers Association, one of the oldest community organizations in the neighbourhood. The primary interests of the Ratepayers Association were encouraging the development of single-family homes in the area, discouraging rezoning for non-residential uses, and protecting property values. It did not see a new neighbourhood house as fitting its vision of Kitsilano. In a letter to city hall, it described itself as "a group of protesting rate payers appealing to you to set aside the decision to use the present buildings on the site of the old Greek Orthodox Church at 7th and Vine as a neighbourhood house." The letter included a number of objections to the rezoning and a petition signed by forty-five local ratepayers. Interestingly, one of the ongoing concerns of the Ratepayers Association was the influx of young people to the neighbourhood – the hippies of Kitsilano. Today, Kitsilano's countercultural history is celebrated in festivals and events, but the hippies were not always welcome. In her history of the Kitsilano Ratepayers Association, Adriane Carr (1980) notes that the association worried that hippies represented the wrong type of resident for Kitsilano. Tensions between the City of Vancouver and youth were high in the early 1970s, peaking in the summer of 1971. That August, the *Georgia Straight* weekly paper called for a countercultural rally in Gastown to protest drug laws and recent drug raids in the city. Estimates range from 1,000 to 2,000 for the number of young people who took part in the rally. The large gathering soon led to clashes with police followed by arrests, and was later memorialized by the artist Stan Douglas. Mayor Tom Campbell came down strongly against the youth and hippies. The Kitsilano Ratepayers shared their concerns over youth bringing an unwelcome element to their neighbourhood.

It was during this period that the NSA began taking steps to form the Kitsilano Neighbourhood House on West Seventh Avenue at Vine Street. At the meeting regarding the rezoning of the new neighbourhood house, Mayor Campbell linked the house with the countercultural movement, de- . claring that it would be a "crash pad" for hippies. Despite opposition from the Kitsilano Ratepayers and Mayor Campbell, the rezoning application passed with support from a more progressive city council. Kitsilano Neighbourhood House never became the crash pad the mayor feared. Instead, it became a key piece of social infrastructure in the neighbourhood.

The origins of the new neighbourhood houses that developed in the 1960s and 1970s show the intertwined ideals of community development and citizen-led initiatives combined with an interest in establishing social infrastructure with lasting impact for the neighbourhood house movement. Unlike Kitsilano Neighbourhood House, most of the new neighbourhood houses established during this period had their origins in community development work that engaged local residents. The case of Kitsilano Neighbourhood House shows that establishing some stability, literally in the physical structures of the neighbourhood house, was also important to the neighbourhood house movement. The securing of physical locations provided the infrastructure that has enabled these neighbourhood houses to persist for more than forty years.

Establishing Formal Organizations with a Community Development Ethos

Since the period of growth in the Vancouver neighbourhood house movement in the 1960s and 1970s, neighbourhood houses have remained an important part of the social infrastructure of local communities. After Little Mountain Neighbourhood House in 1978, six new neighbourhood houses were established in Metro Vancouver: Collingwood Neighbourhood House (1985), Burnaby Neighbourhood House (1996), Oak Avenue Neighbourhood Hub (2004), the new Alexandra Neighbourhood House (2009) in South Surrey, Downtown Eastside Neighbourhood House (2009), and Marpole Neighbourhood House (2019).

In many ways, these new neighbourhood houses have followed a path of development similar to that of Kitsilano Neighbourhood House. For instance, Downtown Eastside Neighbourhood House started as a satellite location of Gordon Neighbourhood House in 2005. After four years of

operating in conjunction with Gordon, a small, independent neighbourhood house was established in a rented storefront on Hastings Street in
2009. Similarly, the new Alexandra Neighbourhood House was operated as
a satellite camp in South Surrey for youth involved in neighbourhood houses
in Vancouver since the opening of the first neighbourhood house in 1938.
What was once a remote area where youth could experience the outdoors
slowly changed and is now a residentially dense part of Metro Vancouver.
Over time, the camp began operating year-round and providing the services of a typical neighbourhood house. In 2009, Camp Alexandra officially became the new Alexandra Neighbourhood House (after the original
Alexandra Neighbourhood House burned down in 1975).

The Collingwood and Burnaby Neighbourhood Houses did not develop
through affiliation, but they did follow from the identification of need in a
neighbourhood for a place-based community organization. In Collingwood,
this need was triggered by development in the lead-up to the 1986 World's
Fair, Expo 86.[7] The SkyTrain commuter rail was proposed as part of a new
state-of-the-art public transit system. The proposal galvanized local residents in Collingwood, leading to a series of meetings with City of Vancouver
planners. The discussions resulted in support for the new Collingwood
Neighbourhood House, initially located in a rented storefront in the neighbourhood. Burnaby Neighbourhood House evolved from the work of a
group of residents and service providers in Burnaby who had experience
working at neighbourhood houses. Antonia Beck led the group and became
Burnaby Neighbourhood House's first executive director. Beck had grown
up alongside neighbourhood houses in Vancouver, attending programs and
summer camps as a youth and becoming a staff member of Mount Pleasant
and South Vancouver neighbourhood houses. A resident of the Vancouver
suburb of Burnaby, she saw the need for a community-based organization
based on the neighbourhood house model in the area. She organized local
residents, found a storefront location in South Burnaby, and established
the new neighbourhood house. Figure 1.1 shows a poster for an information
meeting in its early days. The group also had the support of the Ministry
of Child, Family and Community Services (the predecessor of today's
Ministry of Children and Family Development) community developer and a
handful of service providers who were working in Burnaby but had previously worked at neighbourhood houses in Vancouver.

Today, the new South Burnaby Neighbourhood House is located in a
dense area near a major transit line, and a new North Burnaby Neighbourhood House has been operating for just over a year. Most recently, Marpole

FIGURE 1.1
Poster for an information meeting

Neighbourhood House was initiated by the City of Vancouver, which provided a space in a neighbourhood that was seen as needing this type of community-based organization. The operations of the new house were initially managed by the nearby South Vancouver Neighbourhood House with the intention of turning management over to a local staff and resident board.[8] Each of these affiliated locations that developed into neighbourhood houses continues the model of resident engagement in the operation and direction of the organization.

Today in Metro Vancouver, neighbourhoods that need place-based services are often identified externally by city planners or other leaders in the neighbourhood house movement. Despite this external planning approach, the community development ethos that is a core element of the neighbourhood house movement in Metro Vancouver has driven the development process in all the new houses. A discussion with any neighbourhood house staff member, volunteer, or participant will highlight this essential aspect of practice in the neighbourhood house model. This balance of grassroots engagement and institutional growth developed out of the tension between ground-up and top-down approaches to growing the neighbourhood house movement in Vancouver and the unique contributions and collaboration of Margaret Mitchell and Elmer Helm.

Metro Vancouver Neighbourhood Houses in Comparison with Other Places

How does the history of neighbourhood houses in Vancouver compare and connect with that of other places? Canada was a latecomer to the social settlement movement. By the time the first settlement house opened in Toronto, the centre of the movement had shifted to the United States. The American movement influenced the development of Canadian neighbourhood houses. Thus, when Vancouver established its first neighbourhood house, it took a very different historical route.

Although early Canadian settlement house leaders, particularly those in Toronto, knew of Toynbee Hall and the reform work of Samuel and Henrietta Barnett by at least the late 1880s (Irving, Parsons, and Bellamy 1995), Toynbee Hall's influence on the Canadian social settlement movement was minimal. Instead, the two eastern Canadian champions of neighbourhood houses, James Joseph Kelso and William Lyon Mackenzie King, were influenced mainly by Jane Addams. Addams was no stranger to Canadians, neither in her writings nor in her lectures. In 1909, for example, she gave an address on settlements at the International Congress of Women held in Toronto. The National Federation of Settlements in the United States held its annual conference in Toronto in 1924, and this gathering gave Canadians greater exposure to American settlement leaders, including Addams, Graham Taylor, and Robert A. Woods (Parsons 1986). And while Henrietta Barnett undertook a North American tour in 1920, during which she gave lectures in Canada, Vancouverites seem to have been more influenced by their American rather than British ties, despite their colonial past.

The religious influence in the American social settlement movement did have an impact on the early neighbourhood houses in Toronto and some other Canadian cities. As seen in the example of Libby Carson and the Presbyterian Church, neighbourhood houses growing out of Christian or Jewish missions and charity endeavours were not unusual in the Dominion of Canada. In contrast to the early history of neighbourhood houses in Toronto, Vancouver NHs had a distinct non-sectarian origin, and the first three neighbourhood houses in Vancouver were, from their incorporation, secular. None of them originated as a university settlement, even though the University of British Columbia was founded in 1908. Instead, neighbourhood houses in Vancouver were deeply rooted in grassroots community development. Almost all those established after the 1960s were due to the collaborative efforts of local residents, and some were initiated by professional community developers and social planners.

Unlike many early British and American settlement houses, Canadian neighbourhood houses in general did not have a clear mandate for social reform and political advocacy. This is not to say that they were politically isolated or unresponsive to the concerns of their communities, but they do not appear to have taken the initiative in larger political matters. They did, however, work with civic organizations on matters of family welfare and housing, and provided opportunities for citizens to engage in advocacy of political and social change. They supported, for example, the 1950 Ban the Bomb petition campaign, but controversy arose the same year over the rental of house space for a communist speaker sponsored by the Women's International League for Peace and Freedom. In the end, it was decided that Vancouver neighbourhood houses should not be used for open public meetings of a "political or religious nature," but that groups of different political stances would be allowed to use space even though their positions might offend the sensibilities of some individuals. This non-political tradition was observed in NHs in Vancouver despite their grassroots orientation. Local residents who supported the formation of NHs placed more emphasis on local issues and needs than on the larger social problem.

Right from the beginning, Vancouver neighbourhood houses did not have any outside "settler" residing in the premises. Paid staff were employed to operate the houses. The first one, the original Alexandra Neighbourhood House, was converted from an orphanage. It inherited its infrastructure, including governance and administration, from its predecessor. Professional social workers were the key operators of NHs in Vancouver, particularly at the leadership level, until the 1980s. Operated by paid staff hired to provide services to local residents, NHs in Vancouver tended to focus more attention on facilitating basic social services and community integration than on political reform.

In summary, neighbourhood houses in Vancouver are a continuation of the 130-year-old social settlement movement that started with the establishment of Toynbee Hall in 1884. The movement has evolved and manifested differently in different historical eras and social contexts. As latecomers to the movement, Vancouver neighbourhood houses are largely grassroots-oriented, secular, and professionally initiated and operated. They have kept the spirit and tradition of the Reverend Samuel Barnett's vision of settlement houses as a mechanism of connection. In the following chapters, we examine further how they have actualized this vision and accomplished the settlement house mission of bridging the diverse – not only in terms of class but also in terms of ethnicity and immigrant status – population in the contemporary urban neighbourhood.

Notes

1 See also "The Five Social Settlements of the Presbyterian Church in Canada," available online from the Canadian Institute for Historical Microreproduction Microfiche Series (Monographs). https://www.canadiana.ca/view/oocihm.99423/1?r=0&s=1.

2 Michael Clague has provided the most thorough chronicle of this period in Vancouver's history (Clague 1997, 1988, 1984). Clague was an active community development worker himself and often at the centre of the changes taking place in Vancouver. Being on the ground at the time, he recognized the importance of the changes. His accounts provide important insights into the interrelated roles of political dynamics and neighbourhood house growth. Other accounts can be found in Mitchell 2008 and Meggs and Mickleburgh 2012.

3 This community development work has been documented in Mitchell's memoir, *No Laughing Matter* (2008), as well as in two reports written in part by her (Mitchell 1968, 1975). Clague (1984) also discusses aspects of the community development work done by Mitchell and her team.

4 This work is documented in *Do Not Rest in Peace!* (1975, 17–23).

5 The history of Kiwassa Neighbourhood House is documented in Alleuva 1993.

6 This history of Kitsilano Neighbourhood House is documented in Lauer and Reisz 2012.

7 The development of Collingwood Neighbourhood House is documented in Sandercock and Attili 2009.

8 Marpole Neighbourhood House opened its doors on May 22, 2019, and at the time of writing is still being managed by South Vancouver Neighbourhood House.

References

Abel, Emily K. 1979. "Toynbee Hall, 1884–1914." *Social Service Review* 53 (4): 606–32.

Addams, Jane. 1961. *Twenty Years at Hull House*. New York: Signet Classics.

–. 1999. *Twenty Years at Hull House*. Boston: Bedford/St. Martin's.

Alleuva, Oscar. 1993. "Organizational Change as a Catalyst for Community Development: A Case Study of the Relocation of the Kiwassa Neighbourhood House." Master's thesis, University of British Columbia.

Barman, Jean. 2007. "Erasing Indigenous Indigeneity in Vancouver." *BC Studies* Autumn (155): 3–30.

Bliss, John Donald MacQueen. 1954. "A History of the School of Social Work of the University of British Columbia, 1929–1954." Master's thesis, University of British Columbia.

Boyd, Monica, and Michael Vickers. 2000. *100 Years of Immigration in Canada, Canadian Social Trends,* edited by Statistics Canada. Ottawa: Statistics Canada.

Carr, Adriane. 1980. "The Development of Neighbourhood in Kitsilano: Ideas, Actors and the Landscape." Master's thesis. University of British Columbia.

Carson, Mina. 2001. "American Settlement Houses: The First Half Century." In *Settlement, Social Change and Community Action,* edited by Ruth Gilchrist and Tony Jeffs, 34–53. London and Philadelphia: Jessica Kingsley.

Clague, Michael. 1997. "Thirty Turbulent Years: Community Development and the Organization of Health and Social Services in British Columbia." In *Community Organizing: Canadian Experiences,* edited by Brian Wharf and Michael Clague, 91–112. Toronto: Oxford University Press.

–. 1988. *Creating the Britannia Centre.* Vancouver: Britannia Community Services Centre.

–. 1984. *Reforming Human Services: The Experience of the Community Resource Boards in BC.* Vancouver: UBC Press.

Ehrenreich, John H. 1985. *The Altruistic Imagination: A History of Social Work and Social Policy in the United States.* Ithaca, NY: Cornell University Press.

Ferguson, G. Tower. 1926. "The Relations of a Social Settlement to Community Life." *Public Health Journal* 17 (3): 129–32.

Fraser, Derek. 1984. *The Evolution of the British Welfare State.* Houndmills, Basingstoke, UK: Macmillan.

Gorrie, Kathleen. 1946. "Life Begins at Forty Plus." *Survey Midmonthly: Journal of Social Work* 82: 112–14.

Government of British Columbia. 1891. *Statutes of the Province of British Columbia.* Victoria, BC: Lieutenant-Governor.

Gutstein, Don. 1975. *Vancouver Ltd.* Toronto: James Lorimer.

Harold, Troper. 2013. "Immigration in Canada." In *The Canadian Encyclopedia,* edited by Eli Yarhi. Toronto: Historica Canada.

Helm, Elmer. 1952. "Alexandra Neighbourhood House: A Survey of the Origins and Development of a Vancouver Institution in Relation to its Local Environment." Master's thesis, University of British Columbia.

–. 1967. "Report of the Executive Director." *74th Annual Report of the Neighbourhood Services Association of Greater Vancouver.* Vancouver: Neighbourhood Services Association of Greater Vancouver.

Heyworth, Elspeth, Jean Palmer, and Florence Philpott. 1986. *The Story of the Toronto Settlement House Movement.* Toronto: Toronto Association of Neighbourhood Services.

Hill, Mary A. 2005. "Laura Holland." In *Canadian Encyclopedia of Canadian Social Work,* edited by Francis J. Turner, 180–81. Waterloo, ON: Wilfrid Laurier University Press.

Hunter, Robert. 1902. "The Relation between Social Settlements and Charity Organization." *Journal of Political Economy* 11 (1): 75–88.

International Federation of Settlements and Neighbourhood Centers. n.d. "Members." https://ifsnetwork.org/ifs-membership/members/.

Irving, Allan, Harriet Parsons, and Donald Bellamy, eds. 1995. *Neighbours: Three Social Settlements in Downtown Toronto.* Toronto: Canadian Scholars' Press.

James, Cathy. 2001. "Reforming Reform: Toronto's Settlement House Movement 1900–20." *Canadian Historical Review* 82 (1): 55–90.

Jennison, Mary. 1969. *Study of the Canadian Settlement Movement.* Toronto: McLean Foundation.

Johnston, Susan J. 1998. "Bowes, Sarah." In *Dictionary of Canadian Biography,* vol. 14. Toronto/Quebec: University of Toronto/Université Laval/Canadian Museum of History. http://www.biographi.ca/en/bio/bowes_sarah_14E.html.

Jones, Alexandra Mae. 2019. "Toronto and Vancouver Improve in Cost of Living Survey." *CTV News,* July 4, 2019. https://www.ctvnews.ca/canada/toronto-and -vancouver-improve-in-cost-of-living-survey-1.4483857.

Juliani, Richard N. 2007. "Social Reform through Social Service: The Settlement Movement in South Philadelphia." *Pennsylvania Legacies* 7 (2): 22–29.

Lauer, Sean R., and Maya Reisz. 2012. *A Place on the Corner: Kits House and the Kitsilano Community.* Vancouver: Association of Neighbourhood Houses of BC.

Lissak, R.S. 1989. *Pluralism and Progressives: Hull House and the New Immigrants, 1890–1919.* Chicago: University of Chicago Press.

MacDonald, Norbert. 1977. "The Canadian Pacific Railway and Vancouver's Development to 1900." *BC Studies* Autumn 1977 (35): 3–35.

Matthews, John, and James Kimmis. 2001. "Development of the English Settlement Movement." In *Settlement, Social Change and Community Action: Good Neighbours,* edited by Ruth Gilchrist and Tony Jeffs, 54–68. London and Philadelphia: Jessica Kingsley.

Matthews-Jones, Lucinda. 2017. "Settling at Home: Gender and Class in the Room Biographies of Toynbee Hall, 1883–1914." *Victorian Studies* 60 (1): 29–52.

Meacham, Standish. 1987. *Toynbee Hall and Social Reform 1880–1914: The Search for Community.* New Haven, CT: Yale University Press.

Meggs, Geoff, and Rod Mickleburgh. 2012. *The Art of the Impossible: Dave Barrett and the NDP in Power: 1972–1975.* Vancouver: Harbour.

Mitchell, Margaret. 2008. *No Laughing Matter: Adventure, Activism and Politics.* Vancouver: Granville Island.

–. 1975. *Do Not Rest in Peace!* Vancouver: Neighbourhood Services Association.

–. 1968. *The Red Door: A Report on Neighbourhood Services. Vancouver: Area Development Project and United Community Services.* Vancouver: United Way.

Morrow, Henry McFarlene. 1948. "The Community Services of First United Church: A Case-Study of the Relation of the Ministry of the Church, Social Work, and Neighbourhood Rehabilitation." Master's thesis, University of British Columbia.

Nicols, Elsie. 1898. "The College Settlement Movement." *Vassar Miscellany* 27 (8): 385–90.

Parsons, Harriet. 1986. "Evolution of a Canadian Federation of Settlements." In *Hundred Years of Settlements and Neighbourhood Centres in North America and Europe,* edited by Herman Nijenhuis, 66. Utrecht, NL: International Federation of Settlements and Neighbourhood Centers.

Punter, John. 2003. *The Vancouver Achievement: Urban Planning and Design.* Vancouver: UBC Press.

Purvey, Diane. 1991. "Alexandra Orphanage and Families in Crisis in Vancouver, 1892–1938." In *Dimensions of Childhood: Essays on the History of Children and Youths in Canada,* edited by Russell Charles Smandych, Gordon Dodds, and Alvin A.J. Esau, 107–33. Winnipeg, MB: Legal Research Institute.

Reinders, Robert C. 1982. "Toynbee Hall and the American Settlement Movement." *Social Service Review* 56 (1): 39–54.

Rousmaniere, John P. 1970. "Cultural Hybrid in the Slums: The College Woman and the Settlement House, 1889–1894." *American Quarterly* 22 (1): 45–66.

Sandercock, Leonie, and Giovanni Attili. 2009. *Where Strangers Become Neighbours: Integrating Immigrants in Vancouver, Canada.* New York: Springer.

Scheuer, J. 1985. "Origins of the Settlement House Movement," Excerpted from *Legacy of Light: University Settlement's First Century* by Jeffrey Scheuer. VCU Libraries Social Welfare History Project. http://socialwelfare.library.vcu.edu/settlement-houses/origins-of-the-settlement-house-movement.

Shepherd, William P. 1957. "Genesis of the Montreal Council of Social Agencies." Master's thesis, McGill University.

Tennant, Margaret. 2005. "Race, Class, and Health: School Medical Inspection and 'Healthy' Children in British Columbia, 1890–1930." In *Children's Health Issues in Historical Perspective: International Historical Perspectives,* edited by Cheryl Krasnick Warsh and Veronica Strong-Boag, 267–86. Waterloo, ON: Wilfred Laurier University Press.

Trolander, Judith Ann. 1975. *Settlement Houses and the Great Depression.* Detroit, MI: Wayne State University Press.

–. 1982. "Social Change: Settlement Houses and Saul Alinsky, 1939–1965." *Social Service Review* 56 (3): 346–65.

Vancouver Foundation. 2012. *Connections and Engagement: A Survey of Metro Vancouver.* Vancouver: Vancouver Foundation. https://www.vancouverfoundation.ca/about-us/publications/connections-and-engagement-reports/connections-engagement-report-2012.

Vancouver School Board. 2017. "1891–1910." In *Vancouver School District History.* Vancouver: Vancouver School Board.

White, Gaylord S. 1911. "The Social Settlement after Twenty-Five Years." *Harvard Theological Review* 4 (1): 47–70.

Woods, Robert Archey. 1891. *English Social Movements.* New York: Charles Scribner's Sons.

2

The Eyes and Ears of the Community

Engaging Citizens and Community Advocacy

OLIVER SCHMIDTKE

Governing the Community

At the core of the mission of neighbourhood houses (NHs) is the idea of providing services for the local community while at the same time being a constitutive part of the same community. It is in the latter respect that this chapter investigates the role that NHs in Vancouver play in the place-based governance of communal, public life (Bradford 2008). In this context, I use the term "governance" as an interpretative concept denoting the broader deliberation and decision-making process that communities adopt to address social problems and develop (policy) solutions. This process includes, but is not restricted to, governments and the formal process of policy making. Conceptualizing governance as a practice in which various actors have a voice, take on authority, and contribute to the collective decision making allows for a better understanding of how a plethora of stakeholders in the community address issues of shared concern. Scholarly research has pointed to how such a multi-stakeholder framework that extends into civil society has produced new approaches for solving community problems (Gray 1989; Lawrence, Hardy, and Phillips 2002; Zoller 2000) and shaping "new civic cultures" (Docherty, Goodlad, and Paddison 2001; Saldivar-Tanaka and Krasny 2004). In this respect, the governance perspective also draws analytical attention to the involvement of citizens in communal affairs and participatory policy making (Evans and Shields 2014; Michels and De Graaf 2017; Salamon and Toepler 2015).

Empirically, the most straightforward way in which neighbourhood houses have contributed to this agenda is through the scope and nature of the community services they provide. In 2013, NHs in Metro Vancouver provided a total of 444 programs/activities. Overall, 208,664 participants took part in these activities, many of which catered to newcomers by providing low-barrier and affordable access to services in the community (employment support, daycare, after-school care, senior day activities, parent groups, recreational programs, socio-cultural events, youth leadership, and more). The central question of this chapter is whether and how NHs link this extensive service provision to modes of civic engagement and community advocacy. What are the political ambitions of NHs in terms of working

TABLE 2.1

Overview of semi-structured interviews

Interviewees	Number
Neighbourhood house executive directors	20
Executive directors of Vancouver-based NHs	7
Executive directors of NHs outside Vancouver	3
Executive directors of NHs belonging to ANHBC	5
Executive directors of independent NHs	5
Government interviewees	6
ANHBC interviewees	1
Total	27

Source: service users survey.

Note: NH = neighbourhood house; ANHBC = Association of Neighbourhood Houses of British Columbia

with and on behalf of the community as an independent grassroots civil society organization? How and through what kinds of processes do NHs in Metro Vancouver contribute to governing the community?

I will approach these questions based primarily on a series of semi-structured interviews conducted with executive directors (EDs) from several of Vancouver's neighbourhood houses, other NGOs, and representatives of the city (see Table 2.1 for an overview). In addition, in terms of primary data, I rely on a survey of service users conducted at various NHs, a Clearinghouse Survey on the NHs in Metro Vancouver, and a focus group composed of users and staff members.[1]

First, I analyze how neighbourhood houses envision their role as community stakeholders and the kinds of challenges they have faced in acting as an advocate for the community where they operate. Then I investigate how NHs have worked with different levels of government, most notably at the municipal level, to aid in addressing social problems in the community and in fostering program development and policy making. Finally, attention shifts to the processes by which NHs have contributed to the very substance of local democratic practices, namely, development of social capital and creation of incentives for citizens to take a more active part in the community.

Envisioning the role of Neighbourhood Houses in the Community: The Perspective of Executive Directors

In addressing the question of how neighbourhood houses envision their central mission as grassroots, community-centred organizations, it is worth underlining that NHs do not operate or define their institutional identity uniformly. While studying NHs in Metro Vancouver, it became clear that the leadership provided by the executive directors and the specific challenges of each community shape the profile of individual NHs substantially. Still, it is instructive to begin our discussion by asking about the general evolving nature of NHs as political agencies, if not part of a broader community-based social movement.

The Notion of Place-Based Community

One straightforward way of defining neighbourhood houses would be to focus exclusively on their function as key service providers in the community. Indeed, in the interviews with both the executive directors and representatives of municipalities across Metro Vancouver, there was acknowledgment of the need for "place-based services" and of how well situated NHs were to address this need. From this perspective, NHs have a critical role in identifying what services are required and what infrastructure needs to be put in place to produce an effective support system.

Yet, such an interpretation would not pay full justice to other defining elements of how neighbourhood houses see themselves and are perceived in the community. One critical feature is the basic mode of organization and the grassroots character of NHs: almost all of the executive director defined NHs with reference to having deep roots in the community and the ambition to have their members organize their services independently and proactively. It is at the core of the NH philosophy that members take on responsibility and leadership when it comes to developing and delivering services. One ED argued that a sense of community must remain at the heart of what a NH does: "It needs to remain grassroots and it needs to not be all about service delivery, because that's what makes us different and unique. It's really about community and relationships and people getting involved ... and delivering programs themselves."

This emphasis on self-organization and autonomy is closely linked to the idea that neighbourhood houses provide a sense of place and community that is widely seen as in need of protection. NHs aspire to link citizens to the development of their respective communities and give them a stake in directing it. From this perspective, one executive director described NHs as "mission-driven," as one of the few entities that work with people collectively to have an impact in the community. In a fundamental way, NHs were depicted as representing a "place-based philosophy," whose central mission is the defence and nurturing of a genuine sense of community. On various occasions during our interviews and focus groups, we witnessed a strong desire to address a missing or threatened sense of togetherness and connectedness in the community. From this perspective, NHs were recurrently portrayed as providing a "place to come to, be part of, feel good about, and meet other people." One ED described NHs in this sense as the "living room of the community."[2]

A recurrent theme of our interviews with the executive directors was the expectation that, as their raison d'être, neighbourhood houses reflect the diversity and changing nature of the communities where they operate. In the depictions of those running and working with NHs, what constitutes the community is in constant flux in terms of its constituent groups and the services required. NHs need "to ensure that their programming reflects the dynamics, demographics, and needs of their particular community." An essential part of the NHs' organizational identity is that they develop an astute sense of who forms the community and how NHs can be a vehicle for providing the diversity of this community with services, visibility, and recognition.

In this respect, neighbourhood houses play a fundamental role in empowering the local community with the capacity for self-organization through "building relationships." One interviewee made an explicit link between citizens' engagement in the community and the broader policy process. In her view, NHs allow for a bridging between on-the-ground community participation and the policy-making level: NHs "feed" and connect first-hand experiences of community members with those in positions of political and administrative power. As another executive director put it: "At the core mandate of NHs is the task of fostering a 'web of connection' among community members as well as between community members and government."

An additional defining mark of the community for neighbourhood houses is its inclusive character. The notion of inclusiveness relates to two main features. One of these features speaks to the underlying political objective of NHs to address societal inequality and exclusion. While the leaders of the NHs differ to a certain degree about what this mandate means in practical, political terms, there is widespread agreement with the objective that those who are less privileged in society find support and access to the local community through NHs. Their programs provide services primarily to lower-income citizens who struggle to afford them otherwise or who cannot rely on established communities for support (primarily newcomers to Canada; more on this point later). The second feature speaks again to the mode of self-organization that NHs in Metro Vancouver have adopted. In explicit contrast to the regular mode in which governments operate, one executive director depicted NHs as representing a "broader philosophy of an open, inclusive notion of community and togetherness and cooperation." In this latter respect, NHs represent and practise a particular governance model whose inclusive and cooperative nature challenges established decision-making and power structures governing the community.

Funding Challenges and Professionalizing Neighbourhood Houses

The grassroots, independent way of organizing neighbourhood houses faces considerable challenges, which in turn limit the role that they are able to play as community advocates and agents of change in policy making. From a historical perspective, a former executive director and major player in the Metro Vancouver NH community explained that "we are in a totally different world" in terms of the relationship between government and NHs compared with the late 1970s and early 1980s (see Chapter 1 on this period of expansion and experimentation with regard to community-based initiatives and the NH movement in Vancouver). He described government during the earlier era as being far more willing to support an "experimental and risk-taking" approach from NHs. In his interpretation, NHs now need to be increasingly concerned with costs and legal issues, which ultimately slows the development of new, bold initiatives and makes civil society actors such as NHs far more cautious than in the past. The interviewee contended that NHs are now "living in the night of the risk-managers," mainly driven by their relationship with government funders and an increasingly rigorous legalistic environment.

An additional change in the institutional and political context in which neighbourhood houses operate relates to the broader field of policy and administrative regimes. Following a neoliberal logic in the new public management approach, the field of local service provision has been transformed by the federal and provincial governments' attempts to devolve responsibility to community organizations, harness the involvement of community groups, and seek greater efficiency in the use of public resources by promoting competition and privatization (Evans and Shields 2018; Lane 2000; Moreno, Shields, and Drolet 2018; Andrews and Van de Walle 2013).[3] Settlement services for newcomers to Canada are a good illustration. Not least driven by the downloading of responsibility and some new funding opportunities made available from the province, it is now largely up to the cities to provide essential services for this group (providing newcomers with settlement, employment, housing, health, language training, cultural amenities, engagement in the wider community, and so on). Although there has been considerable variation in the degree to which provinces negotiated agreements with the federal government, provinces and municipalities have generally been empowered to take on this task by expansion of funding schemes directed at local service providers and through greater autonomy in program development (see Biles 2008; Seidle 2010).

Our survey of funding sources for neighbourhood houses in Metro Vancouver shows that their financial resources come primarily from two sources: the provincial government and the fees that NHs themselves collect for their services (these fees are primarily collected for daycare services and are spent accordingly). For instance, for the year 2012, NHs in Greater Vancouver collected almost $16 million from the provincial government in funding and a bit over $10 million from their own services, whereas the federal and municipal governments contributed only around $2 million each to their overall funding portfolio (Dolka and Yan 2019).

When considering the vulnerability and uncertainty that NHs face when securing their financial resources, it is worth looking at the type of funding available to them. On the whole, NHs can rely on a variety of revenue streams, but most of these are relatively small compared with fees and the provincial government. In terms of reliable and continuous funding sources, the provincial government and the service fees collected from their own services constitute the foundation of NHs' budgets. With a view to the funding for their programming, a picture similar to the 2012 snapshot emerges: the federal government has played only a minor role in providing NHs with the needed financial resources to launch and sustain programs over the past two decades (see Figure 7.1 in Chapter 7 and Appendix 1 for details). The municipal level can take on an important role in this respect, indicated by the overall number of programs funded. Yet funding from the city government is predominantly tied to specific projects that, if at all possible, need to be renewed regularly with a duration of no longer than three years. In general, the bulk of neighbourhood houses' financial resources comes from funding schemes and programs that are non-recurrent or require a renewal process on a short-term basis: As Figure 2.1 shows, depending on the type of programming, 30 to 60 percent of the funding is non-renewable. For the NHs' most important funder, the provincial government, almost 90 percent of all funded programs are either not renewable at all or are only renewable for up to three years. Still the provincial government is the only source that provides a substantial amount of ongoing, operational funding. The implication is a relative lack of "core funding" for most NHs and the structural reliance on unpredictable "program funding."

As a result, much of NHs' human resources is tied up in a continuous struggle to secure and renew funding streams. As our interviewees underlined on various occasions, the funding environment has moved decisively toward non-recurrent and short-term opportunities for which NHs are in a continuous competition with other NGOs in Metro Vancouver. The resulting uncertainty about the financial sustainability of the NHs creates, as one executive director noted, a "precarious environment," which has a notable effect on how these organizations operate and use scarce administrative resources. As another interviewee put it: "It's extremely hard to get traction on anything when you're reapplying every year for funding ... In a year, we'll evaluate what you want to change, but you're halfway (through) the year and you're looking for more money."

In the same vein, an executive director with a lengthy career in Vancouver's civil society sector noted how neighbourhood houses had been largely "grassroots" up to the 1980s, and many were consequently "less government savvy" in the initial years of the transition toward contract-based funding. The 1990s offered new opportunities to expand operations at NHs as some of the social services were offloaded onto municipal authorities and then outsourced to community organizations. Yet, with these opportunities also came a greater degree of reliance on external funding and a marked shift toward service delivery. As a result, the previous commitment to political

FIGURE 2.1
Number of Metro Vancouver neighbourhood house programs by stability and duration of funding sources

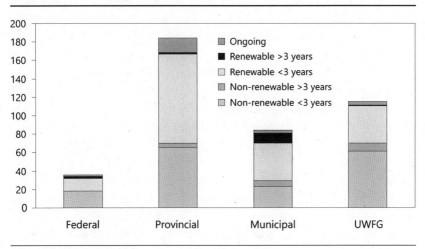

Source: Clearinghouse Survey, 2013

advocacy and far-reaching independence from other agencies has been replaced, at least partially, by a greater degree of reliance on government contracts and on grants provided by private foundations.

How neighbourhood houses operate administratively and financially has
a twofold implication for their role as community advocates. First, the task
of securing government funding and meeting the increased accountability
expectations has become a progressively labour-intensive undertaking that
takes resources and time away from community advocacy. In our interviews, we detected a widely shared frustration with increasingly short-term
contracts and the need to constantly reapply for funding, even for organizations that NHs had long-established relationships with. Several interviewees noted how the short-term nature of government funding made it
difficult for NHs to engage in long-term planning and to guarantee service
stability beyond one- to three-year periods. The economic crisis in 2008–
09 further deepened the sense of financial vulnerability. The consequence of
these changes to the funding relationship, according to some interviewees,
is that NHs have become very "careful" or "cautious" regarding their financial viability and willingness to take on new, riskier initiatives. Second, besides requiring greater amounts of time and resources dedicated to securing
the financial viability of NHs, the evolving funding structure has also had a
politically disciplining effect. As one executive director put it pointedly, in
their growing, albeit varying, reliance on government grants, NHs are conscious of not "biting the hand that feeds you."

When assessing current financial challenges that neighbourhood houses
face, it is worth pointing out that the form and scope of civil society organizations' participation in the delivery of public policy such as settlement
services are in constant flux. For instance, over the past two years, we have
witnessed a reversal of the long-standing trend toward decentralization in
providing settlement services in Canada's system of multi-level governance.
Traditionally, funding for settlement services, which constitutes a significant portion of the financial resources available to NHs, came from the provincial government. Recently, however, the federal government has assumed
a stronger leadership role in designing immigration and integration policies
(Gunn 2019). In particular, during the latter part of Stephen Harper's government, Immigration, Refugees and Citizenship Canada (IRCC) took back
some control over the funds made available to service provider organizations
in the community (see Praznik and Shields 2018; IRCC 2017), a development that Aude-Claire Fourot (2018) describes as the "federal repatriation
of settlement services." British Columbia was significantly affected by this

change in the policy framework, with federal funding opportunities becoming notably more significant for NGOs (including NHs) serving immigrant communities.[4]

As this development shows, service provider organizations such as neighbourhood houses are highly dependent on a political and policy environment that recognizes and supports their work in the community. NHs face a momentous paradox in their efforts to secure a stable funding structure for their initiatives: municipal governments are most familiar with and appreciative of what NHs are doing in and for the community, but at the same time, the local level of government has the most limited funding capacity. Whereas NHs tend to work most closely with municipal governments and administrations, they are dependent primarily on funding schemes made available by the provincial and federal levels of government. It is worth underlining that under Justin Trudeau's government, shifts in the IRCC's funding structure have provided the opportunity to apply for longer, three- to five-year-term funding schemes (easing some of the NHs' concerns regarding short-term and highly competitive funding opportunities). From a provincial perspective, British Columbia's minority NDP government, which has been in place since 2017, has also contributed to a more welcoming governance arena for NHs and their community-based approach.

Nonetheless, government funding is not uncontroversial among neighbourhood house leaders. Some NH interviewees explained that their organizations had avoided becoming tied to funding sources such as service contracts out of a desire to maintain a maximum degree of independence. As one interviewee noted, the financial support offered by government contracts sometimes comes at the cost of the NH's unrestricted ability to act as a voice for their community: "You really had to change the whole approach ... depending who ... who you were to get that money." In short, there is significant tension between NHs' reliance on government revenues to fund their ongoing operations on the one hand and their ability to function as independent community advocates on the other. Still, as I will address in the following section, NHs in Metro Vancouver have played a critical role in shaping their communities and affecting policy development on the ground.

Neighbourhood Houses as Partners in the Local Policy Community: Working with Municipal Authorities as Community Advocates

Given the nature of their engagement in the community as front-line service providers, neighbourhood houses directly interact with different levels of government, most notably at the municipal level.[5] The relationship that

NHs have across Metro Vancouver varies substantially, however. City of Vancouver–based NHs (Cedar Cottage, Collingwood, Downtown Eastside, Mount Pleasant, Gordon, Kitsilano, Kiwassa, Frog Hollow, Little Mountain, and South Vancouver) benefit from a long-established tradition of support from the municipal government, whereas NHs outside the city of Vancouver are at a disadvantage due to other municipalities' unfamiliarity with NHs and the concern that they are merely duplicating services offered by other agencies.[6]

One government representative explained that this difference between Vancouver and its surrounding municipalities regarding NHs was partly attributable to the City of Vancouver's charter, which provides it with powers and capabilities regarding social development and planning currently not possessed by other municipalities. The city can mandate that specific public amenities be included in new development areas. He also noted that Vancouver is also relatively advanced in terms of the infrastructure and the funding it provides for non-profit groups (including its use of a social planning department, which, with the exception of Halifax, does not exist in other major Canadian municipalities).

The long-standing investment of the city into the infrastructure and operational programs of neighbourhood houses reflects an expectation regarding the vital contribution of NHs to municipal governance in Vancouver. NHs have historically had a special relationship with the municipal authorities (see Chapter 1). In particular, the city's Department of Social Planning (later renamed Social Policy and Project) has actively supported NHs for decades, and many have come into existence through the department's active sponsorship, a process that often involves privileged access to office space facilitated by city authorities.[7] A high-ranking administrator at the department argued that NHs tend to regard the city as a key ally with respect to both funding opportunities and broader administrative-political support. The city, in turn, sees NHs as "integral to the whole social service field." In this administrator's assessment, Vancouver's municipal administration, particularly its City Planning Unit, considers NHs as semi-civic facilities – a "kind of civic infrastructure – we don't even see them as very external to what we do."

In this context, it is not surprising that, according to our interviews with administrators and politicians, the City of Vancouver assesses neighbourhood houses according to distinct criteria. While other non-profits are evaluated largely on their service delivery capabilities, NHs are also expected to demonstrate their leadership in the areas of community development, community capacity-building, and community advocacy. The City of Vancouver has acknowledged the distinctive capacity of NHs to build and advocate on behalf of the community through and beyond its service delivery activities. Parts of the city's administration and council explicitly attribute to NHs the ability to represent the local community in a more far-reaching manner politically.

This allusion to an almost symbiotic relationship between neighbourhood houses and the planning unit of the city sheds light on how instrumental NHs are in building community and organizing multi-stakeholder groups at the local level. From the perspective of city administrators, NHs' role in and contribution to governance of the local community has several dimensions. First, a recurrent theme in our interviews and evaluation of the work of NHs is their ability to form multi-stakeholder partnerships that are instrumental for effective public policies. NHs are perceived to be a key component in the processes that bring together government and civil society partners in the community: "Neighbourhood Houses are sponsored by the City of Vancouver, in conjunction with partners from the federal, provincial and non-profit sectors. These facilities seek to meet the needs of local community demographics, and play an important role in building and maintaining healthy neighbourhoods."

The second aspect relates more directly to the contributions of neighbourhood houses to addressing and solving social problems in the community. The City of Vancouver has long recognized and appreciated the role that NHs play within the community and the services they provide, and this understanding and appreciation have only grown over time as other factors, such as social capital and community development, have become priorities of public administrators (particularly as research has pointed to correlations between healthy and vibrant local communities and lower government costs in the areas of crime and community safety, public health, social services, and so on; see Atkinson and Coleman 1992). This approach to governing the city requires strong partnerships and agencies such as NHs that are sensitive to issues in the community and willing to collaborate in a multi-partner framework.

The long-standing collaboration between Vancouver's urban planning unit and neighbourhood houses rests on a key regulative idea: there is a sense of shared values and basic principles in terms of addressing social problems. NHs are very much in line with the goals of the Social Planning

Department in that, as our interviewee from this department stated, NHs provide services that "are accessible to all – they address marginal community members who are most in need and disadvantaged. They are very community and grassroots-driven." This office of the City of Vancouver shares the idea of targeting marginalized societal groups and offering services to them in a self-guided, inclusive approach.

Furthermore, neighbourhood houses provide an essential way of drawing on the experience of, and input from, the community, which municipal governments in particular need to render their program development and policy process effective and legitimate (Fontan et al. 2009). Community consultation, stakeholder engagement, and transparency in decision making are key issues that administrative authorities need to address to demonstrate "good governance" (Connelly 2011; Papadopoulos 2003). In the Vancouver context, NHs are deeply invested in building modes of informal cooperation, mediated through close contact with city councillors and municipal agencies' staff. NHs act as vital intermediaries in the community, as well as sources of information ("link to neighbourhood"). Thus, government representatives portray NHs as integral to the city's planning and community consultation. Particularly in its objective of developing strategies for the city's growth and densification, municipal authorities are dependent on the local community's participation, input, and expertise.

One interviewee from the City of Vancouver depicted neighbourhood houses as "important conduits" that the municipality could contact to learn about issues and challenges in the communities. He noted that in the past, NHs had collaborated with the city and with each other to influence service and policy issues. The contributions of NHs have been important, as they have tended to be "more immersed" in the "realities" of their communities, placing them at the "forefront" of local events and concerns. An executive director also noted that her Vancouver-based NH was "frequently asked to come into council meetings to speak to community issues of importance." In this respect, NHs can play a role of "expert witnesses" and have a stake in deliberations over program and policy formation (regarding such issues as sex workers, homelessness, community planning, low-income housing, and so on).

In a statement in the BC legislature, NDP MLA Jenny Kwan[8] acknowledged "Neighbourhood House Week" and provided a statement on the role of neighbourhood houses in BC communities, framing them as a positive asset, a source of "social capital," a source of important services to vulnerable and marginalized people, and a means of fostering community: "Believe it or not, the Association of Neighbourhood Houses has been serving BC for 122 years. Their members are an integral part of the development of the social service sector and our community safety net. Neighbourhood houses leverage small budgets into mighty programs that build connections with local residents." She went on to say that the "incredible value" that NHs produce goes far beyond the public funds that are invested in them: "They build our social capital. They build our capacity to know, understand and care for each other."[9]

Thus, the involvement of neighbourhood houses in community projects can influence the social planning process at the city level. For instance, by launching projects in the fields of the environment (sustainability projects), provision of health services to local residents, or caring for children or seniors, NHs are a driving force promoting on-the-ground approaches to urgent social tasks. In particular, the City of Vancouver has realized that NHs are important community partners in terms of contributing to place-based program development and connecting municipal authorities with actors on the ground.

In sum, the relationship between the Vancouver city government and neighbourhood houses has evolved organically over decades, with a growing knowledge and appreciation of what NHs contribute to good governance in the local communities.[10] However, while describing the complementary and highly collaborative relationship between the city (and its urban planning unit) and NHs, a word of caution is warranted. Several executive directors pointed out that there are some difficulties in either working with or getting the attention of the city beyond the annual review sessions. As one of them put it, NHs tend to be taken for granted as a constitutive part of the community and consulted in a meaningful way only when it is opportune for city administrators. In the final analysis, there is still a power imbalance in this partnership. In terms of NHs' advocacy role and relationship to municipal authorities, policy makers draw on them primarily in a consultative manner; NHs participate in decision-making processes mainly indirectly; and, to varying degrees, NHs are structurally dependent on the city's funding and support.

Building Community Capacity: Bowling Together

One key element of this research was a survey among users of services and activities offered at neighbourhood houses. Table 2.2 provides an overview of responses regarding individuals' perceived changes in their social skills and their ability to relate to a community setting. The survey is based on a

TABLE 2.2

Perceived changes in social skills through involvement at neighbourhood houses

| | Total (%) | | Place of birth | | | |
| | | | Inside Canada | | Outside Canada | |
Change in social skills	Increased a little	a lot	Increased a little	a lot	Increased a little	a lot
Has your ability to work with people from different backgrounds changed?	42	34	34	29	46	38
Have your decision-making abilities changed?	42	26	30	19	48	29
Have your skills in organizing or managing events and programs changed?	36	21	24	17	42	23
Have your skills in speaking in front of other people changed?	35	27	22	19	42	32

Source: service users survey.

sample of 675 respondents from fourteen NHs comprising Canadian- and foreign-born users (65 percent newcomers, 77 percent women, 54 percent employed, and 30 percent with a university degree).

The results of this survey shed light on the capacity-building of a community-based organization such as neighbourhood houses (Larcombe 2008), at both the individual and collective level. At the individual level, NHs appear to be valuable sites for the formation of social capital in the sense that Robert Putnam (2000, 19) used the term to mean "connections among individuals' social networks and the norms of reciprocity and trust-worthiness that arise from them." Based on the participants' self-assessment, NHs create the capacity to engage with others in the community and to develop skills to do this in a meaningful and competent way. This em-powerment of immigrants and members of the minority community is also facilitated by simple facts. For instance, all NHs operate in a multilingual environment (with a majority of employers being bilingual), and one is widely run by immigrants and minorities themselves. Figure 2.2 indicates

FIGURE 2.2

Languages spoken by three or more staff members at Metro Vancouver neighbourhood houses

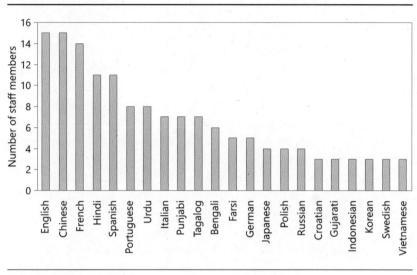

Source: Clearinghouse Survey, 2013.

the degree to which NH staff demonstrate a high degree of linguistic and cultural diversity reflecting the nature of the urban communities they serve.

Thus, the seemingly mundane practice of interacting at neighbourhood houses and participating in community-based activities can enable the learning and practice of important civic and political skills. The effect on the skills and confidence of the respondents is particularly pronounced for those born outside Canada. The local community at an NH validates and recognizes a person's contributions. These civic skills learned through involvement and relating to others are a pivotal resource that contributes to overcoming social isolation and encouraging engagement in the wider community. In Chapter 4, Sean Lauer reports that over 60 percent of respondents stated that they made at least one close friend through the NHs, and he finds a significant increase in civic and community engagement directly related to being involved in NHs.[11] Similarly, qualitative interviews with this group underlined the fact that social isolation is a major concern, and one that can be addressed effectively by NHs.

One critical reason why immigrants and minorities find themselves isolated and unable to contribute to public debates is the absence of low-threshold opportunities for engagement. Neighbourhood houses offer precisely this entry into communal engagement in a non-threatening, service-based environment. The project conducted oral histories with participants about their personal experiences of NHs. One recurrent theme in these interviews is how the use of services gradually built trust and turned NHs into "safe places" (for a detailed account of these findings, see Yan, Lauer, and Riaño-Alcalá 2017; Riaño-Alcalá's and Ono's Chapter 5 in this book). Instrumental in this respect is the reliance of NHs on volunteers: in 2012–13, more than 3,670 people registered as volunteers in NHs in Metro Vancouver. In the same vein, NHs have become socializing agencies that regularly allow immigrants to become leaders in their community and take on prominent roles in public life. In 2013, over 60 percent of staff members at NHs were either current or former resident service users. As an active part of the NGO community at the urban level, NHs pave the path of immigrants toward professional careers with third-sector organizations, community engagement, and leadership.

At the collective level, neighbourhood houses facilitate residents' working together to achieve collective goals. They provide a physical and social framework for social networks, dialogue, and collective-communal empowerment. The skills that community members acquire in taking part in or organizing events can easily be transferred to other forms of active engagement. Through low-cost, family-friendly services and social events, NHs offer tangible incentives to overcome alienation from communal life, particularly for those who have a more precarious social status (low-income people, seniors, immigrants/minorities). These self-governing community associations can be interpreted as entry points and networks that facilitate democratic participation in a basic yet essential way. As Yan (2004, 58) puts it, "motives of democratic participation, sharing, and reciprocity are actualized through services" offered at NHs (e.g., Yan and Lauer 2008).[12]

Social capital researchers have suggested that bridging ties is important for political participation. Our research suggests that neighbourhood houses play such a bridging role in connecting citizens to communal affairs and opening the door for modes of participation (Patsias, Latendresse, and Bherer 2013; Quintelier, Stolle, and Harell 2012). Building on the insight from social capital frameworks, one can argue that NHs bring people together, contribute to overcoming social isolation, convey information about issues in the community, and provide for low-threshold forms of participation in grassroots initiatives. (Regarding the connection function of NHs, please refer to Chapter 3.)

FIGURE 2.3

Types of programs in Metro Vancouver neighbourhood houses

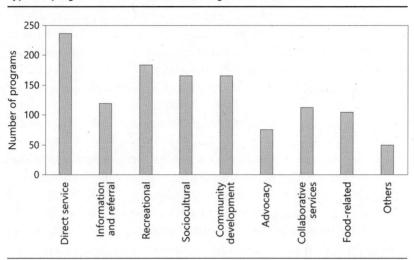

Source: Clearinghouse Survey, 2013.

Considering the nature of program activities at neighbourhood houses in Metro Vancouver (Figure 2.4), it is evident that the most important type of program consists of direct services to the community (e.g., daycare, services for families and seniors), which, as described above, also cover a main part of the NHs' funding scheme. Yet, it is striking to see that a considerable number of those activities are also directly related to community and advocacy-oriented initiatives. In addition, NHs offer a range of programs that, more indirectly, open the door for involvement in community affairs and advocacy. Some of these activities are explicitly designed to serve this purpose; others might start with a local issue and morph into a broader concern for the well-being of the community. Food-related activities are an example. As evidence from multiple NHs suggests, work on a local communal garden project can be a socializing experience, sensitizing NHs participants to and involving them in issues related to food security, urban planning, or healthy living.

The results of the survey provide us with an interpretative lens into the broader socio-political functions that such civil society associations can take on in giving a voice to newcomers and minorities. By investigating the role that neighbourhood houses play in municipal and provincial policy making, our research found consistent evidence of how these self-governing associations in Metro Vancouver establish an institutional infrastructure for building and strengthening urban communities and nurturing their collective capacity (see also Lauer's Chapter 4 on the pivotal role of this infrastructure). The case study of NHs emphasizes the importance of *bridging* social capital – establishing vertical social networks between socially diverse groups or organizations. The experience of these organizations in the urban context is that, when previously unrelated or dissimilar community organizations and groups connect with one another, the created ties strengthen the overall social fabric (e.g., Gittell and Vidal 1998) (see also Yan's Chapter 3). For instance, one prominent initiative of Mount Pleasant Neighbourhood House is the support of a food network (http://www.mpnh.org/food), which has led to the collaboration of a host of stakeholders, such as community groups, NGOs, and city administrators. Thus, bridging social capital also expands the possibilities for inter-sectoral collaboration.

It became clear in our interviews with neighbourhood house executive directors that there is no consensus on whether and to what degree NHs have a mandate to be a political advocate for the community. In practice, however, NHs have proven to be instrumental both as a vehicle for community engagement and as a partner for NGOs and policy makers primarily at the municipal level. In Vancouver, NHs have established themselves as critical for effective policy initiatives and implementation, or, as one executive director put it, NHs are the "eyes and ears in the community." In practice, the demarcation between political advocacy groups and networks of professionals can become blurred depending on the circle of activists and the targets of public campaigns (Bowen, Newenham-Kahindi, and Herremans 2010).

The position of neighbourhood houses in driving the integration agenda is centrally linked to their role as catalysts for community collaboration. In one of our focus group sessions, an NGO representative stated:

> What the NHs have done for us is sort of allow us to network with the community, and brought us into projects that we wouldn't necessarily have been involved in ... and how we, as an organization ... can provide assistance or help or advocate as partners at city hall when we need to advocate for certain things. When we are trying to advocate for certain things, they come and support us.

NHs are the hub of an extensive service network through which untapped community assets are mobilized and nurtured. In this respect, they are an integral part of place-based governance in Metro Vancouver. As our interviews and focus group underline, NHs are in an ideal position to provide an institutional capacity for community governance, to foster mutual learning among community members, and to permit community input and direction in the development and implementation of integration programs. In Metro Vancouver, they have established themselves as a critical link between the people, governments, and private stakeholders that make up communities. They provide social infrastructure and networks of democratic participation, thereby giving voice to those who often feel alienated from government processes. The focus groups and interviews with staff consistently highlighted the role of NHs as a forum for community-based governance, and as an important two-way conduit between community members and the different levels of government. One interviewee characterized this approach as "developing the voice of the community," while another described it as helping the community "mobilize itself to bring these issues forward" to the government.

Empowering Newcomers and Minorities

One critical factor in carving out the governance role for neighbourhood houses is the nature of the policy challenge itself. For instance, it is the task of welcoming newcomers and incorporating them into the fabric of society that has placed cities and community stakeholders in the driver's seat in this domain of public policy making. At its core, integration is a place-based practice that is shaped by territorially specific social, political, and cultural environments (e.g., Bradford 2005). Most importantly, research on the role of the local context has underlined that integration processes are essentially rooted in communal practices and forms of urban or regional citizenship (e.g., Hepburn 2011; Penninx et al. 2004). The local and regional contexts provide a central arena for translation of the need for integration into concrete programs and influences how successful these initiatives are (e.g., Schmidtke 2014; Siemiatycki 2011, 2012; Tossutti 2012). Place plays a critical role in shaping the environment in which legal entitlements need to be realized and, in the case of immigrants, how effective societal integration is promoted. It is the place-specific context that allows, restricts, or prohibits newcomers' actualization of the promise of citizenship in terms of full and equitable inclusion and participation.[13]

However, given the limited fiscal resources and municipal authorities' informal status in the settlement and integration policy process, until recently city governments have remained on the margins of this policy field.[14]

Reflecting on the exceptionally innovative policy responses of urban centres, John Biles (2008) notes how cities have gradually come to play a more active role in the integration process (see also the comprehensive study by the Maytree Foundation [2013]). In his analysis, this development is rooted in the simple fact that new immigrants tend to settle and require services in metropolitan areas.[15] What Biles sees with respect to migrant integration is how the urban context constitutes not only the immediate environment in which the settlement of newcomers is addressed but also the site for facilitating partnerships and modes of cooperation between government agencies and civil society groups (Biles 2008, 163–66). Analyzing Ontario's emergent multipartite immigration and settlement policy framework, Daiva Stasiulis, Christine Hughes, and Zainab Amery (2011, 74) make a similar assessment: they find this policy framework emblematic of "a discernible movement in Ontario's immigrant-receiving centres from *government* to multilevel, multisectoral *governance* in the policy area of immigrant settlement" (see also Andrew et al. 2013).

As the survey indicated, neighbourhood houses in Metro Vancouver have a transformative effect on the lives of immigrants to Canada and minority groups. Indeed, they have assumed a central role in supporting the ambition of municipal authorities to build "welcoming communities" for newcomers to Canada. In 2005, the federal government launched its decentralizing strategy in response to *Canada's Action Plan Against Racism.*[16] The scope of this program was quickly expanded, with the Welcoming Communities Initiative (WCI) being introduced under the leadership of Citizenship and Immigration Canada in 2006. The long-term objective of this program has been to strengthen newcomers' communal participation and equitable inclusion in society. The central goal of the initiative is twofold: first, to establish what successful inclusion of newcomers means on the ground in terms of a place-based, communal effort, and, second, to support locally grounded approaches to settlement and integration. Given the focus on the local context, it is not surprising that, as the program was rolled out as an example of federal-provincial collaboration, municipalities were immediately recognized as key players (Stasiulis, Hughes, and Amery 2011). The program created an institutional opening for NHs to take on a pronounced responsibility in rendering the urban space more welcoming and inclusive.

The WCI promoted a collaborative network of community partners designed to develop, test, and assist in the implementation of settlement and integration strategies. In this respect, the central goal was complex and ambitious: it aimed to gain a better understanding of the intricacy of the integration challenges (Esses et al. 2010) as a task straddling several domains of public policy making and program development. These tasks range from employment and educational opportunities, access to affordable housing, public transport, and suitable health care services to a social environment that endorses cultural diversity and seeks to tackle forms of exclusion for minorities. The complexity of the tasks at hand created challenges but also incentives for municipal authorities to think creatively about their planning tools in terms of multi-service and multi-stakeholder responses.

It is in this context that the engagement of neighbourhood houses with newcomers has had a vital effect on patterns of social inclusion and empowerment at the local level. (For more information on the role of NHs in community-building, see Lauer's Chapter 4 in this book.) From our interviews with NH users, it has become apparent that the low threshold of accessing services and welcoming environment that NHs provide through their services and events (often and very effectively organized around food) is instrumental in integrating newcomers more fully into the fabric of society. Affordable and easily accessible services are essential, particularly for those who seek to settle in Canada and to establish themselves socially and professionally. The grassroots administrative structure of NHs is also important. As demonstrated in Chapters 4 and 5 of this book, NHs provide many openings for engagement, particularly for newcomers to volunteer and take advantage of professional opportunities.

The effects that NHs have also speak to the way in which newcomers and minorities are part of the community's governance structure. One critical outcome of this first round of consultation and capacity-building was the formation of so-called Local Immigration Partnerships (LIPs) in 2008, which provide direct and indirect services to newcomers and aim to strengthen different forms of collaboration at the community level (Esses et al. 2010). At the very core of the LIP initiative is the goal of enhancing the coordination and engagement of multiple stakeholders in planning and delivering the services. LIPs constitute an institutional framework for developing effective action plans and sustainable initiatives that challenge traditional modes of municipal planning and program development. They encourage a response that is fundamentally dependent on the engagement of non-government, local communities (Bradford and Andrew 2010). Cross-sectoral as well as public-civil society cooperation is central to the LIP initiative. Neighbourhood houses have proven to be well positioned to bring stakeholders together and to take on formal responsibility for establishing effective partnerships on the ground.

The mandate of LIPs to use the entire social infrastructure of the community to tackle issues of settlement and integration has had notable effects on the broader governance of migration at the city level. Building these multi-stakeholder partnerships creates opportunities for new, less hierarchical and government-centred modes of governing migration and integration (for a similar argument, see Jørgensen 2012; Schmidtke and Zaslove 2014). In particular, community groups in civil society and migrants themselves have been able to engage more fully in bottom-up grassroots initiatives. In this context, immigrants are not simply objects of the demand for successful integration; rather, they participate in deliberating its meaning and evolving societal practices. A sense of agency for immigrants and minorities emerges from community-based institutional practices and interactions. In particular, the local level has become an arena for negotiating the meaning of what successful integration means on the ground, and what programs successfully promote integration. This governance structure has been instrumental in fostering policy innovation, a more inclusive decision-making process, and urban forms of citizenship (Penninx et al. 2004).

Even though it is difficult to specify the exact impact that neighbourhood houses have on public policy formation in the area of immigrant settlement and integration, I argue that their initiatives have generated marked opportunities for civil society input and initiatives. In this respect, immigrants or minorities gain – as Jamie Winders (2012) puts it in his study of urban politics in the United States – "institutional visibility" in local contexts, thereby enabling them to make political claims. This process, in turn, is likely to strengthen the willingness to see immigrants and minorities included in the deliberation and, in some cases, decision-making procedures regarding integration programs and policies (e.g., Caponio and Borkert 2010; Falge, Ruzza, and Schmidtke 2012; Scholten 2013).

Conclusion

This chapter began with the question of whether, and to what degree, neighbourhood houses in Metro Vancouver have taken on a role in governing the community that goes beyond providing social services. In light of the findings, it seems justified to reword the interpretative lens of this inquiry: it is centrally through the provision of these services and the plethora of initiatives in the community that NHs have a profound effect on shaping the community and advocating on its behalf. From a broader political perspective, our study demonstrates how NHs in Metro Vancouver have become an integral part of the region's governance structure and practice.

The first dimension of this impact on governance is the mode in which neighbourhood houses generate social capital by connecting citizens, helping them to overcome their social isolation, and providing them with the tools to become involved in communal affairs. In this respect, the role of NHs is seemingly basic yet critically important for nurturing democratic and socially sustainable civic communities. NHs are central to addressing widespread alienation in urban communities by reconnecting citizens through communal initiatives. Their service provision serves different purposes. It identifies and addresses the social needs of the community while engaging citizens through place-based activities. Particularly for those who have a more precarious social status (low-income individuals, seniors, immigrants/ minorities), NHs provide low-threshold opportunities for relating to each other and becoming involved in communal affairs.

The services and programs that neighbourhood houses offer can open the door to meaningful interaction and engagement. In the fundamental way that Putnam described social capital as providing the infrastructure for making democracy work, NHs are a key player in nurturing a sense of trust and reciprocity in community life. They are also advocates for their communities as they have a profound effect on the network of interactions and encounters that make up a community. They sustain the capacity to find a voice in the community individually and collectively.

The second dimension speaks more directly to the realm of politics and policy making. Neighbourhood houses provide a critical forum for place-based governance. Ultimately, they operate at a complex intersection between community members and different levels of government. Even though their effect on policy making might be more indirect and informal, they play a significant role in identifying problems in the community, setting the agenda for policy making, and bringing government and civil society actors together. The experiences of Metro Vancouver demonstrate that, with their rootedness in the local community, NHs are critical for effective policy development and implementation. They contribute significantly to joint government–civil society problem solving. One of their key achievements is the facilitation of citizen-government interactions and input, and providing community members with the information, resources, and support necessary for them to advocate for political concerns themselves.

At the same time, the dual role that neighbourhood houses have played as service providers and community advocates over the past decades, specifically in the City of Vancouver, is being challenged. Most importantly, NHs have to face a structurally precarious funding landscape as well as a political-legal environment with time-consuming demands, even as a critical degree of financial independence is indispensable for NHs to operate a grassroots, self-governing organization in and on behalf of the community. In spite of these issues in the broader legal and financial environment, NHs appear well positioned to be a central community player in a place-based governance approach to effectively tackle key challenges of urban politics.

Notes

1 The primary data sources used in this chapter are the Clearinghouse Survey and service users survey (please refer to Appendix 1).

2 In his book on the symbolic construction of community, Anthony Cohen (2013) describes the transformative power of community as a system of identity and meaning based on a system of values, norms, and moral codes. At the same time, he alludes to how such ideas of community can become principles guiding communal and governance practices.

3 There is a certain irony in the fact that civil society actors such as NHs have taken on a stronger role in service provision and local governance structures as a result of a restructuring of intergovernmental cooperation under neoliberal auspices. Elaborating on Lefebvre's concept of "the right to the city," Mark Purcell (2003) describes the aspirations of a locally based citizenship to challenge the very logic of the neoliberal project.

4 On the transformation of immigrant settlement agencies in Canada, see Bushell and Shields 2018.

5 In describing their interactions with provincial funders beyond the application and reporting stages, one executive director said that her neighbourhood house has regular meetings with Ministry of Children and Family Development representatives and other provincial actors, and that the province tries to take a "collaborative approach in terms of ensuring that the services we're delivering reflect their needs and that their priorities are reflecting what's happening in the community."

6 This perception is also reflected in how NHs are funded. For NHs outside Vancouver, most interactions with government and funding schemes are at the provincial rather than municipal level. For instance, a municipality neighbouring Vancouver argued that NHs were ineligible for funding as they did not fit into the city's service delivery model. It took years to "educate" council members and the city administration regarding the benefits that NHs were poised to bring to the community.

7 The *Downtown Eastside Plan* describes the role the City of Vancouver plays in providing facility space and funding to neighbourhood houses to support their

operations and services for the local community: "While only five out of the 11 neighbourhood houses are City-owned, all receive either capital investment or programming grants to ensure space and affordable programs are available" (City of Vancouver 2018, 168).

8 Jenny Kwan was the Member of the Legislative Assembly of British Columbia for the riding of Vancouver-Mount Pleasant from 2001 to 2015, before being elected to the House of Commons. As a member of the Vancouver city council and an MLA, she was an outspoken advocate for less privileged groups in Vancouver's inner city.

9 See http://www.anhbc.org/kuldeep/History%20of%20ANHBC%20final.pdf.

10 One executive director, Antonia, adds that one way South Burnaby overcame the lack of knowledge surrounding NHs in Burnaby was to gradually forge partnerships with other organizations and bring them in to deliver services.

11 Also see a summary of these findings in the research brief by Sean Lauer (2019).

12 Based on their case study of neighbourhoods in Los Angeles, Juliet Musso and Christopher Weare (2017) similarly point to the significance of networked-based social capital in supporting the democratic functions of neighbourhood governance networks.

13 In this respect, I conceptualize these dimensions of citizenship as ways that structure the citizen-state relationship and the mode of inclusion in the broader community (Bloemraad, Korteweg, and Yurdakul 2008).

14 Biles and colleagues (2011) use the term "sleeping giant" when they consider the centrality of municipal leadership in the task of integrating newcomers and the relative absence of municipal government from this field of public policy thus far. Canada's comprehensive "settlement program" has traditionally been organized in the form of a federal-provincial partnership. The current federal settlement budget of over $600 million annually almost exclusively flows through the provinces, which organize the services for immigrants on the ground. It has been only over the past couple of years that more formal agreements with municipalities (mostly with limited responsibilities for housing and social services) have been established. Still the Federation of Canadian Municipalities has been adamant in its quest for fuller inclusion of municipalities in the organization and funding of Canada's settlement services.

15 Similarly, the Federation of Canadian Municipalities (2011) highlights both the role of cities as the first point of contact and integration for newcomers to Canada and the challenges that Canadian cities face in fulfilling this important role, due to their limited fiscal resources and their informal status in the settlement and integration policy process. The report calls on the federal and provincial governments to create a formal role for municipalities, using the tripartite Canada-Ontario-Toronto Memorandum of Understanding on Settlement and Integration as a model.

16 See for an evaluation of *Canada's Action Plan Against Racism* in the 2011 Government of Canada report: https://www.canada.ca/en/immigration-refugees-citizenship/corporate/reports-statistics/evaluations/canadas-action-plan-against-racism/evalution.html.

References

Andrew, Caroline, John Biles, Meyer Burstein, Victoria Esses, and Erin Tolley. 2013. *Immigration, Integration, and Inclusion in Ontario Cities.* Montreal and Kingston: McGill-Queen's University Press.

Andrews, Rhys, and Steven van de Walle. 2013. "New Public Management and Citizens' Perceptions of Local Service Efficiency, Responsiveness, Equity and Effectiveness." *Public Management Review* 15 (5): 762–83.

Atkinson, Michael M., and William D. Coleman. 1992. "Policy Networks, Policy Communities and the Problems of Governance." *Governance* 5 (2): 154–80.

Biles, John. 2008. "Integration Policies in English-Speaking Canada." In *Immigration and Integration in Canada in the Twenty-First Century,* edited by John Biles, Meyer Burstein, and James Frideres, 139–86. Montreal and Kingston: School of Policy Studies, Queen's University and McGill-Queen's University Press.

Biles, John, Erin Tolley, Caroline Andrew, Victoria Esses, and Meyer Burstein. 2011. "Integration and Inclusion in Ontario: The Sleeping Giant Stirs." In *Integration and Inclusion of Newcomers and Minorities across Canada,* edited by John Biles, Meyer Burstein, and James Frideres, 195–246. Montreal and Kingston: McGill-Queen's University Press.

Bloemraad, Irene, Anna Korteweg, and Gökçe Yurdakul. 2008. "Citizenship and Immigration: Multiculturalism, Assimilation, and Challenges to the Nation-State." *Annual Review of Sociology* 34 (1): 153–79.

Bowen, Frances, Aloysius Newenham-Kahindi, and Irene Herremans. 2010. "When Suits Meet Roots: The Antecedents and Consequences of Community Engagement Strategy." *Journal of Business Ethics* 95 (2): 297–318.

Bradford, Neil. 2008. *Canadian Social Policy in the 2000s: Bringing Place In.* Ottawa: Canadian Policy Research Networks.

Bradford, Neil, and Caroline Andrew. 2010. *Local Immigration Partnership Councils: A Promising Canadian Innovation.* Ottawa: Citizenship and Immigration Canada.

Bradford, Neil John. 2005. *Place-Based Public Policy: Towards a New Urban and Community Agenda for Canada.* Ottawa: Canadian Policy Research Networks.

Bushell, Riley, and John Shields. 2018. "Immigrant Settlement Agencies in Canada: A Critical Review of the Literature through the Lens of Resilience." Paper of the Building Migrant Resilience in Cities (BMRC) Project, York University, Toronto. https://bmrc-irmu.info.yorku.ca/files/2018/10/ISAs-A-Critical-Review-2018-JSRB-edits-Oct-9-2018.pdf.

Caponio, Tiziana, and Maren Borkert, eds. 2010. *The Local Dimension of Migration Policymaking.* Amsterdam: Amsterdam University Press.

City of Vancouver. 2018. *Downtown Eastside Plan.* 2nd amended ed. Vancouver: City of Vancouver. https://vancouver.ca/files/cov/downtown-eastside-plan.pdf.

Cohen, Anthony. 2013. *Symbolic Construction of Community.* New York: Routledge.

Connelly, Steve. 2011. "Constructing Legitimacy in the New Community Governance." *Urban Studies* 48 (5): 929–46.

Docherty, Iain, Robina Goodlad, and Ronan Paddison. 2001. "Civic Culture, Community and Citizen Participation in Contrasting Neighbourhoods." *Urban Studies* 38 (12): 2225–50.

Dolka, Tsering, and Miu Chung Yan. 2019. "Funding and Implications on the Neighbourhood House." Research Brief of the Neighbourhood House in Metro Vancouver Project. https://www.yournh.ca/wp-content/uploads/2019/10/nh-funding-tsering -miu-revised-sept.pdf

Esses, Victoria, Leah K. Hamilton, Caroline Bennett-AbuAyyash, and Meyer Burstein. 2010. "Characteristics of a Welcoming Community." Welcoming Communities Initiative. Ottawa: Citizenship and Immigration Canada. http://p2pcanada.ca/wp -content/uploads/2011/09/Characteristics-of-a-Welcoming-Community-11.pdf.

Evans, Bryan, and John Shields. 2014. "Nonprofit Engagement with Provincial Policy Officials: The Case of NGO Policy Voice in Canadian Immigrant Settlement Services." *Policy and Society* 33 (2): 117–27.

–. 2018. "The Third Sector, the Neo-Liberal State, and Beyond: Reshaping Contracting and Policy Advocacy." In *The Handbook of Canadian Public Administration*, 3rd ed., edited by Christopher Dunn, 489–500. Toronto: Oxford University Press.

Falge, Christiane, Carlo Ruzza, and Oliver Schmidtke. 2012. *Giving New Subjects a Voice: Political and Institutional Responses to Cultural Diversity in the Health Care System.* Aldershot, UK: Ashgate.

Federation of Canadian Municipalities. 2011. "Starting on Solid Ground: The Municipal Role in Immigrant Settlement." Backgrounder. http://www.fcm.ca/ Documents/backgrounders/Starting_on_solid_ground_the_municipal_role_ in_immigrant_settlement_Report_Overview_EN.pdf.

Fontan, Jean-Marc, Pierre Hamel, Richard Morin, and Eric Shragge. 2009. "Community Organizations and Local Governance in a Metropolitan Region." *Urban Affairs Review* 44 (6): 832–57.

Fourot, Aude-Claire. 2018. "Does the Scale of Funding Matter? Manitoba and British Columbia before and after the Federal Repatriation of Settlement Services." *Journal of International Migration and Integration* 19 (4): 865–81.

Gittell, Ross, and Avis Vidal. 1998. *Community Organizing: Building Social Capital as a Development Strategy.* Thousand Oaks, CA: Sage.

Gray, Barbara. 1989. *Collaborating: Finding Common Ground for Multiparty Problems.* San Francisco: Jossey-Bass.

Gunn, Alexander. 2019. "Immigration and Integration Policy and the Complexity of Multi-Level Governance: A Case Study of British Columbia." *Journal of Borderlands Studies* 35 (4): 603–18. https://www.tandfonline.com/doi/full/10.1080/ 08865655.2019.1619472.

Hepburn, Eve. 2011. "'Citizens of the Region': Party Conceptions of Regional Citizenship and Immigrant Integration." *European Journal of Political Research* 50 (4): 504–29.

Immigration, Refugees and Citizenship Canada. 2017. "Evaluation of the Settlement Program." Ottawa: Research and Evaluation Branch, Immigration, Refugees and Citizenship Canada. https://www.canada.ca/en/immigration-refugees-citizenship/ corporate/reports-statistics/evaluations/settlement-program.html.

Jørgensen, Martin Bak. 2012. "The Diverging Logics of Integration Policy Making at National and City Level." *International Migration Review* 46 (1): 244–78.

Lane, Jan-Erik. 2000. *New Public Management.* London: Routledge.

Larcombe, Karen. 2008. "Community Capacity Building: A Role for Neighbour-hood Houses in Community Revitalization." PhD diss., University of British Columbia.

Lauer, S. 2019. "Civic and Community Engagement through Neighbourhood House Involvement." Research Brief of the Neighbourhood House in Metro Vancouver Project. https://www.yournh.ca/wp-content/uploads/2019/10/civic-and-community -engagement-reformatted.pdf.

Lawrence, Thomas B., Cynthia Hardy, and Nelson Phillips. 2002. "Institutional Ef-fects of Interorganizational Collaboration: The Emergence of Proto-Institutions." *Academy of Management Journal* 45 (1): 281–90.

Maytree Foundation. 2013. *Good Ideas from Successful Cities: Canada. Municipal Leadership on Immigrant Integration.* Toronto: Maytree Foundation. http:// www.citiesofmigration.ca/wp-content/uploads/2013/03/Municipal_Report_ Canada.pdf.

Michels, Ank, and Laurens de Graaf. 2017. "Examining Citizen Participation: Local Participatory Policymaking and Democracy Revisited." *Local Government Studies* 43 (6): 875–81.

Moreno, Karla Angelica Valenzuela, John Shields, and Julie Drolet. 2018. "Settling Immigrants in Neoliberal Times: NGOs and Immigrant Well-Being in Com-parative Context." *Alternate Routes: A Journal of Critical Social Research* 29. http://www.alternateroutes.ca/index.php/ar/article/view/22447.

Musso, Juliet, and Christopher Weare. 2017. "Social Capital and Community Rep-resentation: How Multiform Networks Promote Local Democracy in Los Angeles." *Urban Studies* 54 (11): 2521–39.

Papadopoulos, Yannis. 2003. "Cooperative Forms of Governance: Problems of Democratic Accountability in Complex Environments." *European Journal of Political Research* 42 (4): 473–501.

Patsias, Caroline, Anne Latendresse, and Laurence Bherer. 2013. "Participatory Democracy, Decentralization and Local Governance: The Montreal Participatory Budget in the Light of 'Empowered Participatory Governance.'" *International Journal of Urban and Regional Research* 37 (6): 2214–30.

Penninx, Rinus, Karen Kraal, Marco Martiniello, and Steven Vertovec. 2004. *Cit-izenship in European Cities: Immigrants, Local Politics and Integration Policies.* Aldershot, UK: Ashgate.

Praznik, Jessica, and John Shields. 2018. "An Anatomy of Settlement Services in Canada: A Guide." Paper of the Building Migrant Resilience in Cities (BMRC) Project, York University, Toronto. https://bmrc-irmu.info.yorku.ca/files/2018/ 07/An-Anatomy-of-Settlement-Services-in-Canada_BMRCIRMU.pdf.

Purcell, Mark. 2003. "Citizenship and the Right to the Global City: Reimagining the Capitalist World Order." *International Journal of Urban and Regional Research* 27 (3): 564–90.

Putnam, Robert D. 2000. *Bowling Alone: The Collapse and Revival of American Community.* New York: Simon and Schuster.

Quintelier, Ellen, Dietlind Stolle, and Allison Harell. 2012. "Politics in Peer Groups: Exploring the Causal Relationship between Network Diversity and Political Participation." *Political Research Quarterly* 65 (4): 868–81.

Salamon, Lester M., and Stefan Toepler. 2015. "Government-Nonprofit Cooperation: Anomaly or Necessity?" *Voluntas: International Journal of Voluntary and Nonprofit Organizations* 26 (6): 2155–77.

Saldivar-Tanaka, Laura, and Marianne E. Krasny. 2004. "Culturing Community Development, Neighborhood Open Space, and Civic Agriculture: The Case of Latino Community Gardens in New York City." *Agriculture and Human Values* 21 (4): 399–412.

Schmidtke, Oliver. 2014. "Beyond National Models? Governing Migration and Integration at the Regional and Local Levels in Canada and Germany." *Comparative Migration Studies* 2 (1): 77–99.

Schmidtke, Oliver, and Andrej Zaslove. 2014. "Why Regions Matter in Immigrant Integration Policies: North Rhine–Westphalia and Emilia-Romagna in Comparative Perspective." *Journal of Ethnic and Migration Studies* 40 (12): 1854–74.

Scholten, Peter W.A. 2013. "Agenda Dynamics and the Multi-Level Governance of Intractable Policy Controversies: The Case of Migrant Integration Policies in the Netherlands." *Policy Sciences* 46 (3): 217–36.

Seidle, F. Leslie. 2010. *The Canada-Ontario Immigration Agreement: Assessment and Options for Renewal.* Toronto: Mowat Centre for Policy Innovation.

Siemiatycki, Myer. 2011. "Governing Immigrant City: Immigrant Political Representation in Toronto." *American Behavioral Scientist* 55 (9): 1214–34.

–. 2012. "The Place of Immigrants: Citizenship, Settlement, and Socio-Cultural Integration in Canada." In *Managing Immigration and Diversity in Canada. A Transatlantic Dialogue in the New Age of Migration,* edited by Dan Rodriguez-Garcia, 223–47. Montreal and Kingston: McGill-Queen's University Press.

Stasiulis, Daiva, Christine Hughes, and Zainab Amery. 2011. "From Government to Multilevel Governance of Immigrant Settlement in Ontario's City-Regions." In *Immigrant Settlement Policy in Canadian Municipalities,* edited by Erin Tolley and Robert Young, 73–147. Montreal and Kingston: McGill-Queen's University Press.

Tossutti, Livianna S. 2012. "Municipal Roles in Immigrant Settlement, Integration and Cultural Diversity." *Canadian Journal of Political Science/Revue canadienne de science politique* 45 (3): 607–33.

Winders, Jamie. 2012. "Seeing Immigrants: Institutional Visibility and Immigrant Incorporation in New Immigrant Destinations." *Annals of the American Academy of Political and Social Science* 641 (1): 58–78.

Yan, Miu Chung. 2004. "Bridging the Fragmented Community: Revitalizing Settlement Houses in the Global Era." *Journal of Community Practice* 12 (1–2): 51–69.

Yan, Miu Chung, and Sean Lauer. 2008. "Social Capital and Ethno-Cultural Diverse Immigrants: A Canadian Study on Settlement House and Social Integration." *Journal of Ethnic and Cultural Diversity in Social Work* 17 (3): 229–50.

Yan, Miu Chung, Sean Lauer, and Pilar Riaño-Alcalá. 2017. "Incorporating Individual Community Assets in Neighbourhood Houses: Beyond the Community-Building Tradition of Settlement Houses." *International Social Work* 60 (6): 1591–1605.

Zoller, Heather M. 2000. "'A Place You Haven't Visited Before': Creating the Conditions for Community Dialogue." *Southern Communication Journal* 65 (2–3): 191–207.

3

Mechanism of Connection

Accessibility and Beyond

MIU CHUNG YAN

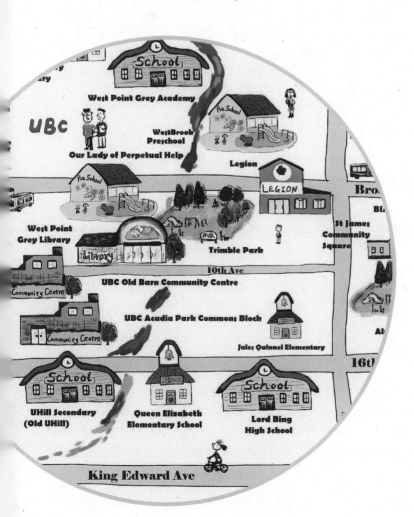

A neighbourhood house (NH) is a place-based community service organization (CSO) that provides services to meet people's needs. In contrast with many other CSOs, NHs have a place-based focus and a strong mandate to serve and advocate for the well-being of residents sharing the same geographical living space. They are also locally governed by a group of elected members mostly from the local community. As a place-based, locally governed multi-service organization in the community, NHs are accessible to local residents in many respects. For instance, being located within walking distance of their service users, they are convenient and safe places that connect local residents. Providing multiple and intergenerational programs, they not only serve the needs of local residents but also facilitate interaction among them. Despite being embedded structurally in the web of social services, which can be intrinsically difficult for people to navigate, NHs serve as a service node connecting local residents to many services within and outside the neighbourhood. In this chapter, we examine how neighbourhood houses, as place-based CSOs, not only enhance their service users' accessibility to their own services but also, through their connections, help local residents navigate and connect to complex service networks. Information presented in this chapter is mainly drawn from the results of the 2013 Clearinghouse Survey, resource-mapping workshops, network-mapping interviews, and focus groups for service users and community partners (see Appendix 1 for details of these research activities).

Accessibility in Social Services: A Perennial Challenge

Social services as a public resource exist to support people, particularly the poor and the socially marginalized, who need help to resolve personal and social challenges. Access to resources not only makes a significant difference by improving these individuals' life chances and living conditions but is also a necessary condition for social inclusion and social justice (Bristow et al. 2009). Service accessibility is impacted by many factors. Individuals' ability to enter, navigate, secure, and exit the system for obtaining the necessary resources has been a major challenge for people wanting to access services (Hernandez et al. 2009). This challenge is exacerbated by how public resources are organized and delivered institutionally. The individual and institutional factors are not mutually exclusive; instead, they inter- actively determine people's access to services (Farrington 2007).

Urban planning scholars have pointed out that the spatial distribution of public resources is a common barrier for people, particularly those who have mobility challenges and those who rely on public transportation to ac- cess services (e.g., Apparicio and Séguin 2006; Farrington 2007). Proximity is an enabling condition that facilitates access to services, particularly for the old, the sick, the poor, and single parents with young children. Govern- ment tends to distribute public resources equally across different districts based on the size of the population, but the equality principle is a one-size- fits-all approach that ignores the unique needs of local residents. In the most deprived neighbourhoods, where social needs are much higher, the equality principle may unjustly further deprive the community of the resources that are needed and available to its residents (Apparicio and Séguin 2006). The unavailability of services in their neighbourhood has forced the most deprived group of people to access services away from home. As one can imagine, this group of people is the one that tends to rely on public trans- portation for access to services, meaning they are burdened with extra costs in money and time.

Availability of resources is not just about the quantity of services. As reflected in the Canadian Community Health Survey, availability is also af- fected by affordability and acceptability (Elliott and Hunsley 2015). Afford- ability is not merely about the financial cost of accessing services; it also entails the cost of temporary support for caring for a young child or sick family member and the opportunity cost of losing work hours. For instance, for many low-income immigrants who need to work long hours to support their families, it is too costly for them to forgo work hours to upgrade their English-language skills. Availability of service is also affected by how the service is delivered. Regular nine-to-five office hours can be a barrier to low-income service users who work long hours with a rigid schedule. The need for services to be language- and culturally sensitive poses barriers for ethno-racial minorities, particularly new immigrants, in accessing services (e.g., Hernandez et al. 2009; Hurley et al. 2013). To some social minority service users, such as LGBTQ youth, societal discrimination and stigmatiz- ation and service providers' lack of awareness and knowledge of their needs can be a deterrent discouraging them from accessing services (Acevedo- Polakovich et al. 2011).

The availability of service is also dependent on potential users' awareness and knowledge of its existence. Despite criticism of inadequacy, there are undeniably numerous CSOs providing a myriad of social services for different groups of people. The problem is that these services are not delivered in a coordinated manner. A study of how African immigrant youth accessed services found that while the service providers agreed that there were many services available to young people, the youth and parent participants reported it was hard for them to know of and to identify suitable programs (Francis 2010). Service providers' control of service availability is diminishing. Driven by neoliberal ideology, governments tend to allocate constantly shrinking public funds to those programs that can remedy the most imminent social issues through a short-term, program-based funding regime (Fabricant and Fisher 2002). The neoliberal funding regime emphasizes competition instead of coordination among service providers (Yan et al. 2017). Most of these short-term programs have a specific target group and cater to a specific need, yet more often than not service users may have multiple needs. The constantly changing and competitive funding environment has also further fragmented the social service landscape and makes it even harder for service users, and even service providers, to navigate.

To resolve the difficult access to public resources due to this fragmentation in social services, John Farrington (2007, 237) suggests a social interaction model that emphasizes the networked nature of social life and recognizes the importance of "co-presence and 'meetingness'" in the functioning and maintenance of social networks. This model echoes the very essence of neighbourhood houses' place-based tradition in connecting public resources to residents' needs.

The Neighbourhood House as a Place-Based Solution:
Accessing Resources Close to Home

Accessibility represents the core feature of neighbourhood houses' place-based approach and efficacy. Located right where people are, NHs are a service hub with long service hours that makes them accessible to local residents, even to those who need to go to school or work. Based on a holistic perspective, they organize and provide low-cost services to different groups of residents to meet individual and collective needs in the community. They also come across as trustworthy and welcoming by opening their doors non-judgmentally to everyone in the community and by employing a group of ethnically diverse staff who share similar lived experiences with the local residents. In NHs, service users are not passive recipients; many also become volunteers to help meet others' needs.

Physical Proximity: Accessible to Local Residents
Neighbourhood Houses follow the settlement house tradition of meeting the needs of local residents in deprived neighbourhoods by bringing in outside resources and building local capacities. They are geographically close to where the needs are. This tradition was initiated by the Reverend Samuel Barnett, the founder of the first settlement house, Toynbee Hall, who in the 1880s brought the well-off and educated university students to settle (i.e., reside) in the deprived neighbourhoods in London's East End. During their stay, students provided services to local residents while learning about their living conditions and challenges. The successful experience of Toynbee Hall in bridging the poor-rich divide soon inspired the wide establishment of settlement houses internationally (Johnson 1995). Following Toynbee Hall, most settlement houses in North America were established in deprived neighbourhoods where immigrants tend to be concentrated (Yan and Lauer 2008).

A similar pattern can be identified in Metro Vancouver, where, with the exception of two, almost all the fifteen neighbourhood houses are located in traditionally immigrant-dominant neighbourhoods with a lower socioeconomic demographic profile. In Vancouver, most NHs serve an area of three to four census tracts. According to Statistics Canada (2015), each census tract has a population of between 2,500 and 8,000. Vancouver is a highly populated urban environment. The geographic area of each census tract is small. Thus, where there is an NH, most local residents can access it within walking distance. Meanwhile, on average, NHs are open for service for over 51.2 hours per week. Eleven of them also provide over 11.5 hours of service in the evening per week and are open during the weekends if needed. The long hours of service enable some hard-to-serve groups, such as working parents, to join their programs. Financially, NHs provide many free and low-fee services to its members, who pay a membership fee of $1–15 each year. Lastly, as place-based CSOs, most NHs have the advantage of having a secure and stable physical infrastructure in the neighbourhood. Their physical presence in the community represents a symbolic figure of the community that is interwoven into the memories of both local residents and their community partners (Yan 2004).

Institutional Proximity: Accessible Programming to Meet Needs

As Martin Stewart-Weeks (1997) suggests, CSOs have the advantage of "institutional proximity," that is, the capacity to respond to the collective needs of the community because of their proximity to the people they serve. However, not all CSOs are place-based. They may have a specific mandate to serve an exclusive group of people who are spread out all over the city. These non-place-based CSOs do not enjoy the full advantage of closeness to the community. As a place-based organization that has a holistic mandate of serving all members of the community, a neighbourhood house utilizes this proximity to respond flexibly to the community's collective needs, particularly the emerging ones. A community partner of Alexandra NH provided a good illustration of the houses' institutional proximity:

> [The] NH can do better than other organizations because it's anchored in the community and has an understanding how those relationships work, the history, the issues ... If someone was to come in with some funding, say, to plant a garden, they may be doing that out of context without understanding some of the issues around vagrancy and theft or whatever, so the NH can provide the infrastructure for that discussion and that allows projects like that to happen.

Many of these partners also noticed that as service organizations anchored in the community, NHs know well what the local needs are. A community partner who worked with Kiwassa NH recalled:

> [I] can't think of how many times we've asked and leaned on the NHs to help donors understand what really happens in the community, and a number of times we've called on XXX, or YYY over at Kiwassa to take a donor through and expose them to a little bit of what families really experience. We know where to come when we need specific information about the neighbourhood ... as much as we like to say we base decisions on evidence, a lot of the evidence just comes from the knowledge that's present in these organizations because they *are* the neighbourhood, they know the neighbourhood from a place-based perspective; they're perfectly situated to have that knowledge.

The institutional proximity also enables neighbourhood houses to see and respond more quickly to the emerging needs of the community than non-place-based CSOs. For example, a community partner credited Alexandra

NH with setting up a Youth Café program for at-risk youth who hung out in local coffee shops and fast food restaurants in downtown South Surrey. Similarly, a community partner who worked with both Collingwood and Cedar Cottage NH observed that neighbourhood houses

> provide a variety of programming to the variety of populations while at the same time – and I see it in both of these neighbourhood houses – they are always looking and seeking and searching: Who are we reaching, who are we getting to, how could we get to them? ... They are always looking out, always focus on the community: What else can we be doing?

To meet the emerging needs of the community, NHs constantly explore new ways to better support local residents. Echoing this spirit, a long-time staff member recalled how Cedar Cottage NH responded to the changing local collective needs:

> Others might be around, things that we've done in the past, kids that are coming from different [ethnic groups], they're maybe new immigrants and say lunch is a challenge. And so working with those children on what would be a lunch that you could bring to school. Another thing might be around kids that are coming to school without food. So working with the school around creating breakfast programs. So these are not necessarily things that are currently happening at the moment but they're things that ... So, I've been here for over twenty years, so during my time here there's been a number of things that we've done depending on whatever needs pop up.

The responsiveness of neighbourhood houses to collective needs also earns them a word-of-mouth reputation as a place in the community where people can always go and ask for help. A service user of Burnaby NH described how she referred people to the neighbourhood house: "If somebody is with a child looking for daycare I would say, 'Go to the NH, go to the drop-in program so your child starts to speak English and feel more comfortable.' If somebody needs to do their tax return, I would also tell them to go to the NH." Word of mouth is the most effective way for CSOs to make themselves known. People prefer to access services that have been used by someone they know.

Neighbourhood houses provide a variety of services to local residents. Unlike many other CSOs, they do not serve only a specific group of people in the community. Instead, they tend to adopt a comprehensive and holistic

TABLE 3.1

Categories of activities accessed by respondents to service users survey

Activities	Respondents who have accessed in last 12 months (%)
Recreational activities	55
Settlement assistance (information, referrals, counselling)	28
Arts and cultural programs	45
Parenting education and support	25
Early childhood (0–6 years) program for children	27
After-school program for children (6–18 years)	11
English language and literacy programs	31
Employment counselling/training	15
Interpretation and translation services	16
Food programs (community kitchen or breakfast club)	43
Health education	34
Leadership and volunteer opportunities	31
Committee and interest group	26
Youth mentorship programs	10
Festival, celebration, or other special events	58
Financial and legal services	18
Family services, including family counselling	15
Drop-in services, such as computer use	30
Dialogue, community consultation, and other civic engagement	23
Self-help and other support groups	28

Source: service users survey.

service model inherited from the early settlement house (Yan 2004). They design and offer programs responsibly to different groups of residents according to the local needs. In the 2012–13 fiscal year, a total of 209,684 people accessed different services provided by NHs in Metro Vancouver. All together, 773 program activities were delivered – 158 for children, 152 for families, 137 for seniors, 107 for youth, and the rest for many other groups. Table 3.1 lists the categories of activities provided by NHs. As shown in Table 3.1, the focus of NHs is not remedial. They provide many recreational, social, and educational programs. Most people in the community will find something useful for them at the neighbourhood house.

Indeed, the physical and institutional proximity of neighbourhood houses has generated a chain effect that shapes many local families' access of their services. Many women service users of NHs share a similar story. They first accessed the NH's child care service, a service offered by almost all NHs. Then they were drawn to other services for their own needs, such as parenting skills, community gardening, language programs, and so on. After a while, they started giving back to the NH by doing volunteer work, such as helping the kitchens prepare lunch for seniors, organizing programs for children, and providing clerical support at the reception desk. Meanwhile, they brought other family members, such as their spouse, and friends to NHs for group activities, social and cultural events, and family outings. Some of them also became staff or board members. (In Chapters 5 and 6, we explore further the pathway followed by service users who became leaders of NHs.) This chain effect may explain why many service users feel that the neighbourhood house is a second home, a sign of psychological proximity.

Psychological Proximity: The Neighbourhood House as an Accessible Welcoming Space

Physical proximity, long hours of service, and low-cost and multiple services make neighbourhood houses accessible. As reflected in the literature, however, although these tangible features may attract service users to access service at NHs, they are not sufficient to retain them. Trust and acceptance are also critical if people are to seek help from strangers and stay in the service. Many studies have shown that feeling judged and not accepted inhibit people from accessing service and support (Acevedo-Polakovich et al. 2011). The formal setting of many CSOs can deter people. Also, due to a restricted mandate, many CSOs open their doors to a specific group of users only, whereas NHs are known as a social hub where everyone in the community is welcome. A community partner of Downtown Eastside Neighbourhood House observed that it was "open to everybody – that is one of the wonderful things about an NH. You've got folks coming from all different places, different levels of income, different ages, ethnicities, backgrounds." One user of Alexandra NH said: "Alexandra NH provides a place-based community ... [it] provides a venue for activities that integrate community and engagement, providing a neutral place for people to meet."

Unlike many other CSOs, which require pre-screening and assessment, neighbourhood houses are open to everyone in the neighbourhood and no intake assessment is needed. "You don't have to be pre-qualified to come into the house," said a staff member from North Shore NH. It is a neutral place for everyone in the neighbourhood where they will not be judged. A service user of Collingwood NH said that "there's a lot of people that come in there, you know, and are just looking for just that little acceptance and help."

Meanwhile, what makes a neighbourhood house welcoming and accessible is not only its physical and institutional proximity but also the people working there. As a service user of Gordon NH experienced, "the teachers in Gordon Neighbourhood House ... are very kind. They help the newcomers a lot. That's not just English, maybe if you have some difficulties, they can just teach you how to solve them." To many newcomers, having to use English to access service can be discouraging. As the second major destination of immigrants to Canada, Vancouver is ethnically and linguistically diverse. NHs have truly reflected the ethnic diversity at many levels. Most NHs serve multi-ethnic groups of residents. Chinese is the most popular group, followed by Latin American, Southeast Asian, South Asian, and eight other different groups.

To meet the language and cultural needs of this diverse group, neighbourhood houses have also hired a correspondingly diverse group of staff members. All together, the staff of all NHs represent twenty-four different ethnic minority groups who speak twenty different languages other than English and French. Meanwhile, close to half of their staff were themselves first-generation immigrants. Many were once also service users of NHs. Their service to NHs is not motivated exclusively by monetary gain. More importantly, many NH staff want to pay back to the community. (For detailed stories of how service users have become leaders of NHs, please refer to Chapters 5 and 6.)

Sharing similar experiences, the ethnically diverse staff of neighbourhood houses can easily earn trust, an important factor contributing to accessibility (Hurley et al. 2013), from their service users, and make them feel welcome to the NHs. As the literature suggests, strangers who access services provided by public institutions can become scared, particularly when they are in a vulnerable situation. Lack of trust is a major barrier for them in accessing social support. Neighbourhood houses are trustworthy places where people can feel understood and accepted by the staff, who share similar lived experiences. As a service user of Burnaby NH shared: "[The NH is] a *trusting* place, so you can come here and feel safe. It's like *home*. It's a warm feeling when you walk in the door ... It's just very comforting to know that you can come somewhere and your kids can hang out together and meet new people in the NH" (italics added). The NH is like a home where people usually feel comfortable and safe enough to stay and relax. As one community partner of Downtown Eastside NH recalled: "Sometimes after we finish our activities somebody will pull out a game of cards and they'll start talking, telling stories. And that's this environment that people automatically said when they came through the door that oh, I feel comfortable here." Another community partner retold the story of a client's experience of accessing service at Frog Hollow NH: "'If it wasn't for Frog Hollow, I am not sure that I'd be alive right now as a single mom, three kids.' And she said, 'we spend more time at Frog Hollow than we do at our house ... that's not programming or courses like that ... that's the extended family.'"

Sense of Ownership: Beyond Passive Service Recipients
The metaphors of home and extended family indicate a sense of ownership among the service users. When comparing neighbourhood houses with local community centres, which provide recreational and sports programs and are owned and run by the municipal government, several community partners of Little Mountain and Mount Pleasant NHs assert that users of NHs have a "sense of ownership, you feel like you belong to this place, it's your extended living room and you take care of it." According to them, "when we're with NH, say, we have a family gathering, they come and have coffee and they're also connected to other programs that are useful. Whereas when we go to Hillcrest [Community Centre], it's such a big facility we're just there for a specific time and we tell them about the programs, but it's less personal."

These community partners also pointed out another major difference between neighbourhood houses and community centres: "People who have used the services [of NHs], once they're a little more familiar with the area, they come back and volunteer, whereas at CCs, they volunteer to get experience so they can get a job. People volunteer in the NH because they want to give back and be part of the community." Just like family members, service users give back to their home – the neighbourhood house – which they care about.

Volunteerism: Expanding Local Resources
Indeed, perhaps the most explicit manifestation of the sense of ownership and belonging is the vibrant spirit of volunteerism. In 2012–13, there were over 3,682 registered volunteers among all fifteen neighbourhood houses. They contributed on average 15,000 service hours to each NH. Most of these volunteers were women (70 percent). Youth (22 percent) and

seniors (22 percent) were another two critical masses. Over half (55 percent) were adults. All together, they spoke eighteen languages, which were similar to those that the service users spoke. Overall, 35 percent of registered volunteers were immigrants, and 52 percent had been service users of NHs.

Volunteers are the service backbone of neighbourhood houses. They provide a variety of support to the staff – sitting on boards and committees, organizing events and activities, teaching and tutoring children, serving at the reception desk, and many others. Volunteers are mostly local residents and service users. Through volunteering, they give back not only to the neighbourhood house but also to the community at large. A staff member at Gordon NH shared the story of a volunteer there:

> I have parents that volunteer. Do you know XXX, you know, a volunteer here [for] different programs that we have like the children ... And some've also gone on to volunteer at other places 'cos I know one of the moms who is a single mom. She's not only a volunteer here. She volunteers for the Salvation Army. She volunteers for a whole bunch of other places as well because her, her thing is that the community has given her so much that she wants to make sure she gives it to the community and she wants to teach her children that.

By promoting volunteerism among service users, neighbourhood houses also nurture a sense of mutual caring and actualize the basic principle of active citizenship, which emphasizes a balance of rights and caring among residents (Drover 2000). As active citizens, volunteers of NHs are no longer passive receivers. They are active participants who give back to other members of the NH and the community at large. A volunteer at Little Mountain NH told this story:

> LM gave me that opportunity ... Through the NH I met incredible people and through that involvement I've been able to put together a concert that brought together the community. With their talents, I have been able to help people outside of our circle. In May I'm organizing a food drive for the Vancouver Food Bank and allowing the community to participate in it. It's a citywide project. What I'm finding as I work on the campaign is that I'm learning a ton about people and other things. And we can all share and impart like that, so I think this NH is particularly welcoming, there's a sense of everybody wanting to pull together.

Accessibility in a neighbourhood house is not only about receiving service and support. It is also about how to give back to the community as a resource to improve the accessibility of others in the community. Indeed, a NH is a one-of-a-kind community capacity-building mechanism (Yan, Lauer, and Riaño-Alcalá 2016). Instead of treating local residents as passive receivers of social support, NHs see them as valuable assets that can benefit other members of the community by nurturing their skills, leadership, and social networks. Volunteers are social resources. By promoting volunteerism as a form of active citizenship, NHs build the capacity of their local communities and generate new social resources among the residents.

These local resources, namely, volunteers in the local neighbourhood, are easily accessible through personal connection to residents who tend not to seek help by directly accessing formal services. As service users themselves, volunteers help break down the barriers that discourage and hinder others in the neighbourhood from accessing public resources. As local residents, they help connect other local residents, particularly those who are socially isolated, to services. For instance, a service user at North Shore NH reflected on her own experience: "Volunteering involves people of different physical and mental capabilities. And it brings the community together and people that would be isolated on their own, and some of them are very shy, this really helps them to find somewhere that they fit in and feel comfortable."

The spirit of reciprocity embraced by volunteerism is reflected in the informal relationship among service users. An earlier study on neighbourhood houses in Vancouver found that service users had successfully established a friendship network among themselves. This network provided them with seemingly trivial but critical daily support, such as childminding and grocery shopping. According to the study:

> Although 26.6% of respondents do not make any exchange (i.e., give or receive help) with people associated with neighbourhood houses, it does appear that the NHs play a role in forging social ties for the reciprocal exchange of favors. Over 50% of respondents make these sorts of exchanges with people associated with neighbourhood houses, while 20% make all or most of their exchanges with people associated with neighbourhood houses. (Yan and Lauer 2008, 239)

NHs are a community mechanism that brings people together and helps them establish functional exchange relationships, which are undoubtedly useful resources for them.

Neighbourhood Houses: An Appreciated Institutional Asset for Local Residents

As discussed above, many service users felt strongly that the neighbourhood house was their home, a place where they felt a strong sense of ownership. One service user of Alexandra NH explained why she cared when the local residents were not involved in neighbourhood houses:

> We've invested in this community because our children go here. We're not just looking at the daycare as an isolated thing. We want to be involved. That's why I started the parents group to get us all together. I think the issue that we all feel is that they [staff] are not communicating effectively even to those that are involved in the NH. They're not telling us where there is a lack of things or what their plans are. What would they like to see? We want to be involved!

Many service users want to be involved because they feel that they are part of the neighbourhood house. Their involvement is also a reflection of the success of NHs as place-based accessible social assets in the community. As publicly funded CSOs, NHs are a social asset "made by the public, society, or group through various forms of dues, fees, donations, and tax exemptions" (Bryce 2006, 315). Meanwhile, service users also invest in NHs through their participation and active volunteering. In other words, they are also shareholders of NHs. They delegate governance to the board of directors, who are the legal entity that owns and governs the NH. Members of NHs, who are largely local residents, elect board members to represent their interests. Unlike at many other CSOs, board members of most NHs are no strangers to NHs. In 2012–13, among the 128 (81 percent) members serving on the boards of all the NHs, 59 were active or former service users, while 88 and 31, respectively, were either residing or working in the neighbourhood served by the NH.

To maintain itself and grow, a social asset must yield results that satisfy the shareholders. As indicated in Table 3.2, among the 675 respondents of the neighbourhood house service users survey, a great majority are pleased with the NHs' performance. Echoing what we have discussed so far, most respondents agreed that NHs were a safe place with trustworthy leaders (board members, staff, and volunteers) who can motivate and inspire them. They also felt strongly that NHs have positive effects on solving community problems, raising resources, and, more importantly, improving their access to services.

TABLE 3.2

Survey respondents' perspective on neighbourhood houses' functions (*N* = 675)

Statement	Strongly disagree (%)	Somewhat disagree (%)	Somewhat agree (%)	Strongly agree (%)
The neighbourhood house has had a part in solving at least one problem in this community.	2.84	7.19	44.31	45.65
Leadership in the neighbourhood house has been able to motivate and inspire.	2.51	4.18	44.98	48.33
In general, people at the neighbourhood house can be trusted.	1.51	4.01	32.27	62.21
In general, I feel safe at the neighbourhood house.	1.00	3.51	22.74	72.74
The neighbourhood house has been able to successfully raise resources to run programs.	4.01	5.85	40.30	49.83
As a result of the neighbourhood house's efforts, the community has access to important information and resources.	1.67	3.34	37.46	57.53

Source: service users survey.

However, the success of neighbourhood houses is always hampered by limited resources. As reflected in the result of the 2013 Clearinghouse Survey, among all fifteen NHs in Vancouver the average budget was $2.5 million, ranging from $171,097 to $6,115,402. Despite this variation, they shared similar funding sources, largely from the different levels of government, and suffered similarly from the neoliberal funding regime. A great majority of their funding is program-based, short-term (three years or less), and non-renewable, which results in unstable employment for most of their staff. In 2012–13, 34.5 percent of the total staff had worked less than three years at NHs and less than 45 percent of staff working at NHs worked thirty-five or more hours per week. Their limited resources have hampered NHs in meeting the major needs of the community. As one service user who has been using the family program at Frog Hollow NH observed: "We talked about the family program, you know, people being turned away because there's not enough space for everybody to come." She understood that the NH has done its best to provide more space but lack of funding has limited what it can do. A service user of Alexandra NH also noted:

> My impression over a number of years is that funding for ANH is so important and I think they look for anything that is going to generate revenue, such as daycare, renting out the cottages or facility here to groups. That's their primary focus and I think other things like doing the community stuff has become secondary because the funding to keep it running is the main thing.

As indicated in Table 3.2, many service users agreed that neighbourhood houses have done well in raising resources to run their programs. In view of the shortage of public funding, NHs have to seek extra resources elsewhere to meet the myriad needs in the community. Most of these additional resources are secured through the vast networks that NHs have strategically nurtured through the years. These networks are the organizational social capital of NHs, the use of which has improved local residents' access to hard-to-reach public resources.

Organizational Social Capital and Neighbourhood Houses: Solution for Wicked Problems

Accessing formal service can be daunting and frustrating, particularly for the marginalized groups of people who lack time, mobility, knowledge, and skills to navigate through the maze-like public service system. Resource allocation and program delivery through this system involve multiple layers of stakeholders, but often these hierarchically positioned stakeholders operate in silos both vertically and horizontally. This generates what public policy scholars call "wicked problems." Wicked problems are social situations or social needs, such as poverty, social exclusion, and an aging population, whose causes and solutions are beyond the capacity of any one organization, including government, to understand and determine (Ferlie et al. 2011, 308). As suggested by Horst Rittel and Melvin Webber (1973), who were credited with articulation of the concept, a wicked problem is difficult, if not impossible, to delineate, define, and resolve. Such problems are the consequences of the institutional disconnect and silo between different layers of public service organizations that are hierarchically immutable (Bradford 2005). In the neoliberal era, the shrinking of public resources and the rise of a new public management mentality have further reinforced wicked problems.

These problems create institutional barriers for people in accessing the public resources they need in order to resolve their predicaments.

In many countries, social services are largely provided by CSOs and funded by the government. Many CSOs are set up for a restricted mandate that limits their scope of service to a specific target group, such as children, families, seniors, immigrants, or people with a particular illness or disability. Often a family may have to seek services from many CSOs to meet the different needs of its members. How to coordinate among different services to provide better support for people to meet their comprehensive needs is important. However, the prevalent neoliberal mentality makes governments across and within nations at multiple levels use the discourse of economic recession to justify a public policy that entails the contraction of public funding, resulting in "budgetary cuts during a period in which local social problems and conflicts have intensified in conjunction with rapid economic restructuring" (Brenner and Theodore 2002, 367). Governments tend to allocate their shrinking funding through short-term, program-based funding regimes. The unilateral top-down nature of funding programs of different government departments means that the programs typically focus only on imminent problems related to their specific mandate. This funding regime leads to competition among service providers rather than valuing or encouraging concerted efforts to address factors causing wicked problems in the first place. It also tends to destabilize the availability and continuity of social services. The constantly changing and fragmented social service landscape is already difficult for service providers, not to mention service users, to navigate.

To address wicked problems, a place-based framework for public policy has been advocated and experimented with in many parts of the world. For instance, Britain's National Health Service piloted the Total Place initiative to minimize duplication and waste by integrating local resources and services (Humphries and Gregory 2010). In the United States, the Clinton administration experimented with a hybrid framework integrating "people-centred" and "place-centred" approaches to tackling issues of poor families in deprived neighbourhoods (Ladd 1994). The European Union initiated Multi-Level Governance and Policy Networking (Börzel and Heard-Lauréote 2009). In Australia, a neighbourhood renewal project was implemented in Victoria (Ferrie 2008). In Canada, a policy framework was also proposed by a civil society think tank (Bradford 2005) and a research unit of the federal government (Shugart and Townsend 2010). All these initiatives point to the importance of networks in resolving wicked problems. In public policy, networks are connections and "interactions of many separate but interdependent organizations which co-ordinate their actions through interdependencies of resources and interests" (Börzel and Heard-Lauréote 2009, 136).

Neighbourhood Houses as Organizational Social Capital

Networking has been part of the settlement house movement tradition. Many early settlement houses, such as Toynbee Hall in London and Hull House in Chicago, networked with universities and churches to provide educational programs to local residents and to conduct social research to improve the condition of the local neighbourhoods (Yan 2002). This tradition has handed on to neighbourhood houses. Indeed, due to their limited resources for meeting the myriad needs in the community, NHs have actively connected with a multi-faceted group of institutional partners. With their physical and institutional proximity, they have also assumed a coordination role among their institutional partners at the local level, which helps break the silo mentality and fragmentation of the formal service system and achieve community involvement, take collective action, raise funds, and disseminate and perpetuate information. These networks have therefore been instrumental in tackling the wicked problems that prevent local residents from accessing public resources. NH networks are beneficial in a bilateral way. On the one hand, through these partnerships, NHs actively mobilize other public resources from inside and outside the community to serve the local community. On the other hand, effective use of functional networks can help integrate and coordinate the unevenly and inequitably distributed public resources and improve their accessibility to people who need the resources. Using the concept of social capital, these networks are instrumental in furthering the goals of NHs (Schneider 2009, 644).

Despite its popularity, there is no one agreed-on understanding of the concept of social capital (Field 2003). From a social resource perspective, social capital is not just about social networks but, more importantly, about the resources that are accessible through these networks and that affect opportunities and outcomes of instrumental actions (Lin 2001; Portes 1998). These instrumental actions are intended to increase the resources for meeting local residents' myriad needs and advocate for their well-being. Economically, as capital, these networks also enable neighbourhood houses and their institutional partners to not only maximize return (i.e., resources available to the community) but also reduce the cost of services. While conceiving of these networks as the organizational social capital of NHs, we can also argue that NHs are themselves organizational social capital serving the need of local residents as well as bridging the gap between them and the NHs' institutional partners.

Neighbourhood Houses as Organizational Social Capital for Service

Apparently, seeking extra resources requires ongoing effort on the part of neighbourhood houses. With proper connections, there are abundant resources in the community. To meet the large and diverse volume of collective and individual needs in the community, NHs in Vancouver have strategically developed and made use of their networks to connect resources inside and outside the community to the local residents. As a service user of Little Mountain NH said:

> The NHs connect with other centres like community centres and businesses like VanCity. And through these connections we get a huge network of support and pretty much being able to access any program you can imagine because they are all networked together through the NHs. And every section of the net gives you access to other parts of the net, so it's a network.

Embedded in multiple networks, a neighbourhood house is a local hub that connects with numerous public and private resources inside and outside the community. Using their networks, NHs improve the access of local residents to the inequitably and unevenly distributed public resources provided by other stakeholders. Remember the Youth Café that Alexandra NH initiated? A community partner said:

> What do we need to do to have a place where kids can come and just hang out[?] So this Youth Café was developed and it would encompass resources – RCMP, Alexandra House, all different support services, employment, crisis assistance – you know kids don't want to be told: "Come next Tuesday," they want a counsellor now, they live in the here and now, so that would be a place where they could go and at least talk to someone and get support that way.

NHs bring together resources from different partners and provide a one-stop access point integrating different services and resources to serve the local needs.

Meanwhile, the connection function of neighbourhood houses also benefits other social service organizations that may not have the physical and institutional proximity to their service users in the local community. Through the connection with NHs, they can detect the unmet needs in the community and effectively deliver their services to the targeted population whom they may find difficult to reach. A community partner of Burnaby NH said: "When we need something or there's a problem or an issue that somebody brings to the table, BNH with their connections will tell us: 'Oh you should be going here.' It's that connecting, the network and that's the whole point ... Our programs go through BNH because they are so well connected."

Another community partner of Burnaby NH echoed this: "It was with the NH linking us with resources that we could either replicate or connect with. It really supported us! We have a really interesting thing going on now where people are like, wow what happened to this community, it's so much better now! I give a lot of credit to the NH." As a hub of the network, neighbourhood houses not only bridge different stakeholders to the local residents' needs, they also bring stakeholders together.

Neighbourhood Houses as Organizational Social Capital for Advocacy

Other than tapping and connecting resources from the networks to serve local needs, neighbourhood houses have also actively engaged in the network of advocacy. All NHs reported that they have actively participated in many coalitions and alliances, members of which share some specific interest and mandate, particularly in advocating for the well-being of local residents. A staff member of Cedar Cottage NH gave this reason for joining the Cedar Cottage Area Service Network: "We can learn from each other about neighbourhood-based services and how they're connected. Get to know people, faces, get to know the different work that people do, and get a sense of how we can collaborate." NHs use these networks to bring like-minded organizations together to advocate for their service users. A community partner of Kiwassa and Frog Hollow praised NHs:

> What the neighbourhood houses have done for us is sort of allow us to network into the community, and brought us into projects that we wouldn't necessarily have been involved in, and allow us to get to know more about who is this community and who lives in this community, and how we as an organization through the BIA [business improvement association] and

through the businesses can be of assistance or help or advocate partner at City Hall when we need to advocate for certain things. When we are trying to advocate for certain things, they come and support us.

A manager of Frog Hollow shared another example of how NHs affect child care policy through networking:

They're a group of large childcare providers, so they're people that have a huge wealth of knowledge in that room. And people have different connections. So some people in that group have connections with politicians, with the city, with licensing. And so what we do when we come around the table, and we all sit on different boards, right, and committees and you know, we all sit on different working groups. And so we each bring that information to each other to share and to strategize on how we can utilize the group as a whole to make the system better for kids. So we will do things like invite Victoria to come and speak on what it is that they, you know, how the subsidy system is working. And so they'll have to speak on what they're doing, and we'll ask a whole bunch of questions. And they'll go away with the questions and figure out how to answer them, which helps the system ... And that helps the big system, but it also helps us because then we get this knowledge about how it works.

Multilateral Connections: Networks in Action

As this manager pointed out, each network is connected to many other networks through the different connections brought to the table by its members. For instance, the fifteen neighbourhood houses have formed their own service network. The web of networks that NHs share is complex. While some NHs have shared partnership with some CSOs, each has a unique set of local partners. Through this web of networks, these unique local partners can be accessible to and by other NHs.

The organizational social capital of neighbourhood houses is complex. Conceptually, we can classify organizational social capital into three different forms (Schneider 2009). Horizontally, "bridging social capital" refers to resources embedded in the network of organizations providing complementary services, while bonding social capital is from organizations with mandate and service. Horizontal social capital is also called structural social capital, which is built through networks "that have collective and transparent decision making processes, accountable leaders, and practices of collective action and mutual responsibility" (K. Bain and N. Hicks, quoted in

Krishna and Shrader 1999, 10). Vertically, "linking social capital" refers to governments and other funding bodies that control the resources. These classifications metaphorically pinpoint the multi-level and multidirectional networks that NHs have and need.

These multi-level and multidirectional networks are built through the concerted efforts of board members, senior staff, front-line staff, volunteers, and service users who are situated in different social positions within a larger social space. In their unique positions, they have their own stock of social relationships and of social capital that they can access and mobilize. The structural differentiation in position and work creates a natural division of labour within neighbourhood houses. While front-line staff are active in building structural social capital (i.e., local service organizations), leaders of non-profit organizations, such as board members and executives, are in a position to invest in linking social capital for funding purposes. Some will even argue that leaders in non-profit organizations have a particular role in identifying and nurturing social capital "in order to recruit and develop board members, raise philanthropic support, develop strategic partnerships, engage in advocacy, enhance community relations, and create a shared strategic vision and mission within the organization and its employees" (King 2004, 471).

In the network-mapping study, we invited a total of sixty-one executive directors, board members, mid-level managers, front-line staff, and volunteers from thirteen neighbourhood houses (on average four to six per NH) to map out the community partners that they linked to their own NH. Together they reported 955 links, with an average of 16 (SD = 4) links per person. Some of these links (n = 197) were listed by more than one participant from the same NH. Close to half (n = 335, 44.2 percent) of these links were reciprocal. They shared projects with 224 (29.6 percent) of these links. Many (n = 233) of the links were classified as long-term by the participants. Table 3.3 shows the classifications of the 758 links.

As Table 3.3 indicates, CSOs and government units (including public libraries, health authorities, community centres, and Members of Parliament) are two important groups of partners, particularly in terms of funding and public resources. Meanwhile, neighbourhood houses have also proactively tried to solicit resources from the business sector. For instance, a Cedar Cottage staff member approached the local liquor store for a donation. The store donated some leftover Christmas bears, which she used as part of a welcoming gift for new families who joined the NH supper programs. Many NHs received food donations from local bakeries, grocery stores, and super-

TABLE 3.3
Network links of neighbourhood houses

Classification	Number of links	Percent (%)
Government	136	18
Community service organizations	214	28
NGOs – non-service	42	6
Business	61	8
Churches	19	3
Coalition/alliance	160	21
Education	59	8
Individuals	51	7
Others	16	2
Total	758	101

Note: The 101 percent total is due to the percentages being rounded up.
Source: Network-Mapping Study.

markets. Besides soliciting tangible items, many NHs also reported that they had actively engaged with the local BIA in community programs. For instance, Collingwood NH partnered with the local BIA to study sex workers in the area. Similarly, Mount Pleasant NH reported that it tried to engage the BIA in a local community development project: "We collaborate, we might participate in their festivals. They support us with letters when we do a joint festival in June with the community. They have been extremely active with our community development project ... to get residents engaged in revitalizing Broadway East and in trying to get people connected with the implementation of the community plan."

Indeed, as part of the community development efforts, neighbourhood house members have actively taken part in various coalitions and alliances (e.g., Networks of Inner City School, Literacy Table) for service coordination and advocacy work. For instance, the North Shore NH has been a long-time member of the North Shore Homelessness Task Force:

It's been around for about twelve years. Started out because the community saw, you know, the issue of homelessness becoming more serious on the North Shore and how was the community going to address that. So they created a steering committee and North Shore Neighbourhood House was one of the original members because we saw a lot of homelessness in this specific area.

Interestingly, many participants also pointed out that, besides institutional partners, some individuals in the community are also important links to them. One participant of Cedar Cottage NH shared the story of a senior in the community:

> She's a senior but she knows everybody. So we have a workshop this afternoon. It's a health and wellness workshop. She's gonna be bringing probably fifteen Chinese seniors with her ... She does fantastic outreach. She's also a great "bridger" and "welcome" if people are brand new and say they're very nervous about coming, she's the ultimate person to help bridge people to the program or to the NH as a whole.

However, people come and go, particularly in neighbourhood houses, which tend to have a high turnover of staff due to the short-term, program-based funding. It is therefore unrealistic for NHs to depend solely on their individual members to create and maintain their networks. As one community partner of Burnaby NH worried: "How do I make sure that when I leave, the relationships don't come to an end? It's a huge challenge, especially in organizations that are very lean, like the NH, there's not a lot of people at the senior level ... even front-line workers build relationships in communities and when they go, what happens to those relationships?"

As Jo Anne Schneider (2009) contends, an organization is itself an organic entity that will form its own networks and operate like social capital. Indeed, past success, reputation, and the commitment of neighbourhood houses are all key elements that make them successful in generating organizational social capital (i.e., functional relationships with other organizations). As Robert Putnam (2000) suggests, social capital comprises functional networks through which people can generate trust, mutual support, and co-operation. In return, these normative features, which are also key to the success of NHs in engaging with other organizations, reinforce the function of the networks. Indeed, the foundation of social capital – trust and credibility – of NHs is beyond individuals' relationships. A community partner who worked with both Kiwassa and Frog Hollow explained why organizational partners are keen on working with NHs:

> So when we are, like with the community policing centre, policing-related, people hear the word "police" and already some people are, you know ... someone like Kiwassa or Frog Hollow or you know, a lot of places that lead the work credible, you know, their *credibility*, so when we invite them to

something, there is *trust* that's already there and we can access and without that it's way longer, takes way longer to be able to try to help people, right? And we do it for each other as community partners but the neighbourhood houses really do that. They build the *credibility* for the other partners. (Emphasis added)

The trustworthiness and credibility of neighbourhood houses, not simply the involvement of individuals, have made them a reliable ally of community partners as a form of organizational social capital. Such trustworthiness and credibility are an accumulated asset of NHs that take time and many people's efforts to foster, earn, maintain, and grow.

Conclusion: Neighbourhood Houses as a Mechanism of Connection

The Reverend Samuel Barnett, the founder of the first settlement house, Toynbee Hall, conceptualized the settlement house as a mechanism of connection (Meacham 1987). Barnett and many of his successors brought rich students and others to settle in deprived neighbourhoods. The settlers brought resources, knowledge, skills, and political influence to bear on meeting the needs of local residents. However, settlement houses have never been merely charitable service providers, and the connection between rich settlers and local residents was not a one-way street. Instead, each benefited from the other.

Today, neighbourhood houses in Vancouver do not have rich settlers, but they have inherited the service tradition of their predecessors. NHs are key service providers in many deprived urban communities. They are accessible to local residents and responsive to emerging needs in the community. Their multiple generational services, provided by ethno-racially diverse staff members who also came from the local community, have made them psychologically accessible. Their proactive approach in nurturing leadership among local residents fosters a strong sense of ownership among their service users. They have successfully built and integrated local assets into the community service infrastructure and expanded the sources of formal and informal resources that residents in the community can access.

More importantly, neighbourhood houses have strategically and institutionally connected different stakeholders of public resources, which are so siloed and fragmented that the general public finds them difficult to access. As members of many service networks, NHs help coordinate these different partners and bring them to the local residents. As place-based civil society service organizations, they are the one-stop shop through which people will be referred to the services they need without getting lost in the maze-like service networks. As a form of organizational social capital, NHs are service assets to the local community. They can also use their network to advocate for policy changes. Meanwhile, NHs are the local hub through which other organizations can reach their targeted service recipients scattered in different neighbourhoods. In short, neighbourhood houses are a local place-based mechanism of connection that facilitates local residents' access to resources not only inside but also outside their community.

References

Acevedo-Polakovich, Ignacio David, Bailey Bell, Peter Gamache, and Allison S. Christian. 2011. "Service Accessibility for Lesbian, Gay, Bisexual, Transgender, and Questioning Youth." *Youth and Society* 45 (1): 75–97.

Apparicio, Philippe, and Anne-Marie Séguin. 2006. "Measuring the Accessibility of Services and Facilities for Residents of Public Housing in Montréal." *Urban Studies* 43 (1): 187–211.

Börzel, Tanta A., and Karen Heard-Lauréote. 2009. "Networks in EU Multi-level Governance: Concepts and Contributions." *Journal of Public Policy* 29 (2): 135–51.

Bradford, Neil. 2005. *Place-Based Public Policy: Towards a New Urban and Community Agenda for Canada.* CPRN Research Report. Ottawa: Canadian Policy Research Networks.

Brenner, Neil, and Nik Theodore. 2002. "Cities and the Geographies of 'Actually Existing Neoliberalism.'" *Antipode* 34 (3): 349–79.

Bristow, Gillian, John Farrington, Jon Shaw, and Tim Richardson. 2009. "Developing an Evaluation Framework for Crosscutting Policy Goals: The Accessibility Policy Assessment Tool." *Environment and Planning* 41 (1): 48–62.

Bryce, Herrington J. 2006. "Nonprofits as Social Capital and Agents in the Public Policy Process: Toward a New Paradigm." *Nonprofit and Voluntary Sector Quarterly* 35 (2): 311–18.

Drover, Glenn. 2000. "Redefining Social Citizenship in a Global Era." *Canadian Social Work (Social Work and Globalization: Special Issue)* 2 (1): 29–49.

Elliott, Katherine P., and John Hunsley. 2015. "Evaluating the Measurement of Mental Health Service Accessibility, Acceptability, and Availability in the Canadian Community Health Survey." *American Journal of Orthopsychiatry* 85 (3): 238–42.

Fabricant, Michael B., and Robert Fisher. 2002. *Settlement Houses Under Siege: The Struggle to Sustain Community Organization in New York City.* New York: Columbia University Press.

Farrington, John H. 2007. "The New Narrative of Accessibility: Its Potential Contribution to Discourses in (Transport) Geography." *Journal of Transport Geography* 15 (5): 319–30.

Ferlie, Ewan, Louise Fitzgerald, Gerry McGivern, Sue Dopson, and Chris Bennett. 2011. "Public Policy Networks and 'Wicked Problems': A Nascent Solution?" *Public Administration* 89 (2): 307–24.

Ferrie, Damian. 2008. "Social Inclusion and Place Based Disadvantage: What We Have Already Done That Is Valuable for the Future." Paper presented at Social Inclusion and Place Based Disadvantage Workshop, Victoria, Australia, June 2008.

Field, John. 2003. *Social Capital.* London: Routledge.

Francis, Jenny. 2010. "Missing Link: Youth Programs, Social Services, and African Youth in Metro Vancouver." Metropolis Working Paper, Vancouver, BC.

Hernandez, Mario, Teresa Nesman, Debra Mowery, Ignacio David Acevedo-Polakovich, and Linda M. Callejas. 2009. "Cultural Competence: A Literature Review and Conceptual Model for Mental Health Services." *Psychiatric Services* 60 (8): 1046–50.

Humphries, R., and S. Gregory. 2010. *Place-Based Approaches and the NHS: Lessons from Total Place.* London: King's Fund.

Hurley, Catherine, Georgia Panagiotopoulos, Michael Tsianikas, Lareen Newman, and Ruth Walker. 2013. "Access and Acceptability of Community-Based Services for Older Greek Migrants in Australia: User and Provider Perspectives." *Health and Social Care in the Community* 21 (2): 140–49.

Johnson, Christian. 1995. "Strength in Community: Historical Development of Settlements Internationally." In *Settlements, Social Change and Community Action: Good Neighbours,* edited by Ruth Gilchrist and Tony Jeffs, 69–91. London: Jessica Kingsley.

King, Nancy K. 2004. "Social Capital and Nonprofit Leaders." *Nonprofit and Voluntary Sector Quarterly* 14 (4): 471–86.

Krishna, Anirudh, and Elizabeth Shrader. 1999. "Social Capital Assessment Tool." Paper presented at Conference on Social Capital and Poverty Reduction, Washington, DC June 1999.

Ladd, Helen. 1994. "Spatially Targeted Economic Development Strategies: Do They Work?" *Cityscape* 1 (1): 193–218.

Lin, Nan. 2001. *Social Capital: A Theory of Social Structure and Action.* Cambridge, UK: Cambridge University Press.

Meacham, Standish. 1987. *Toynbee Hall and Social Reform 1880–1914: The Search for Community.* New Haven, CT: Yale University Press.

Portes, Alejandro. 1998. "Social Capital: Its Origin and Applications in Modern Sociology." *Annual Review of Sociology* 24 (1): 1–24.

Putnam, Robert. 2000. *Bowling Alone: The Collapse and Revival of American Community.* New York: Touchstone.

Rittel, Horst W.J., and Melvin M. Webber. 1973. "Dilemmas in a General Theory of Planning." *Policy Sciences* 4 (2): 155–69.

Schneider, J.A. 2009. "Organizational Social Capital and Nonprofits." *Nonprofit and Voluntary Sector Quarterly* 38 (4): 643–62. http://www.doi.org/10.1177/0899764009333956.

Shugart, Ian, and Thomas Townsend. 2010. "Bringing 'Place' in: Exploring the Role of the Federal Government." *Horizons (Sustainable Places)* 10 (4): 4–6.

Statistics Canada. 2015. *Census Dictionary.* Ottawa: Government of Canada.

Stewart-Weeks, Martin. 1997. "Voluntary Associations: Social Capital at Work or Post-Modern Romance?" In *Social Capital: The Individual, Civil Society and the State,* edited by Andrew Norton, Mark Latham, Gary Sturgess, and Martin Stewart-Weeks, 85–113. Sydney, Australia: Centre For Independent Studies.

Yan, Miu Chung. 2002. "Recapturing the History of Settlement House Movement: Its Philosophy, Service Model and Implications in China's Development of Community-Based Centre Services." *Asia Pacific Journal of Social Work and Development* 12 (1): 21–40.

–. 2004. "Bridging the Fragmented Community: Revitalizing Settlement Houses in the Global Era." *Journal of Community Practice* 12 (1/2): 51–69.

Yan, Miu Chung, Chun-Sing Johnson Cheung, Ming-Sum Tsui, and Chi Keung Chu. 2017. "Examining the Neoliberal Discourse of Accountability: The Case of Hong Kong's Social Service Sector." *International Social Work* 60 (4): 976–89.

Yan, Miu Chung, and Sean Lauer. 2008. "Social Capital and Ethno-Cultural Diverse Immigrants: A Canadian Study on Settlement House and Social Integration." *Journal of Ethnic and Cultural Diversity in Social Work* 17 (3): 229–50.

Yan, Miu Chung, Sean Lauer, and Pilar Riaño-Alcalá. 2016. "Incorporating Individual Community Assets in Neighbourhood Houses: Beyond the Community-Building Tradition of Settlement Houses." *International Social Work* 60 (6): 1591–1605. http://doi.org/10.1177/0020872816633889.

4

Social Infrastructure for Building Community

SEAN LAUER

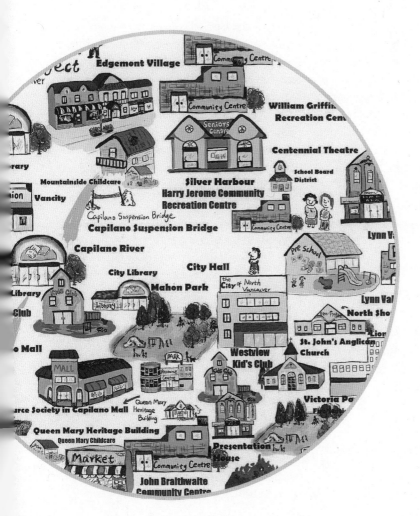

The mention of infrastructure does not typically cause crowds to roar; students don't sit up in their seats, and readers don't typically find their interest piqued. Social infrastructure is not all that different. Despite this, the term *social infrastructure* is commonly used in discussions of social life. Mark Zuckerberg, for instance, used social infrastructure as a guiding concept for the direction of Facebook over the next decade in his 2017 address to its users: "For the past decade, Facebook has focused on connecting friends and families. With that foundation, our next focus will be developing social infrastructure for community." We also mention social infrastructure in our introduction to this book, proposing that neighbourhood houses (NHs) are a form of social infrastructure that can contribute to the ideal of a welcoming community, potentially helping to ameliorate challenges associated with the community problem in Vancouver and the wider society. The term *social infrastructure* is commonly used, often in ways that suggest its potential for improving community life. For this reason, it is worth looking at the idea more closely, asking what it means to say that a neighbourhood house is a form of social infrastructure.

In this chapter, I will outline an approach to thinking about social infrastructure and clarify how it can contribute to community-building. By *community building*, I am referring to the development and maintenance of relationships, and the development of social capacity in a neighbourhood. A key part of this discussion will address the role of organizations as forms of social infrastructure, and the unique potential of organizations for community-building. Following this discussion, I will examine neighbourhood houses as social infrastructure and explore their contributions to community-building. This part of the chapter will draw on survey research to examine how participation in neighbourhood houses contributes to community-building through the development of relationships with friends and neighbours.

Social Infrastructure and Community-Building

Developing and Maintaining Relationships
In his book *Palaces for the People*, Eric Klinenberg (2018, 16) defines social

infrastructure as the physical places and organizations that shape the interactions of people in a community. Examples include public spaces like local parks and public markets, cafés and other commercial establishments, and community organizations such as libraries. In these locations, social infrastructure brings people together, sometimes for extended periods of time, and sometimes supporting engagement in collective activities. This guiding of interactions is the key mechanism for relationship development. By providing a venue for interaction, the presence of social infrastructure in communities allows new relationships to form and helps existing relationships to persist. When we think of community-building, that relationship development within a neighbourhood is perhaps the first thing that comes to mind.

The concept of social infrastructure has roots in a number of theoretical and research traditions in the social sciences. Social relationships have been on the minds of social scientists for some time in discussions around social capital, so it is worth noting that social infrastructure is not the same as social capital. As Klinenberg points out, there is a distinction between these two concepts, with social capital referring to the interpersonal networks people hold and social infrastructure referring to the conditions that guide social interaction and contribute to building social capital. Klinenberg (2018, 5) suggests that robust social infrastructure "fosters contact, mutual support, and collaboration among friends and neighbours." Perhaps the most direct antecedent of discussions of social infrastructure lies in the discussion of place making in geography and urban planning (Jacobs 1961; Whyte 1988). Here, the emphasis is on the potential of *public spaces* to support social interactions. Elijah Anderson (2011), for instance, has recently proposed that certain public spaces provide the conditions for positive interactions across divisions of race, class, and gender. In his research, he examines social life in Philadelphia at public spaces including the Reading Station Market, the Gallery Mall, and Rittenhouse Square. He sees them as public spaces that bring a wide cross-section of the city together in interaction. Anderson finds that public spaces like theses enable individuals to set aside their particular racial and ethnic identities and to learn more cosmopolitan ways of interacting and communicating.

Social infrastructure, however, has a broader scope and potential than place making because of the inclusion of organizations in addition to public spaces. Like public spaces, organizations bring people together in interaction. Some organizations, such as retail and commercial establishments, are similar to public spaces – dominated by short-term and anonymous interactions. These locations can help to build community by providing a venue for the maintenance of existing relationships. Ray Oldenburg's (1989) description of third places as locations that are neither the workplace nor the home and that provide an alternative place where people make friends and connect with neighbours is well known. The participation in third places and the relationships that form sometimes last over very long periods of time. Many sociologists have documented the dynamics of these third places. In his book *Slim's Table*, Mitchell Duneier (1992) made the See Your Food Cafeteria in South Chicago famous by documenting the strong relationships among a group of men of different ages, races, and classes who met there regularly for dinner. Duneier documents how these bonds provided care and respectability while crossing lines of race and class. Carrie Yodanis (2006) documents the relationships among a group of women who met for coffee every day at the same café in a small rural town. Here, rather than breaking down barriers of class, the interactions at the coffee shop provide a location for demonstrating, creating, and reinforcing class differences among the women in town. Colin Jerolmack (2013) finds a local pet store to be the location of community life among a group of pigeon enthusiasts. Public spaces and commercial establishments can contribute to the maintenance of relationships. They are less commonly associated with the formation of new relationships, but other organizations do provide a context for relationships to form.

Some organizations provide a context where people interact over extended periods, often with shared interests or a shared focus. Workplaces and schools are classic examples of formal organizations that bring people together and create opportunities for long-term interactions. Being involved in an organization also suggests shared experiences and motivations for being involved. Students at school are similar in age and typically live in the same or similar neighbourhoods, for instance. Involvement in organizations often leads to participation in shared activities, as well.[1] This participation in shared activities can increase the regularity of interaction, produce shared experiences, and enable people to get to know one another.

It is worth looking more closely at what is going on at organizations that can lead to relationship formation and community-building. Perhaps Mario Small (2009) has done the most to explicate this process in the development of his concept of *organizational embeddedness*. Small begins with the question of how people form relationships. The most common understanding suggests that people form relationships on purpose, because they want to make a friend or a connection. We probably all know someone who is a good networker – good at making connections that are useful to them down the road. Small points out that, though many relationships are formed on purpose for instrumental reasons, many relationships are not formed on purpose – they simply happen under certain circumstances. For instance, a relationship may form while people are pursuing some other goal, such as taking a class to learn pottery making. Attendance at the class may lead to regular interactions that lead to relationship formation – a new friend, for instance. Many relationships form like this, when people are pursuing other goals. Relationships also form without the pursuit of a goal at all. Imagining that same pottery class, two students might realize they both prefer the same pottery-making technique or share another interest, such as supporting a local sports team. That shared interest might spark ongoing conversation and sharing of knowledge and skills, but supporting the same local team was not done on purpose. Or perhaps a student accidentally drops a pot and another acts without thinking and catches it before it falls to the ground. That act – almost instinctual – may lead to conversation and to the formation of a relationship. While many new relationships do form from purposeful acts on the part of at least one person, the key insight here is that there are many relationships that form when people are pursuing other goals, and almost by accident.

The distinction between purposeful and non-purposeful relationship formation is an important one, and Small's contribution (2009) to our understanding of social infrastructure comes from his observation that organizations often guide the non-purposeful processes of relationship formation. This is where the contributions of organizational embeddedness take shape. The first contribution is that organizations bring people together into contact, creating the opportunity for relationships to form. Having more social interactions increases the likelihood of making a new friend, for instance. These patterns can also influence the types of relationships people are likely to form – or not form. The chances of my making a new friendship with a billionaire are quite low, given that I have never come into contact with one and I do not participate in any formal or informal organizations frequented by billionaires. In addition to opportunity, a second contribution of organizations is that they bring people together into frequent contact. Frequent interactions between individuals make the formation of a relationship more likely. Repeated interactions between people can increase trust and affection, and make the formation of a friendship more likely. Finally, organizations contribute to community-building by providing opportunities for people to work together on shared activities. The effect of frequent interaction on relationship formation grows when people are engaged in a shared activity of some kind. Engaging in a shared activity provides an entry point for more meaningful conversations and commitments. It is also helpful when these shared foci of attention involve activities that require cooperation.[2] When an activity cannot be accomplished alone, commitment is intensified and the potential for relationship formation increases.

Small points out that many of the contributions of organizations, and by extension social infrastructure, to community-building comes through the playing of a brokerage role. Brokerage involves connection among actors that were not previously connected. It is an important concept in social theory (Simmel 1950), one examined extensively by Ronald Burt (2004). Organizations play two types of brokerage roles. First, they act as brokers between individuals when, for instance, a service agency arranges a support group for immigrant new mothers. Here, new mothers may meet other mothers with whom they share similar experiences. Or perhaps the group brings together some mothers who already have met, but provides a venue for their relationship to develop further. In this sense, we might consider the brokerage a purposeful act of connection and community-building on the part of the organization. Second, organizations act as brokers between institutions, as when an immigrant mother is referred to the local school district in order to enroll her children. At the new school, the mother will meet other families with children of similar ages. Remembering our earlier discussion, the community-building outcomes of institutional brokerage are potentially non-purposeful – the outcome of the referred organization's activities.

One of the strengths of Small's organizational embeddedness approach is how it demonstrates the possibility and importance of non-purposeful routine activities in organizations that contribute to relationship development. This approach shows that how an organization structures these activities may have unintended consequences for relationship development. A daycare centre, for instance, may or may not structure activities like child pickup in ways that allow parents to meet and interact with each other. These decisions are not made with parental relationship development in mind.

It is just a small step to go beyond Small's attention to how organizations structure interactions and consider how other aspects of organizations, such as their stated missions, governance structures, and even particular leadership styles, may influence relationship development outcomes. Michael McQuarrie and Nicole Marwell (2009) have pointed out that these institutional structures – the formal and informal rules of the organization – add a complexity and dynamic understanding of the contributions of organizations to community life. Taking this seriously directs our attention to how organizations contribute to community-building purposefully. An organization's strategic mission or the priorities of its leaders may make relationship development a priority and result in programs and activities with this explicit goal in mind. A university might provide funds for projects that encourage collaboration across disciplines or across universities, for instance. When considering the contributions of social infrastructure through organizational embeddedness, we also need to consider how organizations structure programs and activities with the purpose of relationship development in mind.

Developing Social Capacity

I believe it is an easy extension of the social infrastructure hypothesis from relationship development to social capacity development. Though it has not previously been developed explicitly, I argue in this chapter that social infrastructure contributes to community-building through the development of social capacity among community members. By social capacity I am referring to a person's ability to work with others to achieve shared goals (Mattessich and Monsey 1997; Lichterman 2006; Chaskin et al. 2001). We have already seen that social infrastructure brings people into contact, sometimes over time and around shared activities. For an initial connection to become a more established relationship, including collaboration on shared goals, requires certain social skills such as communication across differences (including age, race, ethnicity, class, and gender). Other skills like decision making, managing groups, and organizing activities and events are part of social capacity as well. Here, organizational embeddedness remains important by providing opportunities for social capacity development.

One way we can approach these social capacity outcomes is to extend Small's concept (2009) by showing how organizational embeddedness also contributes to social capacity development. First, like relationships, social capacity can be developed both purposefully through intentional actions and non-purposefully through participation in organizations. A volunteer or employee, for instance, may develop social capacity purposefully by taking an organization-sponsored leadership development program. In this example, skills that contribute to social capacity are addressed directly and perhaps motivated by the acceptance of a new position or role within an organization. Social capacity may also be developed non-purposefully through regular participation in an organization's activities. Consider a neighbourhood group dedicated to cleaning up a local park. The purpose of the group, and the motivation for most who join, will be the instrumental goal of neighbourhood improvement. That group may require some members to take leadership roles and organize the group's activities. The group itself may attract diverse members of the community, which requires communicating across differences and motivating around shared interests. These experiences develop social capacity, although members of the group may not have intended that. They may have remained motivated by the larger goals of the group, including improving a local park. Like relationship development, social capacity can develop both purposefully and non-purposefully.

Continuing the extension of the social infrastructure mechanism to social capacity, we can outline the specific aspects of organizations that lead to social capacity development. Fortunately, like the sociology of relationship formation, there is a research tradition that considers the capacity development of individuals involved in organizations. These themes are most commonly discussed in the tradition of Alexis de Tocqueville ([1840] 2003) that has been revived contemporarily by Stanley Verba, Kay Schlozman, and Henry Brady (1995). The research in this tradition has found that organizational involvement provides opportunities for capacity development for those individuals involved. These opportunities include experiences that develop social capacity skills, and opportunities to practise those skills (ibid.).[3] Matthew Baggetta (2009), in a study of the social capacity development of members of choral groups in the Boston area, finds that choral groups provide opportunities for interpersonal interactions outside primary social networks. Through regular meetings and collaboration in activities, participants interact regularly with individuals different from themselves. This is similar to the insights around relationship formation discussed above – organizations bring people together in interaction. But here the emphasis is on interactions that span difference and as a result provide opportunities to learn and practise communication across those differences. This contribution dovetails nicely with the classic work of Gordon Allport (1954; Pettigrew 1998) on contact theory. Contact theory is primarily interested in positive relationship development, including tolerance and understanding, across divisions of race, ethnicity, and gender. Here again, the key mechanism is interaction over time while working on shared activities. Research in contact theory finds that shared time working on collective activities, and the interactions that take place during that work, provides the opportunity for people to recognize similarities that break down typical dimensions of difference. In this way, contact theory is similar to research showing capacity development through intergroup communication skills, which results from organizational participation.

To this point, we have seen that social infrastructure, particularly in the form of organizational embeddedness, can build community through relationship development and social capacity development. Organizations provide opportunities for individuals to come together in regular interactions around shared activities. Those interactions may lead to relationship formation, and they may also lead to social capacity development as individuals learn and practise skills associated with communication across differences. Baggetta (2009) reports that the choral groups he studied showed two additional types of activities that provided opportunities for social capacity development. First, they provide governance opportunities – the opportunity to practise decision-making and organizational management skills. This might be as simple as choir members planning a series of practice sessions leading up to a performance, and organizing times, locations, and perhaps the agenda for those practice sessions. It may also suggest larger questions of leadership and group direction – managing discussions and implementation around accepting new members and planning choral repertoires. Second, participating in these groups provide opportunities to interact with other organizations and institutions in the wider community, including those from business, government, and non-profits.

The research on social infrastructure and social capacity development in political science and contact theory emphasizes the non-purposeful aspects of community-building. Baggetta's research on choral groups, for instance, does not see the skills surrounding communication across difference, governance practices, and connections with local institutions as the explicit goals of the groups. Rather, participants develop these capacities non-purposefully through their participation in the groups and pursuit of their goals. Recognizing these non-purposeful capacity-building outcomes of participation in organizations is valuable because they are often overlooked. But there are purposeful activities in organizations that contribute to social capacity–building. Social capacity development can often be an explicit goal of an organization, being part of the strategic mission and therefore including activities with the explicit goal of developing capacity. Contact theory, with its interest in how positive relationships across cleavages develop, is one area of research where this purposeful action on the part of organizations is recognized. This approach considers organizational authority figures and their direction and values for developing social capacity an important factor in the capacities being developed. When intergroup interaction is supported by organizational authority figures, it is more likely to develop among participants.

Having developed an approach to thinking about social infrastructure, we can see that its presence in neighbourhoods, including public spaces, commercial establishments, and community organizations, can contribute to community-building by providing opportunities for relationship and social capacity development. The key mechanism here is the guiding of social interactions, particularly the regular interactions of neighbours over time while engaged in shared activities. Community organizations are a notable type of social infrastructure because of their ability to guide interactions focused on shared activities. Many of the opportunities for community-building follow from non-purposeful interactions, but community organizations also include an institutional dimension that can lead to purposeful actions geared toward relationship and capacity development among neighbours. Neighbourhood houses are one example of social infrastructure operating at the neighbourhood level.

Neighbourhood Houses: Social Infrastructure Building Local Communities

Neighbourhood houses in Vancouver are place-based, multi-service community organizations. They emerged from the settlement house movement that had its roots in well-known organizations such as Toynbee Hall in London and Hull House in Chicago (Fabricant and Fisher 2002; Irving, Parsons, and Bellamy 1995; Trolander 1987; Yan 2002). As community-based organizations, they are a good example of social infrastructure as described by Klinenberg (2018). In the remainder of this chapter, I will examine neighbourhood houses as examples of social infrastructure with community-building potential. Following the example of Small's organizational embeddedness approach, and the organizational autonomy approach of McQuarrie and Marwell (2009), I examine the unique organizational structure and institutional approaches of neighbourhood houses that may have implications for their role in developing relationships and social capacity.

My examination is based in part on research that is ethnographic in nature, drawing on participant observation and organizational documentation. The primary source of data, however, consists of survey data that we collected from participants from all fifteen neighbourhood houses in Metro Vancouver in February and March 2014. Our target population was all neighbourhood house users in Metro Vancouver. No sampling frame exists for this population, nor could one be reasonably constructed.[4] Instead, we recruited respondents from the fifteen NHs on randomly selected times and days in order to reach our target population. In total, we collected 687 questionnaires and the final sample size includes 675 respondents due to missing data and other problems uncovered in the data cleaning. Questionnaires were completed by respondents at the time of their selection, and respondents could choose from among six languages to complete the questionnaire.[5]

Place-Based Organizations: Diversity of Activities and Participants

One of the distinguishing features of a neighbourhood house is its mission to serve the needs of the local neighbourhood. Like other community organizations, neighbourhood houses provide programs and activities geared toward their mission. The focus on the local neighbourhood and the diversity of local residents lead to a wide variety of activities that take place at the neighbourhood house. Other organizations are sometimes organized around a particular interest and/or type of activity, such as choral groups. With a focus on the local place-based community, neighbourhood houses do not focus on one type of activity, but rather must address multiple interests and activities. One easy way to see this variety is to look at an activities bulletin board at a local neighbourhood house.[6] Most neighbourhood houses have such bulletin boards at their entrances in order to let all those who pass through know what is going on there. Figure 4.1 shows a photo of the bulletin board at Little Mountain Neighbourhood House in Vancouver taken in November 2018. It does not include all of the activities taking place at the neighbourhood house, but a close look shows the variety of activities.

The bulletin board promotes activities such as self-defence classes, a philosophy night, citizenship test preparation, employment coaching, and a multicultural winter festival – all taking place at the neighbourhood house. These activities provide opportunities for regular and routine interactions arranged around a shared activity. These are the types of activities that social infrastructure organizations support and that we expect would contribute to community-building. They bring local members of the community together with a shared focus and engagement that can lead to relationship formation and capacity development. What is unique here is the variety of activities taking place within the same community organization. With a focus on the whole community, the neighbourhood house provides a variety of programs with both expressive and instrumental goals geared to different members of the local community.

FIGURE 4.1
Activities bulletin board at Little Mountain Neighbourhood House,
November 2018

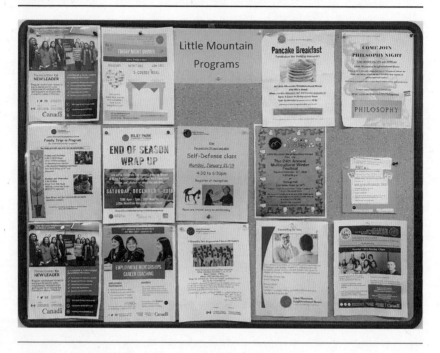

Another way to get a sense of the variety of programs that are a part of regular neighbourhood house activities comes from our survey data. We asked participants to tell us what types of programming they participated in at the houses. When preparing our questionnaire, we wanted to get an exhaustive list of types of activities, so we turned to the staff at the neighbourhood houses to help us prepare that list. They provided twenty-one different types of activities available at the neighbourhood houses in Metro Vancouver.

Table 4.1 lists all these types of activities and the rates of participation our respondents reported. It captures the wide variety of programming that takes place at neighbourhood houses, from recreational activities and arts and cultural programming to employment counselling and legal services. Neighbourhood houses respond to the local needs of the neighbourhood. Each of these activities provides opportunities for relationship development through social infrastructure. A literacy program, for instance, brings people together around a shared interest in improving English-language

TABLE 4.1

Types of activities respondents engaged in at neighbourhood houses in Metro Vancouver (*N* = 675)

Activity types	Participation rate (%)
Recreational activities	55
Settlement assistance (information, referrals, counselling)	28
Arts and cultural programs	45
Parenting education and support	25
Early childhood (0–6 years) program for children	27
After-school program for children (6–18 years)	11
English language and literacy programs	31
Employment counselling/training	15
Interpretation and translation services	16
Food programs (community kitchen or breakfast club)	43
Health education	34
Leadership and volunteer opportunities	31
Committee and interest group	26
Youth mentorship programs	10
Festival, celebration, or other special events	58
Financial and legal services	18
Family services including family counselling	15
Drop-in services, such as computer use	30
Dialogue, community consultation, and other civic engagement	23
Self-help and other support groups	28
Attended workshops	44

Source: service users survey.

literacy. That repeated interaction focused on improving English-language proficiency provides opportunities for individuals to work together, recognize similarities, and develop affinities that may lead to new relationships.

Table 4.1 also captures variation in participation in activities. More people join in at festivals and celebrations than at employment counselling, for instance. In addition to variety in programming and variety in participation rates, individuals themselves also exhibit variety in their experiences, participating in multiple types of activities at neighbourhood houses, with some participating in a wider variety of programing types than others. We allowed respondents to check all types of activities they participated in, and the histogram in Figure 4.2 shows that variety of experiences was common among them. Higher bars show that a higher proportion of respondents chose a particular option. It was most common for respondents to

FIGURE 4.2

Number of different activities that respondents participated in

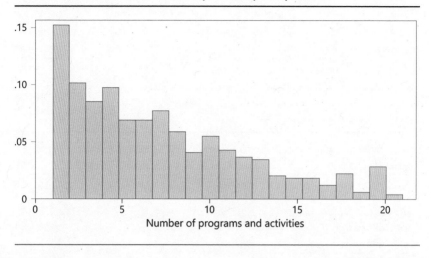

Number of programs and activities

participate in more than one type of activity, and 50 percent of respondents participated in more than the median of six activities.

Considering these varied experiences of participants, it is possible to imagine a *pathway of participation* through the neighbourhood house. Participants do not typically arrive at the neighbourhood house for the first time and join six different types of activities. Rather, a new participant might first join one group, a mother-and-toddler drop-in program, for instance, and later learn about other activities they are interested in joining – a cooking club or a self-defence course, perhaps. These pathways of participation are also evident in the participant stories presented in Chapter 6. It is worth considering the relationship-building potential that participation in six different activities might provide. The relationship-building opportunities accumulate as a person passes through each activity, spending time with a different set of people focused on a different shared activity. Continued participation at the neighbourhood house also provides opportunities for relationship maintenance as people meet in one activity and continue that relationship by joining a new program together. These pathways increase the density of personal relationships at the houses and in the neighbourhood, as more people from the local community make friends and acquaintances, and meet the friends of friends.

This variety of participation at the neighbourhood house also suggests opportunities for social capacity development, particularly by bringing together people with diverse characteristics and from diverse backgrounds through interaction around a shared activity. Some organizations are geared toward a particular demographic group, such as a seniors' centre. With a focus on the local place-based community, neighbourhood houses reach out to and accommodate a variety of ages, education levels, genders, and ethnic diversity. For example, 77 percent of our survey respondents were female, 31 percent had a university degree, 65 percent were born outside Canada, nearly 60 percent had a first language other than English or French, over 40 percent were seniors, and 10 percent were under thirty years of age. Our protocol did not allow sampling of respondents under eighteen, but we know that many of the programs and activities at neighbourhood houses are for youth. While we may explore these differences in future analysis, my current interest is in showing the variety of different backgrounds the neighbourhood house model attracts.

With this demographically varied participation at the neighbourhood house, participation in any one program or activity makes interacting with someone who is different in some important way very likely. That experience provides the opportunity to develop social capacity skills in working with and communicating across differences. Following a pathway of participation, and engaging in more than one program or activity, makes these capacity-developing experiences even more likely. It also raises the possibility of transferring the skills learned in one program to the new context of a different activity. These experiences make social capacity development of neighbourhood house participants likely, and potentially increase the social capacity in the wider context of the neighbourhood.

A Community Development Mission

We have seen that neighbourhood houses provide opportunities for interaction within local place-based communities, and this interaction provides opportunities for relationship development and social capacity development. That discussion focused primarily on opportunities for community-building that are non-purposeful. The proposal is that the unique structure of programming and activities at the neighbourhood house provides opportunities for community-building even if that is not the goal of the neighbourhood house in organizing those activities, or the motivation of participants who engage in those activities.

But providing community-building opportunities is often done purposefully by the neighbourhood houses, which operate with a community development mission. This approach has an impact on community-building in two ways. First, the community development mission provides a set of guiding values and principles that govern many of the activities at the neighbourhood house. This approach is documented from the point of view of executive directors in Chapter 2. It results in the implementation of programming and activities directed at making new connections and maintaining existing ones. For example, consider community get-togethers like the Friday Night Dinner promoted on the bulletin board of Little Mountain Neighbourhood House (Figure 4.1). It is billed as an opportunity to "meet new people and find out what's new in the neighbourhood." This and similar events are organized by the neighbourhood house with the goal of making new connections among neighbours and maintaining exiting connections. They are designed with the goal of bringing people together to form new relationships, and attracting individuals who share that goal.

Neighbourhood houses also support programs and activities that follow from stated values of making connections across differences in the neighbourhood. An example of this is the participation of neighbourhood houses in the City of Vancouver's Dialogue Circles Project (2011). This project had the goal of bringing together members of three communities: First Nations, urban Aboriginals, and new immigrants to Canada. Nine events were held to enable them to have preliminary conversations about living together in Vancouver. Three of the events took place at Kiwassa, Mount Pleasant, and South Vancouver Neighbourhood Houses. Dialogue circles are used in many circumstances at neighbourhood houses, including projects like Building Welcoming and Inclusive Neighbourhoods (BWIN), a provincially funded program working with neighbourhood houses to help new and established immigrants adapt to and integrate with their communities, and to address problems of exclusion. The Dialogue Circles and BWIN projects are two examples of the types of programming neighbourhood houses support that reflect the goals of making connections across differences and building skills for communicating across those differences.

A second aspect of the community development mission that purposefully builds community comprises the day-to-day practices of the neighbourhood house staff. These are more mundane aspects of the work of neighbourhood houses than dialogue circles and the BWIN program, but they include capacity development strategies for working with participants, such as encouraging participants in one activity to consider getting involved in other activities at the neighbourhood house, and encouraging participants to run and initiate programs and activities at the neighbourhood house. By recognizing the interests and abilities of participants and

TABLE 4.2

Participation of respondents in social capacity–building activities at neighbourhood houses (N = 675)

Activity type	Participation rate (%)
Volunteered time at the neighbourhood house	56
Participated in planning and organizing a program or event	44
Responsible for running a program or event	26
Helped start a new program or event	27
A member of an advisory committee or board	15

Source: service users survey.

encouraging them to join other programs that follow from this, staff are purposefully trying to expand the variety of participation experiences among users. As discussed above, this varied participation contributes to capacity development. The average participant at the neighbourhood house is engaged in multiple program and activity areas, and this variety of participation among users is, in part, a reflection of the encouragement they receive from staff.

Neighbourhood house staff also encourage participants to get involved in running or starting programs, and to participate in governance activities at the neighbourhood house. This might include a weekly Laughing Yoga class initiated and run by a participant at South Vancouver Neighbourhood House, or serving on the Seniors' Advisory Committee at Kitsilano Neighbourhood House. Our survey asked respondents about these types of participation, and Table 4.2 shows the rates at which they engaged in these more complex types of participation at neighbourhood houses.

These higher-level types of participation require time, skills, and commitment and thus are less common among users of neighbourhood houses. Most of those who engaged in these activities were first drawn by participating in programs and activities at the houses. Over half volunteered to help at a program or activity, and many helped plan or organize programs and activities. It is less common to run an event, start a new program, or serve on an advisory committee, but these types of participation still occur at notable rates.

Neighbourhood houses in Metro Vancouver are a unique form of social infrastructure. All forms of social infrastructure provide opportunities for community-building through relationship development and social capacity development. The neighbourhood house model is unique for its place-based approach and community development mission, which provide opportunities for participation in a variety of programs and activities and a variety of participation types – all of which we would expect to contribute to community-building for participants.

Community-Building Outcomes of Neighbourhood House Participation: An Empirical Examination

In the remainder of this chapter, I will pursue an empirical examination of what might be considered two social infrastructure hypotheses. The first is that using social infrastructure contributes to relationship development and maintenance among users. This hypothesis has been considered at some length in previous theory and research. The second hypothesis is that using social infrastructure contributes to social capacity development among users. This hypothesis is addressed less frequently in the literature, but I have developed the logic of the hypothesis above. For both hypotheses, I use participation in neighbourhood houses to indicate use of social infrastructure, so my primary interest is in community-building in the neighbourhood as a result of neighbourhood house participation. To examine these hypotheses, I use survey data discussed above.[7]

Comparing Neighbourhood House Users

I will make comparisons among users who differ in important participation dimensions. Our primary dimension of comparison will be along the variety of participation among users. This dimension follows directly from the discussion above: an increase in the variety of participation increases the opportunity for both relationship development and social capacity development. Up to twenty-one different types of programs and activities were included.[8]

In addition to the variety of participation, I will examine two aspects of participation that change the opportunity for relationship and social capacity development among users. Figure 4.3 shows the length of time that respondents had participated at the neighbourhood house in response to the question of how long it had been since a respondent's first visit to the neighbourhood house (less than 6 months, 6–12 months, 1–2 years, 3–5 years, 6–10 years, and more than 10 years). The longer a person participates in a neighbourhood house, the greater the potential for experiences that bring the person into contact with others, and experiences that allow for learning and practising capacity-building skills. The responses to this question capture a unique aspect of the neighbourhood house model, that of

FIGURE 4.3

Length of time respondents had participated at the neighbourhood house

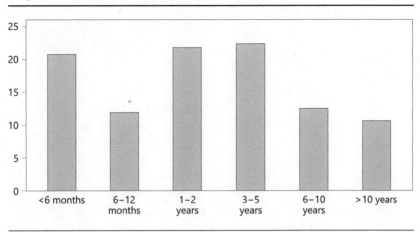

Source: service users survey.

engaging participants over long periods of time – as long as ten years or more. Figure 4.3 shows that the length of participation can be short-term, with 21 percent participating for less than six months, or long-term, with 11 percent participating more than ten years.

I also consider the intensity of participation as measured by responses to the question of how often respondents visited the neighbourhood house in the past year (more than once a week, about once a week, 2 or 3 times a month, about once a month, about once every 2 months (6 times a year), and less than 6 times a year). Here again, intensity of participation makes opportunities for repeated interactions leading to relationship formation more likely, and reinforces new skills with repeated opportunities for practice. We would expect greater intensity of participation to be associated with more relationship formation, relationship maintenance, and social capacity development. Figure 4.4 shows rates of intensity from least intense (less than six visits a year) to most intense (more than one visit a week). There is notable variation in intensity of participation. Figure 4.4 shows that over 50 percent of our respondents participated in activities more than once a week.[9] Some participated less often (every other month or even less frequently) but still engaged in some activities at the neighbourhood house during the course of a year.

In the remainder of the chapter, I will examine the community-building outcomes associated with participation at the neighbourhood houses in

FIGURE 4.4

Respondents' frequency of visits to the neighbourhood house

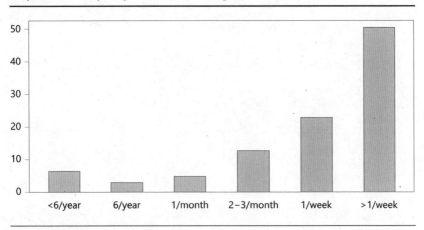

Source: service users survey.

TABLE 4.3

Friendship patterns exhibited by respondents (*N* = 675)

Responses		Percent (%)
Met at neighbourhood house	0	40
	1	14
	2	17
	3–5	17
	6–10	6
	>10	7
Get together with friends	Every day	5
	A few times per week	27
	Once per week	27
	More than once per month	20
	Once per month	11
	More than once per year	6
	Once per year	1
	Less than once per year	3
From different ethnic groups	0	35
	1	16
	2	21
	3–5	21
	6–10	4
	>10	4

Source: service users survey.

Metro Vancouver. My focus will be on the variety of participation in particular, comparing this with the length of time respondents were involved and the intensity of participation. I will look first at friendship development, and follow this with an examination of relationships in the neighbourhood.

Friendships among Neighbourhood House Users

Perhaps establishing a new friendship is the clearest example of the kind of relationship we think of when we consider possibilities of developing and maintaining new connections through social infrastructure. Friendships are a form of intimate relationship that includes an emotional intensity that develops over time. Not every new connection leads to friendship, but we would expect that participation in a neighbourhood house would provide the opportunity for regular interaction over time while one is engaged in shared activities, and this interaction provides a context for friendships to form. Our questionnaire asked three questions about friendships: 1) Of your close friends, how many did you meet through the neighbourhood house? 2) How often do you get together with your close friends? 3) Of your close friends, how many are from a different ethnic group than your own? Table 4.3 summarizes the responses to these questions.

Meeting Friends at the Neighbourhood House

Meeting friends at the neighbourhood house addresses the first social infrastructure hypothesis directly. By participating at the neighbourhood house, neighbours come together in regular interactions around shared activities, and those interactions may lead to relationship formation. The most common response (40 percent) was that respondents made no friends at the neighbourhood house. This may reflect the difficulty of achieving the level of intimacy associated with a close friend. Of course, 60 percent of respondents did make at least one friend, and some reported making more than ten.

The simple descriptive finding that many people do make friends at the neighbourhood house supports the social infrastructure hypothesis, but we can look more closely at friendship formation and the three dimensions of participation at the neighbourhood house. Figure 4.5 shows the association between making friends at the neighbourhood house and these three dimensions. All three dimensions of participation led to more friends made at the neighbourhood house. Length and intensity of participation are similarly associated with new friends met, but it is variety of participation that stands out with the largest association with new friends met. Moving through a pathway of different programs and activities at the neighbourhood house

FIGURE 4.5

Association between friendships made and length, intensity, and variety of participation in the neighbourhood house

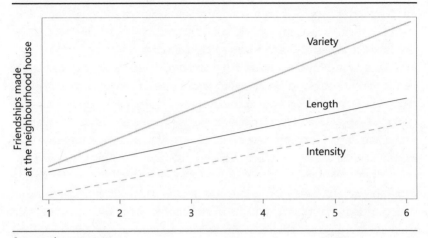

Source: service users survey.

brings individuals into contact with a greater number and diversity of other participants. This alone may account for the greater likelihood of making a new friend at the neighbourhood house.

Getting Together with Friends

Table 4.3 shows that our respondents tended to get together with friends regularly. Most (59 percent) got together with friends every week. Figure 4.6 shows the association between getting together with friends and the three dimensions of participation. Here again, we can see different associations between these dimensions and getting together with friends. Length of involvement is not strongly associated with how often respondents spend time with friends. As length of involvement increases, there is little increase in frequency of getting together with friends. On the other hand, variety and intensity of participation are associated with getting together with friends. As participants participate more frequently, and as they participate in a greater variety of programs and activities, there is a greater frequency of getting together with friends.

Having Cross-Ethnic Friendships

Looking at cross-ethnic friendships introduces a new dynamic to our analysis. Making friends that cross differences such as ethnicity draws on both

FIGURE 4.6

Association between getting together with friends and length, intensity, and variety of participation in the neighbourhood house

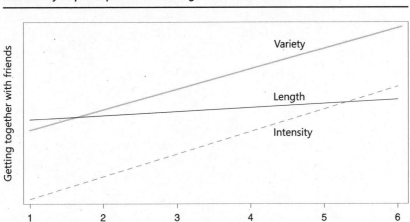

Source: service users survey.

social infrastructure hypotheses discussed above. These friendships are in part a result of opportunities provided by the programs and activities that take place at the neighbourhood house. Forming these friendships also draws on social capacity skills, particularly skills related to understanding and communication across these differences. Friendships that cross differences can be difficult to form, in part due to homophily – the tendency for friendships to be based on similarity. The neighbourhood house respondents reflect this: the majority report having at least one cross-ethnic friendship, but very few have more than five cross-ethnic friends.

Figure 4.7 shows that the variety of participation experiences is particularly important when looking at cross-ethnic friendships. Intensity of participation is not associated, and length of time participating is only slightly associated, with having cross-ethnic friendships. Variety of experiences offers increased opportunities to meet people from different backgrounds, interact with them regularly over time, and develop the skills to move a loose connection toward friendship.

Our analysis of friendships has shown that differences in participation at the neighbourhood house are associated with differences in friendship formation and maintenance. New friendships are made through participation at the houses, and friendships are maintained by getting together with friends. In each case, participation in a greater variety of programs and activities is

FIGURE 4.7

Association between cross-ethnic friendships and length, intensity, and variety of participation in the neighbourhood house

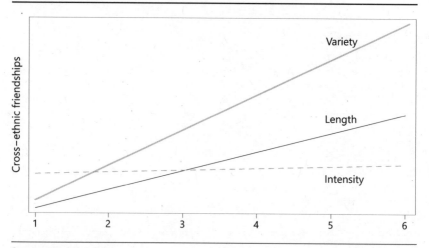

Source: service users survey.

associated with higher levels of relationship formation and maintenance. Having cross-ethnic friendships reflects a specific type of friendship, one that may require the ability to make connections across differences, including the capacity for communication and understanding. We do not know that these friendships were made at the neighbourhood house or after participation there, but we do see that as a wider variety of programs and activities are participated in, the number of cross-ethnic friendships reported increases.

Relationships in the Neighbourhood

Social infrastructure can play a role in the friendships of an individual, but the broader idea behind including such infrastructure in neighbourhoods is that the presence of an organization like a neighbourhood houses will facilitate relationship development and maintenance in the neighbourhood. We asked our respondents five questions to help us gauge their relationships in the neighbourhood:

1 About how often do you have a conversation with your neighbours – more than just a casual hello?

2 Do you know the first names of at least two of your neighbours?

3 In the past 12 months, did you get together with any of your neighbours for coffee or tea, dinner, a barbecue, or some other kind of get-together?

4 How often do you voluntarily give help to your neighbours?

5 How often do you receive help voluntarily from your neighbours?

These are all common questionnaire items used to gauge community integration.

Table 4.4 shows a summary of these responses. A first look suggests that our respondents are individuals who are well integrated into their local communities. Knowing names and having conversations are quite common. Over 80 percent of respondents knew the names of at least two of their neighbours, and 65 percent had conversations that were more than a simple hello once a week or more. These types of interaction suggest a level of neighbourliness that can increase feelings of belonging in a neighbourhood, but they are less intimate and do not ask much from participants as other

TABLE 4.4

Neighbourhood integration of participants (*N* = 675)

Responses		Percent (%)
Conversations	Every day	17
	A few per week	34
	Once per week	14
	A few per month	15
	Once per month	8
	A few per year	6
	Once per year	1
	Less than once per year	6
Know names (yes)		81
Get-togethers (yes)		55
Give help	Never	16
	Occasionally	53
	Often	26
	Very often	5
Receive help	Never	22
	Occasionally	58
	Often	17
	Very often	03

Source: service users survey.

FIGURE 4.8

Relationship between getting together with neighbours and intensity
of participation in the neighbourhood house

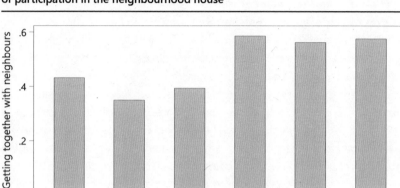

Source: service users survey.

types of interaction. Getting together for coffee, dinner, or a barbecue suggests more intimate relationships with neighbours. Fifty-five percent of respondents had had a more intimate get-together, such as these, with a neighbour in the past year.

Looking back at our dimensions of neighbourhood house participation, the length of time participating, the intensity of participation, and the variety of participation are all associated with higher levels of neighbourhood engagement. For instance, Figure 4.8 shows that the proportion of respondents reporting that they get together with neighbours for coffee, dinner, and so on increases with intensity of participation at the neighbourhood house. For those reporting less intense participation – once a month or less frequent participation – the rates of having dinner or coffee in the past twelve months are around 40 percent. As participation becomes more intense – from two to three times per month up to multiple times per week – the rates of having coffee or dinner with neighbours jumps to around 57 percent.[10]

We can see a similar dynamic between participation and neighbourhood relationship development when we look at the day-to-day support neighbours provide for each other. Table 4.4 shows that over 80 percent of respondents had volunteered help to their neighbours, and over 75 percent had received help from neighbours. These supportive relationships have a

FIGURE 4.9

Association between reciprocal help with neighbours and length, intensity, and variety of participation in the neighbourhood house

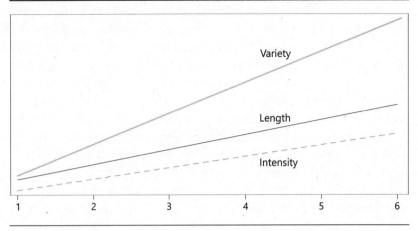

Variety

Length

Intensity

1 2 3 4 5 6

Source: service users survey.

higher cost for participants than knowing names and having conversations. They include time, effort, and perhaps resources when helping, and obligations for reciprocity when receiving support. Perhaps not surprisingly, these responses suggest reciprocal support, with those giving commonly receiving help, although giving and receiving help are not perfectly reciprocal. For instance, over 90 percent of those who give help very often receive at least some help from neighbours as well, but only about 30 percent of these heavy givers also receive help very often. They are more likely to report receiving help occasionally or often. Despite this, it is possible to combine these two questions to get an overall measure of reciprocal support among neighbours ranging from low levels of giving and receiving help to high levels of giving and receiving.[11] Figure 4.9 shows that higher levels of participation in each of our three dimensions are associated with higher levels of reciprocal support.

In Figure 4.9, the association is particularly strong for variety of participation. This may reflect the social capacity development that takes place through the greater variety of activities that a person participates in. Developing reciprocal helping relationships with neighbours would likely require skills of communication and coordination, capacity development that would follow from opportunities to learn and practise these skills through increased scope of participation at the neighbourhood house. These results complement research we conducted in June and July 2005 at nine neighbourhood houses in the city of Vancouver (Lauer and Yan 2013; Yan and Lauer 2008). In that project, our target population was neighbourhood house participants who were also newcomers who migrated to Canada in the ten years prior to data collection. We examined the reciprocal exchanges of voluntary help among neighbours, but with an emphasis on cross-ethnic helping relationships. We found that increased neighbourhood house participation was associated with more cross-ethnic helping relationships, and that intensity of participation was particularly important for this. While this research focused on a unique population within the neighbourhood – newcomers to Canada – it further supports the hypothesis that participation in neighbourhood houses contributes to relationship development among neighbours.

Social Capacity Development

The empirical examination above has focused primarily on the first social infrastructure hypothesis, namely, that participation at the neighbourhood house contributes to relationship development and maintenance. The analysis included some indirect evidence for the second social infrastructure hypothesis, that participation at the neighbourhood house contributes to social capacity development.

As discussed above, social capacity refers to a person's ability to work with others to reach shared goals. We asked our respondents about self-reported change as a result of participation at the neighbourhood house in four different skills that would contribute to this ability: 1) the ability to work with people from different backgrounds, 2) decision-making abilities, 3) the ability to organize and manage events, and 4) the ability to speak in front of others. Respondents reported whether these skills stayed about the same, increased a little, or increased a lot.[12] The questions are meant to capture capacity development that is attributable to neighbourhood house involvement. They also reflect individual perceptions of the neighbourhood house as capacity-building organizations. Table 4.5 presents the percentages of respondents that reported increases of a little and a lot.

Most respondents reported increases in these four skills through their involvement at the neighbourhood house, especially working with people from diverse backgrounds. This is not surprising, as working with people from diverse backgrounds is a typical aspect of daily activities at the neighbourhood house. The lowest reported increases involve the skills of organizing and managing programs and activities. While a majority still report

TABLE 4.5

Change in social capacity of respondents as a result of participation at the neighbourhood house

Skill	Self-reported change (%)	
	Increased a little	Increased a lot
Work with diverse others	42	34
Decision making	42	26
Organizing and managing	36	21
Speaking in front of others	35	27

Source: service users survey.

increases here, this kind of experience is not as common among participants in neighbourhood houses.

The three dimensions of participation are associated with social capacity development in ways that are consistent with some of our findings concerning relationship maintenance and development. To examine this, I combine the four items into a single index that captures overall variation in social capacity development through participation at the neighbourhood house.[13] Figure 4.10 shows the association between the three dimensions of participation and the social capacity index. The graph shows a modest association between social capacity development and length of involvement as well as intensity of involvement. Here again we see that the variety of programs and activities a respondent participated in is associated with reporting of higher levels of social capacity development through participation at the neighbourhood house. In our earlier analyses of relationship development and maintenance, we also saw a consistent association with variety of participation. In those instances, I proposed that the variety of participation would increase the density of interactions within the context of the neighbourhood house, leading to more opportunities for new relationship development. When considering social capacity development, there are likely two mechanisms operating. On the one hand, the variety of participation experiences likely increases exposure to varied experiences that provide opportunities for skill development. In addition, variety of participation also provides opportunities to practise skills developed in the context of one program or activity within the context of a new program or activity. These experiential learning experiences that use recently developed skills in new contexts and settings are well-known approaches to successful learning.

FIGURE 4.10

Association between social capacity and length, intensity, and variety of participation in the neighbourhood house

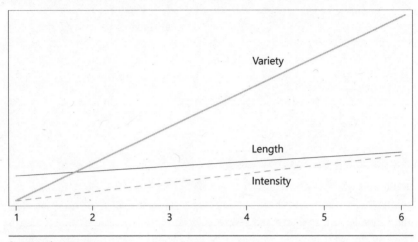

Source: service users survey.

Conclusion

In this chapter, I have developed a conceptual approach to social infrastructure that emphasizes its contributions to community-building. Social infrastructure comprises the physical places and organizations in a neighbourhood that attract and guide interactions in the neighbourhood. I have argued that social infrastructure contributes to two important aspects of community-building: the development of relationships and the development of social capacity. In each case, social infrastructure is a vehicle for opportunities – opportunities for relationships to form and opportunities to learn skills for working collectively. In the case of relationship development, the key mechanism is regular interactions, over time, which provides opportunities for connections to develop. In the case of social capacity development, the key mechanism includes working together with a shared focus or activity that provides opportunities to develop skills for working collectively, such as communication across differences, coordinating and managing others, and practising deliberation and governance.

I have also argued that neighbourhood houses are a unique form of social infrastructure due to their place-based and multi-service approach to serving the neighbourhood. Neighbourhood houses make a unique contribution to community-building in two ways. First, the focus on the whole neighbourhood results in a wide variety of programs and activities and a diverse demographic profile of the users of neighbourhood houses. These two aspects of the houses provide opportunities for users to form and maintain relationships and to develop social capacity skills without pursuing those goals purposefully. Community-building is an outcome of the structure without needing to be a specific goal of the houses or the users. The second unique contribution to community-building is the neighbourhood houses purposeful engagement in the development of relationships and the development of social capacity. They offer a variety of programs and activities with the stated goal of building community and attracting users who are interested in making connections and developing capacity.

Finally, I have provided an empirical analysis that examines friendships and relationships in the neighbourhood, and social capacity development among neighbourhood house users. Looking at different types of participation, particularly the variety of programs and activities participated in, we have seen that friendships and relationships in the neighbourhood, as well as social capacity development, are associated with the varied participation of users.

Notes

1 Scott Feld (1981) in particular has demonstrated the importance of a shared focus of attention in building meaningful friendships and connections.

2 This emphasis on activities that require collaboration is consistent with research in the contact theory tradition (Allport 1954), discussed more below. It also contributes to my definition of social capacity as the ability to work cooperatively to accomplish shared goals (Lauer and Yan Forthcoming).

3 This research is primarily located in the political science and political sociology tradition and calls these skills civic capacity. For our purposes, the difference between civic and social capacity lies in the uses of the skills – civic for political purposes and social for community-building. The development of the skills is the same, and is not dependent on the uses.

4 Neighbourhood houses do keep track of the number of people who use programs and activities, and many users are formal members of the neighbourhood houses. However, they do not always collect contact information, and could not share membership information at the time of this research.

5 Respondents in the primary study could choose from Chinese, English, Farsi, Punjabi, Spanish, and Vietnamese. We selected these languages based on the demographics of the target population in order to accommodate the greatest number of respondents.

6 The variety of programming at neighbourhood houses can also be seen in the monthly newsletters many produce. An example is the newsletter from Gordon Neighbourhood House (https://gordonhouse.org/news-events/newsletter-archive/).

7 Because we sampled NH participants at one point in time, there is a potential bias toward those who are more intensely involved with the NH and away from those who participate irregularly. In addition, there is a potential omission of participants who were once involved but have stopped participating in NHs.

8 The measure was adjusted to a range of one through six in order to simplify comparison with the other two measures of involvement. Analyses were conducted with both the adjusted and unadjusted variety measure, with no notable differences found.

9 Our sampling strategy, by selecting respondents participating at the neighbourhood house, has a known bias toward more intensely participating members.

10 These are significant differences at the bivariate level, and the finding is confirmed using a multivariate model including all dimensions of participation and key control variables.

11 These two indicators have a Cronbach's alpha over 0.71, and a confirmatory factor analysis shows one strong component.

12 The four-item scale of self-reported changes in social capacity is adapted from McMillan et al. 1995.

13 For the multivariate analysis, scores were combined using principal components analysis, with high scores signifying greater skill increases (alpha = 0.86).

References

Allport, Gordon. 1954. *The Nature of Prejudice*. London: Addison-Wesley.

Anderson, Elijah. 2011. *The Cosmopolitan Canopy: Race and Civility in Everyday Life*. New York: W.W. Norton.

Baggetta, Matthew. 2009. "Civic Opportunities in Associations: Interpersonal Interaction, Governance Experience, and Institutional Relationships." *Social Forces* 88 (1): 175–99.

Burt, Ronald. 2004. "Structural Holes and Good Ideas." *American Journal of Sociology* 110 (2): 349–99.

Chaskin, Robert J., Prudence Brown, Sudhir Venkatesh, and Avis C. Vidal. 2001. *Building Community Capacity*. New York: Aldine de Gruyter.

City of Vancouver. 2011. *Vancouver Dialogues: First Nations, Urban Aboriginals and Immigrant Communities*. Vancouver: City of Vancouver.

de Tocqueville, Alexis. (1840) 2003. *Democracy in America*. New York: Doubleday.

Duneier, Mitchell. 1992. *Slim's Table: Race, Respectability, and Masculinity*. Chicago: University of Chicago Press.

Fabricant, Michael B., and Robert Fisher. 2002. *Settlement Houses Under Siege: The Struggle to Sustain Community Organization in New York City*. New York: Columbia University Press.

Feld, Scott. 1981. "The Focused Organization of Social Ties." *American Journal of Sociology* 86 (5): 1015–35.

Irving, Allan, Harriet Parsons, and Donald Bellamy. 1995. *Neighbours: Three Social Settlements in Downtown Toronto*. Toronto: Canadian Scholars' Press.

Jacobs, Jane. 1961. *The Death and Life of Great American Cities*. New York: Random House.

Jerolmack, Colin. 2013. *The Global Pigeon*. Chicago: University of Chicago Press.

Klinenberg, Eric. 2018. *Palaces for the People: How Social Infrastructure Can Help Fight Inequality, Polarization, and the Decline of Civic Life*. New York: Crown.

Lauer, Sean R., and Miu Chung Yan. 2013. "Voluntary Association Involvement and Immigrant Network Diversity." *International Migration* 51 (3): 133–50.

Lauer, Sean R., and Miu Chung Yan. Forthcoming. "Neighbourhood Houses in Vancouver; Developing Social Capacity among Newcomers to Canada." *Journal of International Migration and Integration*.

Lichterman, Paul. 2006. "Social Capital or Group Style? Rescuing Tocqueville's Insights on Civic Engagement." *Theory and Society* 35 (5/6): 529–63.

Mattessich, Paul W., and Barbara R. Monsey. 1997. *Community Building: What Makes It Work? A Review of Factors Influencing Successful Community Building*. St. Paul, MN: Amherst H. Wilder Foundation.

McMillan, Brad, Paul Florin, John Stevenson, Ben Kerman, and Roger E. Mitchell. 1995. "Empowerment Praxis in Community Coalitions." *American Journal of Community Psychology* 23 (5): 699–727.

McQuarrie, Michael, and Nicole P. Marwell. 2009. "The Missing Organizational Dimension on Urban Sociology." *City and Community* 8 (3): 247–68.

Oldenburg, Ray. 1989. *The Great Good Place: Cafes, Coffee Shops, Community Centres, Beauty Parlors, General Stores, Bars, Hangouts, and How They Get You Through the Day*. New York: Paragon House.

Pettigrew, Thomas F. 1998. "Intergroup Contact Theory." *Annual Review of Psychology* 49: 65–85.

Simmel, Georg. 1950. *The Sociology of Georg Simmel*, translated by Kurt H. Wolff. New York: Free Press.

Small, Mario L. 2009. *Unanticipated Gains: Origins of Network Inequality in Everyday Life*. New York: Oxford University Press.

Trolander, Judith A. 1987. *Professionalism and Social Change*. New York: Columbia University Press.

Verba, Stanley, Kay L. Schlozman, and Henry E. Brady. 1995. *Voice and Equality: Civic Voluntarism in American Politics*. Cambridge, MA: Harvard University Press.

Whyte, William H. 1988. *City: Rediscovering the Center*. Philadelphia: University of Pennsylvania Press.

Yan, Miu Chung. 2002. "Recapturing the History of Settlement House Movement: Its Philosophy, Service Model and Implications in China's Development of Community-Based Centre Services." *Asia Pacific Journal of Social Work and Development* 12 (1): 21–40.

Yan, Miu Chung, and Sean R. Lauer. 2008. "Social Capital and Ethno-Cultural Diverse Immigrants: A Canadian Study of Settlement Houses and Social Integration." *Journal of Ethnic and Cultural Diversity in Social Work* 17 (3): 229–50.

Yodanis, Carrie. 2006. "A Place in Town: Doing Class in a Coffee Shop." *Journal of Contemporary Ethnography* 35 (3): 341–66.

5

Trajectories of Life and Belonging in the Neighbourhood Houses of Metro Vancouver

PILAR RIAÑO-ALCALÁ AND ERIKA ONO

Structural challenges such as racism and poverty, as well as everyday obstacles related to lack of inclusion, discrimination, and other social attitudes of dominant members of society toward new immigrants, have historically impacted immigrants' economic, social, and political incorporation (Alba and Foner 2015). This chapter considers neighbourhood houses (NHs) as place-based organizations that have played a unique role in immigrants' pathways toward incorporation in the economic and social life of the city. Based on life history interviews with forty staff, volunteers, and board members from NHs in Metro Vancouver, we trace two complementary dynamics and functions of the NHs: 1) as places for meaningful social, family, and civic engagement, and 2) as hubs for exchange, career path, and self-development.

Applying holistic place-based approaches to the understanding of civic engagement and to Arjun Appadurai's notion (2004) of individual and collective aspirations as a navigational capacity, we argue that in the context of a settler colonial country such as Canada, immigrants have played a central role in the envisioning and maintenance of NHs as places of social and racial inclusion, place-based learning, and leadership. Drawing on first-person testimonies, we analyze how those engaged in building and sustaining NHs narrate inclusion, community engagement, and the fostering of a sense of place. We further interrogate this dynamic of inclusion and engagement from the lens of a racialized architecture of power where racially minoritized staff and volunteers have scant presence in the decision-making roles and systems of the neighbourhood houses.

Locating and Contextualizing the "Place"

The neighbourhood houses in this study are located in Metro Vancouver, also known as the Lower Mainland, in British Columbia, Canada. The Lower Mainland is located on the unceded territories of the Hwlitsum, Katzie, Kwantlen, Kwikwetlem, Matsqui, Musqueam, Qayqayt, Semiahmoo, Skxwú7mesh, Tsawwassen, and Tsleil-Waututh peoples (Metro Vancouver 2019). As mentioned in the Introduction, Vancouver has one of the largest immigrant populations in Canada, with over 40 percent of metro-area residents classified as immigrants to Canada. Ethnicity demographics of Metro Vancouver in 2016 were 49 percent white settlers, 48 percent racialized, and 3 percent Indigenous (Statistics Canada 2017).

The Vancouver Foundation's first (2012) *Connections and Engagement* report concluded that 65 percent of participants in its study did not see diversity as an opportunity to make meaningful connections. In this report, 35 percent of participants had no close friends outside of their own ethnic group (Vancouver Foundation 2012). These responses and the 20 percent of participants who chose not to answer questions related to whether they would "welcome recent immigrants or refugees from certain regions of the world" suggest some of the troubling attitudes that underlie dynamics of racial exclusion and discrimination at the local level. Despite the report's conclusion that more research was needed to further explore these findings, the Vancouver Foundation's latest report (2017) does not mention the themes of diversity and racism even once. Questions remain about the dynamics of community fragmentation and racialized groups marginalization in the neighbourhoods of Vancouver.

Research shows that immigrants, particularly racialized immigrants, face additional challenges to local integration and engagement, such as language barriers, barriers to information, barriers to health and social care access, barriers to equal job opportunities, cultural differences, racism, and discrimination (Alba and Foner 2015; Kalich, Heinemann, and Ghahari 2016; Phan et al. 2015). Moreover, as El-Lahib (2016, 759) posits, these barriers are historically linked in Canada to dominant discourses on migration as "opportunity" and immigration policies and practices that "have intensified the marginalization experiences of specific social groups; historically, immigration policies have been shaped by economic priorities and have aimed to serve colonial, racist, sexist and ableist agendas by constructing immigrants to meet these aims."

Neighbourhood houses offer a unique site and history to further inquire about the dynamics of inclusion/exclusion and engagement within the context of a large city in a settler colonial nation. One of the unique features of NHs is that their staff, volunteers, and users are from highly diverse ethnic, age, and social class backgrounds, with, for example, a staff profile of 49 percent immigrants and 44.7 percent racial minorities in Metro Vancouver (Yan, Lauer, and Riaño-Alcalá 2017, 1599). Furthermore, and as we will explore in this chapter, users, volunteers, and staff consider the NH as a place of meaningful engagement and inclusion but locate these social dynamics in a contradictory landscape of unstable program funding and job insecurity and a form of racialized glass ceiling within the organizational structures of the NHs. Based on forty oral history interviews, we examine here the ways in which NHs constitute places of social and racial inclusion, place-based learning, and leadership that break down fragmentation and provide opportunities to racialized immigrants for personal, social, and economic development.

Methodology

As part of the larger Neighbourhood Houses in Metro Vancouver study, life history interviews were conducted with research participants who started as users of programs and are now service providers, volunteers, or board members. Forty people were interviewed from fourteen NHs. Twenty-three self-identified as immigrants and three as second-generation immigrants. Nineteen were women and four were men. Participants had immigrated from fourteen different countries, from Asia, Europe, Latin America, and Africa. Engagement with NHs ranged from four to thirty years.

The life history interviews are based on an oral history framework, which is the interviewing of eyewitness participants in the events of the past for the purpose of historical reconstruction (Grele 1996) and the valorization of the voices of ignored and oppressed groups (Berger Gluck and Patai 1991). A life history is defined as a story about the life of a person that is told to another; it recovers the person's identity and legacy for the future (Portelli 1991). It seeks to understand the interviewee life trajectory in relation to broader social processes of – for example, in this project – migration, urbanization, and social inclusion (Riaño-Alcalá 2013).

Life histories offer a narrative about a person's life paths and the manners in which this person relates it to the experiences of others and to the social context in which it takes place. Anna, a journalist and filmmaker who immigrated from Romania in 2009 with her partner and five-year-old daughter, and who runs the Aboriginal Family program at Collingwood Neighbourhood House in East Vancouver, illustrates this process by stating: "My story is part of the neighbourhood house story because they all overlap to create the neighbourhood house."

Holistic Place-Based Approaches

This chapter is informed by discussions about the relationship between experiences of place and place attachment in neighbourhood settings and community development. It draws on holistic place-based approaches and theories of place, space, and community to explore how place attachment and sense of community within neighbourhood houses constitute critical elements of how interviewees see their work and history in these places. (Please also refer to the introduction of the concept in the Introduction.) According to Lynne Manzo and Douglas Perkins (2006, 335): "As we are all inextricably embedded in a physical context, we are compelled to understand the nature of our relationship to place." One of the elements that differentiates NHs from other community organizations is the focus of NHs on providing place-based services. Additionally, the NH service delivery model recognizes attachment to place as a key component of developing a sense of community, social participation, and civic engagement. Thus, the interpersonal and socio-political dimensions of "place" are integral to an analysis of participants' life stories in relation to the NHs.

Research on place-related attitudes, behaviours, and emotions by environmental psychologists and geographers conceptualizes the relationships to place as critical components of lived experience (Altman and Low 1992; Proshansky, Fabian, and Kaminoff 1983; Tuan 1974). Yi-Fu Tuan (1974, 33) observed the ways in which people attach meaning to place to describe how what starts as indistinguishable "space" transforms into "place" as people become acquainted with places and ascribe value to them. Places therefore attain deeper meaning through the "steady accretion of sentiment." The granting of emotional and experiential significance to the experience of place informs notions of place attachment and place identity, and constitutes core concepts weaving our discussion of the place-based dimension of community engagement in NHs (Korpela 1989; Pretty, Chipuer, and Bramston 2003; Proshansky 1978; Ryden 1993; Twigger-Ross and Uzzell 1996).

Place attachment is characterized as an affective connection between people and places (Altman and Low 1992). Place identity includes the meaning and significance of places for individuals and how such meanings influence individuals' conceptualizations of self (Proshansky, Fabian, and Kaminoff 1983). Place attachment and identity affect individual and group behaviours and also influence the relationship developed between a sense of community and the everyday life in neighbourhoods. Bondedness and rootedness (Riger and Lavrakas 1981; Vitek and Jackson 1996) and the valuing of community places (Cobb 1996; Hummon 1992) are important components of how people come to ascribe importance to their relationships with place and their community involvement. As Manzo and Perkins (2006, 337) assert: "If people's identity and values are indeed informed by places they deem significant, then it follows that people's bonds with those places will impact their engagement in such places, whether it be to maintain or improve them, respond to changes within them, or simply to stay in that place."

Community-level place attachment studies look at ways in which emotional bonds to place can result in community participation (Hester 1993; Shumaker and Taylor 1983). This is because people's attachments to place are usually linked to their sense of community (Pretty, Chipuer, and Bramson 2003). According to Manzo and Perkins (2006, 339), a psychological "sense of community" includes "feelings of membership or belonging to a group, including an emotional connection based on shared history, as well as shared interests or concerns ... [and] both sense of community and place attachment manifest themselves behaviourally in participation." For example, Barbara Brown, Douglas Perkins, and Graham Brown (2003) conducted a study of neighbourhood revitalization and place attachment in a suburban neighbourhood experiencing deterioration that demonstrated that place attachments and sense of community are important contributors to neighbourhood revitalization efforts.

Literature on place attachment, identity, and sense of community has tended to disregard how larger social and economic forces, including forces of globalization, neoliberalism, settler colonialism, and environmental degradation, impact the experience of and attachment to places (Tuck and McKenzie 2015). As Eve Tuck and Marcia McKenzie (2015, 1) posit, we need to grapple with how "places and our orientations to them are informed by, and determinants of, history, empire, and culture." In the context of a white settler–dominated society like Canada, where immigrants, particularly refugees and immigrants of colour and countries in the Global South, encounter discrimination and marginalization (El-Lahib 2016), the more inclusive space facilitated by neighbourhood houses becomes a key element of their experiences of place attachment and may open spaces for contestation. As Jennifer Carter, Pam Dyer, and Bishnu Sharma (2007, 755) suggest: "Structural forces shape sense of place, rendering the specifics of each place-meaning open to contestation by alternative voices within class, gender, or race divisions at any locality." Place identity and meaning making of place is connected to and influenced by history and colonial powers. Although historically community-building in the settlement houses was rooted in a vision of building bridges across differences, it was also embedded in a model of "the house" as a place of immigrant adaptation and assimilation into a white mainstream society (Lyon 2017; Yan, Lauer, and Riaño-Alcalá 2017).

A holistic place-based framework considers personal everyday experiences, attachments, and meaning, along with socio-political, historical, economic, and environmental contexts. Additionally, and as we will explore here, the presence of vital social networks also shapes people's attachment to place, and, in the case of neighbourhood houses, is linked to the development of a sense of individual and collective agency by staff and volunteers of neighbourhood houses. Sense of agency, in this context, refers to the values and beliefs of people in their individual and/or collective capability to act and produce a desired effect (Monroe 2012; Trujillo and Tanner 2014). This holistic place-based framework is used in this chapter to analyze how particular preferences, perceptions, and emotional connections to place relate to community social cohesion, organized participation, and community development in the context neighbourhood houses.

Places for Meaningful Social, Family, and Civic Engagement

Lynn is the community kitchen coordinator at Burnaby Neighbourhood House. Her relationship with neighbourhood houses goes back forty years, when a neighbourhood house staff member visited her elementary school to promote a camp for kids. As a second-generation immigrant, both of whose parents had immigrated to Canada from rural communities in China, Lynn shares her excitement about getting her first job outside of her parents' grocery store, at South Vancouver Neighbourhood House. Speaking about her ongoing connection to NHs, she reflects:

> And for a while I was thinking that, you know, most of the people I see are living in poverty, but the neighbourhood house sees so many other people so it's neat when people come together. Because some people have things to share and give too, and somebody who's living in hard times has things to share with people who are doing really well, and people who are doing really well have things to share with other people. I see the neighbourhood house as a commons place where people come together so I hope more of that happens.

Lynn's reflection on the neighbourhood house as a commons place introduces a major theme that emerged from the life story interviews: how engaging community and connecting people across differences in income or race are central to the task of inclusion, civic-mindedness, and capacity-building. In this section, we describe the rich and varied ways in which NHs create these commons. Staff and volunteers interviewed believe that NHs foster a sense of place by enlarging the "boundaries" of the NH as a place for services, community-building, and leadership. NHs are experienced as a shared place: a commons for knowledge, resource sharing, and community. This is felt through place-based forms of association and participation, in the everyday life of participants as parents, volunteers, leaders, or staff and through the intergenerational endeavours that occur in neighbourhood houses.

Place-Based Connection and Engagement

The relationships that staff participants establish with neighbourhood houses go far beyond job satisfaction and are associated with the deep meaning they grant NHs as places that build community and place identity. A common theme among the oral history interviewees is the link interviewees see between job and community experience and the affective and historical connections they have established with the NHs. Therefore, this place-based relationship shapes the way staff members understand the role of the NHs and their manner of engagement in the communities. It is foundational as it shapes their relation to the NHs as identity-based and based on place attachment. Carmen, recreation coordinator at Collingwood Neighbourhood House, immigrated to Canada from Colombia with her husband and three children in 1998. She describes the ways in which the programs at the NH invite people into a relationship:

> I find for people in the neighbourhood, who aren't living in Canada for many years and they find a place to stay to talk with people, to have a program. They have seniors' program, sometimes they are very lonely at home. They come in and they feel happy, find someone to hug. Say welcome, you know coffee and tea. Chat with somebody. Yesterday we had seniors' community lunch. I saw the faces. Oh my god those people are so happy to see each other ... You know songs and food and you can see their faces. You need to talk to them. They are feeling so welcomed and many people from staff you know we have a team. We have some special event everybody helps, other person will help set up tables, other people help decorate. We have a very good team, support each other. And other people who live in the neighbourhood they come to us. But I think for the immigrants it's more important than anybody else because they don't have friends and it's the only house you can go to.

Carmen's description of what happens when immigrants come to some of the programs in the house suggest the important role of neighbourhood houses as connectors. Interviewees provided a rich variety of examples and reflections on this connector function and its power to break isolation for those with weak networks of relations or those who have experienced exclusion and discrimination in public places. This, we heard from interviewees, is particularly significant for newer immigrants. Andrea, who moved to Vancouver thirteen years prior to her life history interview and works as the community connections coordinator at Collingwood Neighbourhood House, sees this connecting role anchored in the support and information resources the NHs offer. According to her:

> Our lives are newer and so it's just to find ways of getting to know each other, you feel safer and then you have a support system because a lot of us don't have families here necessarily. And there's always, you find that you hear about a lot of things, it's kind of like an information centre as well. So that's all important for people too, in the city. It makes the city more livable.

Andrea provides in her own reflection a key analytical connection when she links the knowing of others to feeling safer and to making the city more livable. Ana, who, as mentioned earlier, immigrated to Canada from Romania and now runs the Aboriginal Family program at Collingwood Neighbourhood House, further elaborated on neighbourhood houses' connector role as having the potential to trigger a transformative experience: "People they can come from outside, from the street then just change their life inside the neighbourhood home. This is another power. This is another thing I love about the neighbourhood house. You just step in and all of a sudden everything changes."

Maheen, the family programs manager at Burnaby Neighbourhood House, also discusses neighbourhood houses as places of connection. She and nine family members arrived in Canada in 1986 as refugees from Iran via Pakistan. They joined eight family members who were already in Vancouver. At the time, Maheen's daughter was two years old; her son was born nine months later. One year later, Maheen began looking for preschool classes and found herself at Mount Pleasant Neighbourhood House (MPNH), in the community where she lived at that time. The first person she met was the program director, Sharon, who became her mentor and one of her closest friends. From the start, Sharon encouraged Maheen to share her plans and to become more involved with the NH, suggesting: "Every so often, come to my office and we will talk about how life is going, and what you would like to do." Meanwhile, Maheen's daughter began preschool at MPNH. Maheen talks about how the quality of the relationships and the feeling of community drew her into becoming more involved:

> It was the warmth of the staff, and all the programs that were happening in this one hall ... There was a preschool in the morning, then they would stack the tables and make the room ready for seniors to come for lunch. And then at five in the afternoon everything changed again, and persons with disabilities arrived for the evening program. And youth were coming for different programs. There was such an amazing feeling of community. I was drawn in – I wanted to be more involved.

Wen Ling is an art therapist who volunteers at Kitsilano Neighbourhood House. She immigrated to Canada from Taiwan in 2010. In describing how she became involved with neighbourhood houses, she reflects on the meaning of the connections that NHs offer:

> I was attending an occupational counselling program at a local immigrant serving agency and one day an email went out that mentioned a support program for immigrant women at Kits Neighbourhood House. I joined the group and from that point on, things started to get better because I realized that many immigrants had gone through what I was going through. I felt less lonely and less alone in my situation. At the time, I was a little bit depressed because if you imagine you have no one to talk to and the only connection you have to people is going to the library or grocery store, it's very lonely ... Coming to Kits Neighbourhood House was great. At least I had someone to talk to!

In each of these stories we find a link between a personal story of relative isolation or lack of connection and the change experienced when the interviewee's participation in an activity brought opportunities to relate to other people and the desire to engage in community work. This, Andrea stated, grounds the person: "It's just feeling more grounded in the neighbourhood and having an outlet which you knew was always here." The place-based and relational opportunities offered by the neighbourhood house moved them in a short time from program users to active participants in the life of the NH. This engagement was possible, as Andrea suggested, because NHs are experienced as safe spaces.

Neighbourhood houses are places where people feel supported and comfortable, contributing to the feeling of safety. Agata, the program director at Gordon Neighbourhood House, immigrated with her family to Canada from Poland when she was a young child. She became connected to neighbourhood houses in 2000 when she was studying psychology at the University of British Columbia, starting at South Vancouver Neighbourhood House, where she worked in the Homework Club program, then working in the Nobody's Perfect parenting program at Gordon Neighbourhood House. Agata explores the topic of NHs as safe spaces: "It helped me get through. Because it was stable, it was always a safety place, it was a place where I could be myself and get support! Because you know that everyone is working together, not one staff person will tell you that they haven't felt supported here." This association between getting support and feeling safe is further elaborated by Carmen:

> I was feeling safe in this place. Finally, when you find a place like Collingwood that you find support, and you find like one family, the right place to go. Or the orientation. You are very connected, a very strong connection ... And I feel it's safe, and in this place, I feel support. And I feel that it doesn't matter if your English is not good, it doesn't matter. I just had lots of support. So, for me it's like the place that people need to belong I say, one place that people are looking for to feel safe.

In the two previous narratives, safety is associated with the quality of the relationships and support. Cassandra, second-generation, with parents who immigrated to Canada from Vietnam, further elaborates on the impact on new immigrants of having a safe and supportive place. At twenty-one years of age, she is a board member of Collingwood Neighbourhood House and has been involved with neighbourhood houses for over ten years, starting with her introduction to Kiwassa Neighbourhood House when her mother enrolled her in several after-school programs. Reflecting on her experience as a young person participating in the NH, Cassandra realizes that the program benefited not only her but also her parents. When her parents arrived in Canada, they spoke only Vietnamese and Cantonese, so the NHs were instrumental in helping them navigate the Canadian educational system and meet new people. Cassandra notes that the after-school programs not only met her need for fun, engaged learning, and social interaction but also helped her parents. She highlights:

Neighbourhood houses really allow families to just be comfortable in a welcoming space. I remember my mom would be comfortable leaving us at the
neighbourhood house. She would go home and then come back to pick us
up later. Her feeling comfortable to let us be alone there sent us a really
strong message that a neighbourhood house is a safe place to be.

This idea of safety and support for Cassandra is at the core of what neighbourhood houses offer to service users and to the creation of a sense of
"ownership that community members have in the neighbourhood houses."
This demonstrates how NHs are safe spaces that provide not only support
but also a sense of belonging and a place for people to share with others.

Anna shares her experiences of how neighbourhood houses have provided her with a sense of belonging and importantly, changed her life: "It's a
place you can go where you connect. It's a place where you learn resources.
It's a place where you share joy. It's a place where you share your problems.
It's a very special place. For me, as you see, it changed my life."

Patricia is a family support worker at Kitsilano Neighbourhood House. She
immigrated to Canada from Peru in 2007 with her husband and two young
daughters. She became connected to a neighbourhood house through first
attending a parents-and-tots group and then working in various jobs for the
NH since 2008. She is now an assistant in the Families program. She describes
the ways in which she sees access to programs like lunch meals as a means
of breaking down feelings of isolation and disconnection: "But it's not only
coming to eat, it's also connecting with other people. Not being isolated, not
being alone at home. Not being disconnected with the community, the other
things happening in the community. Because human beings need to be connected! We need to be in touch with each other." This idea of neighbourhood
houses as sites that bring people into relationships with each other for the
purpose of connecting them with others in the community provides the basis
of the NHs' place-based notion of engaging communities.

Interviewees in the role of program coordinators, volunteers, or facilita-
tors understand well that their work addresses critical social issues and that
a critical component of this is to create a community to work with. As Agata
explains, this is linked to the neighbourhood houses' ability to provide a
sense of belonging by creating a sense of community in place: "I see neighbourhood houses as addressing social issues and advocating for people, but
also about creating community in a place where it's hard to feel in a community sometimes if you don't know many people."

Participants' life stories show how engaging individuals and connecting people are central to the task of inclusion, civic-mindedness, and capacity-building. As described in previous chapters, neighbourhood houses emerged from the settlement movement that was deeply rooted in the idea that change is achieved through collective engagement and organizing (Yan, Lauer, and Riaño-Alcalá 2017). Over time, the work and mandate of NHs have become more service-oriented in part, and, as we elaborate later in the chapter, as a consequence of competitive tendering funding systems and monitoring models based on market efficiency and performance appraisal (Kenny 2002). This reinforces a climate that erodes work toward collective empowerment and social change, and leads rather toward social mainten-ance of service delivery. During the interviews, staff reflected often on this climate and the fears it creates. Jane and Maheen both reflected and de-scribed the uncertainty it creates. Jane used to volunteer and work in family programs at Alexandra Neighbourhood House. She immigrated to Canada from Scotland in 1957, when she was three years of age, and is still con-nected to Alexandra NH. According to her: "Then there was, you know, the thought that we were all gonna get fired because we didn't have any funding. However, it's always dependent upon funding." Maheen states:

> So be able to sustain what we have. And you know, like staff being comfort-able and not worry about, you know, six months and a year ... Every year we have to fight for the same money, and every year we don't know we're gonna get it. Imagine the position you put the staff in. I see people who are paid paycheque to paycheque, and I feel for them.

However, the staff continue to envision their work outside a service deliv-ery model and use principles of community engagement and solidarity as the basis for creating strong communities and building capacity to seek avenues for change on critical issues. According to Agata:

> I think the movement for me, it's part of the movement of getting out there and letting people know who we are and what we do. And I love the fact that we're moving away from providing services to fix a problem. There's a parenting workshop if you're having trouble parenting. Or here's this program to fix this problem. It's about engaging a community and making people in a big city feel like they're part of a community. I think that's the biggest ... all the time that I've seen such a huge shift from providing a ser-vice to engaging people in a community and making them part of it.

From service to engagement to fix the problem, Agata stresses, and this she sees as critical to community-building. Tatiana, a youth worker at Kiwassa Neighbourhood House, highlights that another way in which neighbourhood houses build community capacity is by creating space to include the voices of all community members. Tatiana is a second-generation immigrant, the daughter of Chinese immigrants. Her first connection to NHs was when a couple of Kiwassa youth workers visited Hastings Elementary School to promote their programs, after which she began volunteering in the Junior Leadership program, which was part of their Preteen program. She became a Junior Leader when she was twelve and her first job was assisting the Summer program leaders at Pandora and Oak Street Parks. Since then she has worked in several programs, including Cultural Buddy (now known as Youth Settlement), Eastside Teens, and Eastside Power Mammas. Tatiana shares:

> We are very open with the youth and we encourage their input in what we program and what the service gaps are. And so, like I said, like management's very open-door and so we're like that with our youth and we try and kind of work with that to better. We always try to better the program. So yeah, it's a circle.

Participants' narratives emphasize the importance of place-based connections, social networking, and inclusive participation that is experienced at neighbourhood houses. From the theme of place-based connection and engagement, the subthemes that emerged from the life stories include NHs as places that provide connection, establish safe spaces, create a sense of belonging, engage communities, and build community capacity. In sum, NHs build community beyond a service delivery or needs-based framework; it is the working of social networking and place-based engagement that opens space to create a movement for developing a sense of community and collective agency. These are the core elements that participants saw as central to building an inclusive community, civic-mindedness, and the capacity to address larger issues and envision collective horizons in a localized manner.

Embeddedness in the Everyday Lifeworlds of Participants
Another way in which neighbourhood houses exemplify being places for meaningful social, family, and civic engagement is in how they become part of the everyday lifeworlds of community members. Interviewees shared

various stories of family interaction, activities, and use of child care/family programs through which they came into relationship with other neighbours and families and found lifelong friends. In describing their everyday lives as embedded in the life of the NHs, they often used relatedness metaphors of NHs as second homes and the people in NHs as second families.

Participants see neighbourhood houses as places for family interaction and importantly where children do everyday home-like activities, such as chores and homework, with entire families volunteering as a result of the leadership, volunteer, or work-related engagement of one of their members. Ana talks about bringing her child to the NH and the activities she soon joined: "I brought my child. She was in the childminding room, and she loved it because she loves babies. She said: 'Mommy, I want to come back here.' She's nine now. She came here when she was almost five. She reads, and she writes, and she's making her own comics and she's writing stories and she loves that place." Maheen too talks about her family's growing connections with the NH over time and how these experiences shaped her feeling of the house as "part of our family":

> My family was very involved with the neighbourhood house. I became part of any community event that the neighbourhood house was involved in ... Both of my kids were closely involved with the neighbourhood house. Both went to preschool and summer camp, attended leadership programs, and volunteered with summer programs. They kind of grew up in MPNH – they were always there. If I didn't finish work on time, they would walk to the neighbourhood house from school and we would go home together. It was our second home. My mom also came to a lot of the family nights and multicultural nights. My husband came if he had time. My sister-in-law volunteered. My nieces and nephews got involved in the leadership program and they also volunteered. The neighbourhood house was part of our family.

These descriptions highlight both the very practical contributions that neighbourhood houses make to families with the services and programs offered and also the way routines often associated with private family space take place in a communal realm, and in time come to shape participants' attachment to place.

For many participants, particularly immigrant mothers, not only had their families and children been involved with neighbourhood house activities but their first interaction and their entry into the NHs was due to their use of child care programs. Several participants said that they first became aware of NHs because they accessed child care services, which started their journey of involvement with the houses as service users to service providers. Theresa leads a drop-in program for parents of young children at Frog Hollow Neighbourhood House. She first came to Canada from Taiwan in 2000, and studied English in Kamloops for three years. She returned to Canada on a few occasions to continue practising English, and during one of her visits to Vancouver she met her husband, who had come to Canada from China. In 2005, he sponsored Theresa to come to Canada permanently. Three years later, she had her first child. It was only in 2008 that Theresa learned about NHs. She recalls her first encounter with Frog Hollow Neighbourhood House:

> We lived just a few minutes away, but we didn't know the neighbourhood house had services for different people. We thought it was only a preschool or a place for seniors to hang out. But after I had a baby, the community nurse came to visit me at home and told me: "You know, just down the hill there is a neighbourhood house. You should bring your baby there." She gave me information about what they offer at Frog Hollow, such as the programs for parents and children. So, I went to Frog Hollow Neighbourhood House for the first time after my son was three months old, I decided to bring him to Frog Hollow Neighbourhood House because I felt isolated at home ... we started coming to the drop-in. I met other parents and my son found friends to play with and he was very happy here.

Satinder also reflects on her first interaction with neighbourhood houses and the manner in which finding the daycare and other services was vital in her job search. She is currently the family program coordinator at Collingwood Neighbourhood House, where she has worked since 1990. Satinder shares how she first became connected with the NH:

> The day is etched in my memory because when I and my family came to Canada from Bahrain, we didn't know a single soul here. My husband and I wanted to look for work, but first we needed daycare for our two children, who were ten and six years old. We didn't know where to start. Fortunately, Collingwood Neighbourhood House was at that time doing a community research project to find out what the needs were in the community. A researcher from South Asia, Rashmi, came to know about me and when we met she told me about the neighbourhood house and the daycare and other services.

In addition to family interaction and use of child care programs' contribution to the neighbourhood houses as sites that are part of participants' everyday lifeworlds, the meaningful connections they make once they are involved with NHs also play a role. Along with such connections comes finding lifelong friends. Agata illustrates this experience:

> And I still have Jessie and Linda, which they've been here since the beginning with me. So, they're like my family, my second family. So, I love everyone else I work with obviously, but they, I've known them for so long. It was such a great place to work. We had so much fun. Yeah so, it's like a big family you know. And there's staff, participants, volunteers, you get attached to these people. I have this amazing job. But I also have friends at my workplace. I go out for dinner or for drinks with people that I work with! It's like a social life as well, you know what I mean?

Antonia, the executive director of Burnaby Neighbourhood House, began her journey with neighbourhood houses when she joined the Cedar Cottage Neighbourhood House leadership program at Camp Wallace, now known as Sasamat. She has been connected to NHs for forty years. She also sees a close link between family involvement, working in the NH, and developing a sense of family: "You really become close, connected and family, they become your family, you're with them so much, and your family gets involved, too." Participants further emphasize how these lifelong friends and feelings of second families make NHs a second home. According to Cassandra: "I think I would still very much be involved in the activities around there. Because Collingwood Neighbourhood House is pretty much my second home." Maheen speaks about how the NH is a second home not just for her but also for her family:

> [My children] grew up in neighbourhood houses. They were always there, they would come. If I didn't finish the job, they walked to the neighbourhood house, we would go home together. My kids became ... it was a really homey feeling. It was our second home. A lot of the evening events we did, I would bring my other family. My mom was here. She came to a lot of the family nights and multicultural nights. My husband would come to some of them.

The blurring of boundaries between home, work, and service in participants' narratives suggests also how their understanding of community-building is linked to place. Participants' narratives about place-based connections and support, experiencing everyday lifeworlds through the neighbourhood houses, and undertaking intergenerational endeavours at the NHs show in this manner how the NHs apply a holistic place-based approach to community-building and work. The connection we have traced between everyday life, family interaction, and ideas of home illustrate a key aspect of place-based approaches and their "call for a return to the everyday lifeworlds of lived experience, and a move away from the objectification of place and its meaning" (Manzo and Perkins 2006, 337). The idea of the NH as a place of everyday family interaction and activity and as associated with ideas of home suggests the sense of attachment to the NHs as a place for dwelling.

Neighbourhood houses build community beyond a service delivery or needs-based framework. Such community-building is the working of social networking and place-based engagement that opens space to create "a movement" for developing a sense of community and collective agency. These are, at the same time, the core elements that participants saw for building an inclusive community, civic-mindedness, and the capacity to address larger issues and envision collective horizons in a localized manner.

Hubs for Exchange, Career Path, and Self-Development

The pathway that participants, many as first- or second-generation immigrants to Canada, follow in neighbourhood houses is one where they start as service users and then transition into volunteers, then community workers or service providers, and finally into leadership roles. (For further information on building of community capacity by neighbourhood houses, please see Chapter 4.) In this section, we examine how these pathways of engagement and employment in neighbourhood houses contribute to self-development and strengthen the capacity to aspire for those involved in NHs by providing support, mentorship, and opportunities. Thus, we also apply holistic place-based approaches to Arjun Appadurai's (2004) notion of individual and collective aspirations as a navigational capacity in the analysis of participants' life stories in relation to NHs.

Appadurai (2004) understands capacity-building to be a socio-cultural category instead of an individual motivational trait. Aspirations are "complex understandings of the future pathways available to people" (Bok 2010, 164), and as Appadurai (2004) explains, they are unevenly distributed in society along lines of social class, gender, and race. The capacity to aspire is organized by social, cultural, and economic experiences, and by the avail-ability to navigate information; it is, in Appadurai's words (2004, 76), an ability to read "a map of a journey into the future." Appadurai (2004, 67) argues that aspirations can be fostered through collective action and move-ment: "Aspirations are never simply individual (as the language of wants and choices inclines us to think), they are always formed in interaction and in the thick of social life."

Understanding such social and cultural domains of aspirations illumin-ates the role that neighbourhood houses have played in strengthening the capacities of participants, many of whom experienced social isolation and exclusion. In what follows, we further examine participants' perspectives on how their experience and work in NHs contribute not only to their self-development but also to their capacity to explore the future and to their very sense of individual and collective agency. NHs play this role of navigation by providing opportunities for new immigrants, offering first jobs, creating job opportunities for volunteers, offering leadership programs, enriching experience and skills through different programs, supporting participants to develop and facilitate new programs, recognizing participants' skills and strengths, providing support and mentorship, and promoting training and professional development.

Capacity to Aspire in Place

Julio reflects on the personal and professional learning that occurred from his everyday presence in neighbourhood houses throughout childhood and adolescence, learning that he suggestively describes as occurring "through osmosis." He shares:

> My social skills were really heightened by watching the social workers and my mother, who later became a family worker and worked with seniors and other groups, interact with community members. Quite a number of people who came in had mental health issues, so I learned to navigate around their stresses and coping mechanisms. That gave me the confidence to engage in conflict resolution in the work that I did afterwards. I learned how to de-escalate and talk to people in crisis because all the social workers did that; I watched and repeated their behaviour. A lot of learning happened just from being around, and it also gave me a really strong appreciation of community and interpersonal relationships later in life. I've always had a curiosity and desire to understand the causes and meanings of poverty, and I think that

came from growing up in the neighbourhood house where those conversations were always happening. I don't believe it was innate in me; I think the nurture piece was most prevalent. I followed my mother's trade because that's the environment I was in. My participation with neighbourhood houses hugely influenced my education and my career choice. It's also enabled me to connect and make friends with people who are also my colleagues in community social services. It's been a reciprocal process: my education affected my work here and vice versa, so the neighbourhood house has really affected my whole life.

Julio explains how his presence in neighbourhood houses affected the way he thinks and the stands he takes on social issues and the formational nature of this presence. Other participants further connected this idea of self-development to the opening of new employment paths. Jessy immigrated to Canada from India in 2003 with her husband. She started volunteering at Gordon Neighbourhood House soon after arriving in Vancouver. She has had many responsibilities, including reception, payroll, accounting, assisting the operations manager, planning seniors' trips, and organizing workshops and special events lunches. In India, Jessy had worked in high-end hotels, and she shares how working at the neighbourhood house represented a new career and contributed to self-development:

In the hospitality industry, it was all about the money. When I moved here I thought to myself: "I should just work with normal people, where money doesn't dictate all the terms." However, I had no experience with this kind of work! I didn't even know that this kind of place existed to provide so many services to so many different people. It's just really amazing. I'm so glad I found Gordon Neighbourhood House ... For me, small events are big things in my life. If I can make somebody feel that this is a place that they can come to feel safe, and feel comfortable talking to somebody, or if I can just listen and give them an ear or shoulder to cry on, that's something big for me.

Mehak is a family support worker at Little Mountain Neighbourhood House. She immigrated to Canada from India with her family when she was six years old and first became involved with the neighbourhood house when she was in elementary school. She talks about her experiences at the neighbourhood house and how one opportunity led to another:

Little Mountain Neighbourhood House sent me to a community capacity-building class through Capilano University. That laid the foundation for community development for me and put theoretical frameworks in my head about how to work with people and how to work with communities. During that year I made a bridge between the work that I was already doing and the work that I wanted to pursue, and so that's why I went into social work.

In addition to training, neighbourhood houses provide opportunities where service users and providers can increase their skills. Many participants who immigrated to Canada as adults experienced NHs as the site of their first job. Despite the credentials they had obtained before immigrating, many participants experienced barriers in gaining employment. According to Wen Ling:

When I arrived, I was totally alone. At first I was lost, not knowing where to go, what to do. I had assumed that I would just find a job and that I would get to know my neighbours and people at my work, but it was not that easy. I felt a sense of failure because I had two master's degrees, yet I couldn't secure a job at all, at least nothing close who what I knew or had done before. I didn't know where to turn to because I didn't have any connections at all.

A common path that interviewees described was that from a first experience with a position in the neighbourhood house that then led them to increase their skills – and led some of them to leadership positions (Figure 5.1). For example, Carmen shares:

We have memories, we have pictures from when we arrived to Canada, how the people grow and now they are in different positions and I think it's amazing. And the people have opportunities to arrive and feel that you are, you can put some of your skills in this place. And I feel it's safe and, in this place, I feel support. And I feel that it doesn't matter if your English is not good. I just had lots of support. And I find that at Collingwood Neighbourhood House I get the opportunity to show my qualifications and it was for me a really big event for me to find this kind of job.

Patricia comments on her experience: "I think it's important that when you are an immigrant and you are coming to a new place, to just have the

FIGURE 5.1
Immigrant pathways to employment and leadership in the neighbourhood houses

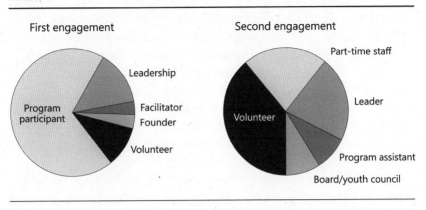

opportunity. Just have one opportunity and you will show whatever you are able to do. And that's what I got from the neighbourhood house."

Having a Voice and Aspirations

By offering training and providing opportunities for self-development, civic life, and career paths, neighbourhood houses are also places that strengthen participants' capacity to have a voice. For Appadurai (2004, 66) to exercise "voice" relates to the capacity of the oppressed, "to debate, contest, and oppose vital directions for collective social life as they wish." Maheen exemplifies the NH's role in her self-development and connects it to the strengthening of her voice and her ability to stand up:

> It was through my involvement with the neighbourhood house that I started becoming strong and able to stand up and have a voice and be able to look for things that I wanted. The first five or six years in a new country, you don't even know who you are. It's like being a singer without a voice. That's all you are because you were ripped out of what you knew and thrown somewhere. I remember when our plane landed in Canada that I felt like I would be okay here. But you still have to learn the language and culture, look for a job, earn money, bring up your children, and go through the struggles that I see people going through every day. The neighbourhood house saved me because being a part of anything at the neighbourhood

house gives you some sense of how the world works, how Canada works. You can't put a value on that. I am lucky, my kids are healthy and happy. I'm able to work and live in a country where I don't have to worry about people taking my husband away every night. The neighbourhood house helped me to be grounded here and to realize that Canada is a great country. It has a lot of challenges, but I feel like these are my challenge now because I am part of this country. I'm grateful to the neighbourhood house for giving me the opportunity to help myself and also help others, for helping me to be part of the solution ... As my kids were growing up, the neighbourhood house allowed me to figure out what I am capable of, the neighbourhood house was key to finding myself. They allowed me to frown at my own pace.

Najia also speaks of her experience with the neighbourhood house that supported her in finding a voice. She immigrated to Canada from Morocco twenty-two years ago, and she is the community kitchen leader at Collingwood Neighbourhood House. Najia shares:

When I came to Canada, I had problems from the first day I came. I went through abuse: physical abuse, mental abuse, everything. I had been told so many times that I was nothing, that I was worthless. At that moment those people [at the neighbourhood house] changed my life. Everybody stood up for me. I realized: "Oh my gosh, I'm not what that person told me I was. Now I'm back to me!" It took just that moment to give me "me" back. They gave me the courage to believe in myself. I was myself from that time and I've never left that program.

The faculty of voice, Appadurai (2004) argues, is reciprocally linked to the capacity to aspire. Maheen's description of and reflection about her involvement in neighbourhood houses illustrates this. Najia's reflection also makes this connection to voice and describes her own pathways of navigation from living in the isolation of an abusive relationship to engagement in community; it gave her back to herself, as she powerfully says. Through training, increasing skills, and strengthening voice, participants view NHs as providing avenues for employment and leadership.

Providing Avenues for Employment and Leadership
For participants who had been involved with neighbourhood houses since they were young, often having been service users in youth and leadership programs, NHs were their first place of employment. These participants

discuss their positive experiences with the NHs' leadership program. They speak about how their involvement with these programs led to jobs at the NHs. As Wei illustrates: "After that [leadership] training, we actually got jobs as day camp leaders. So, I worked here for my very first job as a day camp leader at South Van."

Tommy immigrated to Canada from Hong Kong with his parents when he was six years old. He spent eight years volunteering and working at Cedar Cottage Neighbourhood House. He first heard about neighbourhood houses at age fifteen when a youth worker from Cedar Cottage went to his high school to let the students know about the youth leadership programs. He recalls:

> I walked into this big room and there were around twelve other people from my high school. I didn't know them because I wasn't really connected in my high school either. In that first session, I definitely did not have the experience or confidence to speak up, I just didn't know what to say. That's one of the things that has changed since then, that's one example of how the neighbourhood house helped me to grow up and learn to speak and socialize in social settings. I completed the program [and] at the end of it there was an opportunity to work in the Summer Fun program with kids.

Tatiana also reflects:

> I started volunteering in the Junior Leadership program ... I became a junior Leader when I was twelve. One of my first jobs was assisting the summer program leaders ... I remember that the leaders really appreciated how I connected with the youth during the time I was there. They asked me to come back for training and then I was offered work in the summer day camps when I was about fifteen.

Leadership as a subtheme arose both in reference to specific leadership programs, in general showing neighbourhood houses as places that mentor youth into becoming leaders and provide leadership capacity development. For example, some participants mentioned how they felt supported and given chances to develop and facilitate new programs. Anna highlights:

> After I finished the film and Jennifer asked me if I want to run a program, an art program because I was talking about the power of the story and people. I believe in that. I've been involved, my fifth year with Collingwood

Days, coordinated with the Collingwood Policing Centre and the Collingwood Business Improvement Association. And, I work now, my contract
has expanded to work on celebrations and create connections, so connecting community members with, or connecting them together through arts
and performance.

Carmen also shares:

I start to get experience and I show my supervisor. My qualifications I
showed him that I finished PE classes in Colombia and that I had experience and he looked at everything and said: "Well why don't you prepare
some classes for teaching children?" Because I feel the supervisor gave
me freedom to create new programs. So, from the last years I find that
the department is growing, and our funder provide us more money because the program that we provide is good quality.

Participants illustrate how such opportunities for creative engagement,
training, and professional development give meaning to their work and
leadership. Providing opportunities for immigrants and second-generation
immigrant youth by offering first jobs, creating job opportunities for volunteers, creating leadership programs, enriching experiences and skills
through different programs, supporting members to develop and facilitate
new programs, recognizing skills and strengths, providing support and
mentorship, and promoting training and professional development are all
ways in which youth and volunteers are encouraged to aspire in place for
change in their lives and to explore the future. The charts in Figure 5.1 are
based on the analysis of interviewees' forms of participation within neighbourhood houses, from their first engagement mostly as volunteers and
program participants to their most recent engagement as staff or in leadership positions in the NH. They provide a visual illustration of the career
paths and self-development that participants reflected on in interviews.

In summary, those interviewed see that their work and life satisfaction is
tied to the meaningful work they do and to their engagement in the neighbourhood houses. This satisfaction is limited, however, by the structural dynamics of a neoliberal regime that has severely impacted the non-profit and
community sectors in the last two decades. As mentioned earlier in the
chapter, the work of NHs has become more focused on service delivery in
part as a result of unstable funding systems and monitoring models (Kenny

2002; Yan, Lauer, and Riaño-Alcalá 2017). This reinforces a climate that erodes efforts toward collective empowerment and social change and instead leads toward social maintenance of service delivery and the status quo. Taking this context of uncertainty and precarious work as a contextual background, we explore further in the next section the connection between job satisfaction and meaningful work.

Pathways of a Journey

In many ways, participants have grown alongside neighbourhood houses as they transitioned from various stages in their lives. Their life stories highlight the ways in which NHs are an essential part of their life journeys and how they would not be able to share stories about their lives without including the role of NHs. Several images and metaphors associated with "paths" surfaced, demonstrating the association of paths to a journey. Through the process of learning and developing at the NHs, several participants also strengthened their ability to balance work and their personal lives, which came with practice as the houses were often "more than a job" to them. However, what they learned through their work also appeared to influence how they coped in their personal lives and how they navigated the balance between work and everyday life. Consistently, participants see that their work and life satisfaction are tied to the meaningful work they do and to their engagement with NHs. For example, Anna shares:

> I changed a lot because of my work with the neighbourhood house. Back home I was a very career-driven person, and I had a lot of success ... I had everything that a journalist could want but I didn't feel complete. I was kind of stuck ... Here, it's totally different. I feel so happy with what I am doing, and I feel it has meaning. I feel in touch with people in a way that I couldn't be as a journalist; now I am part of the people, part of the life that I am looking at; I'm on the inside rather than looking in from the outside. I changed my life and the path of my job. The neighbourhood house was the place where I discovered where my career is going and, having established that, my career is guiding my personal life.

Jessy also reflected:

> Every single moment of my life here at Gordon House is a small achievement in a certain way. I try bringing a smile to someone's face at least a

couple of times a day ... I have these small things that I carry on. People say: "Work is to get money." I say: "My work feeds my soul." It really does. I really enjoy the small moments.

According to Maheen:

As my kids were growing up, the neighbourhood house allowed me to figure out what I am capable of. The neighbourhood house was key to finding myself. They allowed me to grow at my own pace ... Ultimately, I learned, and I contributed too. The neighbourhood house allowed me to develop skills that I might not even have had the confidence to try because they let you develop at your own pace, but encourage you to move forward too.

Participants highlight the impact that neighbourhood houses have had on their lives and on whom they have developed into as individuals. Part of the role of NHs in their life journeys is the significant role they have played in participants' personal growth and their own sense of agency. For example, Anna comments:

My first project working with the neighbourhood house, and from that moment, so many things came. I don't know I just opened up a lot and I was proposed to go to this school called community development, this course from Capilano University. And, that place was so the scene for me, that was the place where I just opened so much, everybody around saw what I am able to do when they ask me to do it. I was hired last year to do so many videos for so many places because of the videos I made for the neighbourhood house and for the Inspired project. Oh yeah, I changed a lot. I feel so happy with what I am doing, and I feel it has meaning. I mean, it changed my life, changed the path of my job. I kind of like myself now more than I liked before. I think the neighbourhood house was a place where I kind of discovered where my career is going and having established that, I think your career is guiding a little bit your personal life. I think so. That's what I found about myself.

Part of personal growth through neighbourhood houses is participants' increased empathy due to their experiences of being and working at the houses. Several participants highlight how working in NHs enhanced their empathy and non-judgmental attitude toward others. According to Anna:

It's true because I changed my values. I changed the way how I look at people. I changed the way how I judge people or not judge people, you know. And I needed that, but now I feel so, it's amazing. It's just a big change. And I think part of the change is the fact that I was there, and I was listening to people's stories. And I was empowering myself from the people's stories.

Jessy also comments on this: "I've learnt that I cannot take anyone for ... I've found that I just stopped making ... To not to pass judgment on people. And that is one thing I've stopped judging people. That was a huge thing. I think not judging people is the biggest for me. And that's just my personal."

Participants not only illustrated how they enhanced their empathy and non-judgmental skills, they also voiced how through their work and engagement with those who came to the neighbourhood house, they learned to place more value on such traits as empathy, non-judgment, and understanding of people's differences and circumstances. These constitute core values and skills in enacting inclusive and non-discriminatory attitudes to working and respecting others and providing services. The life stories demonstrate how during their involvement with NHs, participants began to understand how meaningful inclusive community practices can be and increased the value they placed on them. For them, NHs are places that provide a space where people can build significant relationships, and by experiencing this, place greater value on having and belonging to a community. Participants discussed how meaningful they believed this to be for service users and for themselves, and how being service users and service providers/community workers at NHs brought meaning to their lives. According to Agata:

And I would say the best part of my job is seeing first-hand the difference we can make in people's lives. There's been numerous examples over the years where there was a single mom or a family that just moved, like newly immigrated to Canada that came here for help. And we were able to support them and connect them to other services. So that is I would say the most satisfying part of my job is to be able to make a difference. Sometimes you can't, sometimes you try and there's only so much, so far you can go. But when you can make a difference then it's my favourite part of the job.

Participants shared how they could not imagine what their lives would look like without neighbourhood houses and the richness that being involved with the houses brought to their lives. Seeing the difference they can make in service users' lives brings joy to their work. Multiple participants commented that as service users, they had experienced the same kind of support, which added to the meaningfulness of their current work as service providers. Through their experiences of growth, self-discovery, learning work/life balance, improving self-confidence and social skills, enhancing empathy and non-judgment, and experiencing the value of community, participants spoke about how their involvement with NHs changed their lives and shaped who they had become so far in their lives. As Cassandra shares:

> And then I eventually developed a really strong passion for food security and food-related social justice work and I really enjoyed that. It's given me a lot. I've learned to become more patient, understanding, supportive, working with community members and really learning from them, a lot of the learning experiences that I've had with neighbourhood houses is learning directly from them, community members ... Being involved in neighbourhood houses has given, has taught me a lot because I want to give back and support the community members that had taught me, and so I find the beauty of neighbourhood houses is that reciprocating knowledge and experiences and sharing of skills and just everything together is what makes me continue to love neighbourhood houses and spend so much time there. I am grateful for being able to learn from them all of that.

Neighbourhood houses are part of participants' pathways and life journeys, both personally and professionally, and, as Cassandra explains, continue to provide opportunities to engage in social justice–relevant work in a variety of areas. They share how crucial the role of a safe community network is for themselves and for everyone, especially during a time and place where racism and classism continue to impact the everyday life of residents of larger cities and are embedded in the materiality of places (e.g., in the upsurge of walls, borders, surveillance, and gentrification [Razack 2018]).

Conclusion

These life stories provide a picture of what neighbourhood houses are, what their role is, what they provide, what they represent, and how individuals and communities experience their presence in NHs. Participants' narratives demonstrate how vital it is for communities to have holistic place-based services, how NHs evolve alongside changing populations and changing needs, and how they have sustained community relationships throughout their history. It is evident from these stories that NHs are not only sites that provide supports and services but also the glue that holds together communities by fostering collective capacity and social inclusion.

In this chapter, this positive outlook on the significance that staff encounter in their engagement with work and community in neighbourhood houses was situated in a broader context under which the transformative potential of community work and movements toward job equity and stability continue to be under threat. The life stories demonstrate how in the context of a settler colonial country such as Canada, immigrants have played a central role in the envisioning and maintenance of NHs as places of social and racial inclusion, place-based learning, and leadership. Our analysis indicated some of the structural threats in which these place-based practices of engagement and inclusion operate under a neoliberal regime. Amid these structural constraints and risks, NHs continue to function as places for meaningful personal, family, and civic engagement, and as hubs for exchange, career path, and self-development. Those engaged in building and sustaining NHs narrate inclusion and community engagement as a place-based task that nurtures collective aspirations.

References

Alba, Richard, and Nancy Foner. 2015. "Mixed Unions and Immigrant-Group Integration in North America and Western Europe." *Annals of the American Academy of Political and Social Science* 662 (1): 38–56.

Altman, Irwin, and Setha M. Low. 1992. "Human Behavior and Environments: Advances in Theory and Research." In *Place Attachment,* edited by Irwin Altman and Setha M. Low, 1–12. Boston: Springer.

Appadurai, Arjun. 2004. "The Capacity to Aspire: Culture and the Terms of Recognition." In *Culture and Public Action,* edited by Vijayendra Rao and Michael Walton, 59–84. Palo Alto, CA: Stanford University Press.

Berger Gluck, Sherna, and Daphne Patai. 1991. *Women's Words: The Feminist Practice of Oral History.* New York: Routledge.

Bok, Derek. 2010. *The Politics of Happiness: What Government Can Learn from the New Research on Well-Being.* Princeton, NJ: Princeton University Press.

Brown, Barbara, Douglas D. Perkins, and Graham Brown. 2003. "Place Attachment in a Revitalizing Neighborhood: Individual and Block Levels of Analysis." *Journal of Environmental Psychology* 23 (3): 259–71. https://doi.org/10.1016/S0272-4944(02)00117-2.

Carter, Jennifer, Pam Dyer, and Bishnu Sharma. 2007. "Dis-placed Voices: Sense of Place and Place-Identity on the Sunshine Coast." *Social and Cultural Geography* 8 (5): 755–73. https://doi.org/10.1080/14649360701633345.

Cobb, John B. 1996. "Defining Normative Community." In *Rooted in the Land: Essays on Community and Place,* edited by William Vitek and Wes Jackson, 185–94. New Haven, CT: Yale University Press.

El-Lahib, Yahya. 2016. "Troubling Constructions of Canada as a 'Land of Opportunity' for Immigrants: A Critical Disability Lens." *Disability and Society* 31 (6): 758–76. https://doi.org/10.1080/09687599.2016.1200460.

Grele, Ronald. 1996. "Oral History: Method and Theory." *Radical History Review* 1996 (65): 131–35. https://doi.org/10.1215/01636545-1996-65-131.

Hester, Randolph. 1993. "Sacred Spaces and Everyday Life: A Return to Manteo, North Carolina." In *Dwelling, Seeing and Designing: Toward a Phenomenological Ecology,* edited by David Seamon, 271–97. New York: State University of New York Press.

Hummon, David M. 1992. "Community Attachment: Local Sentiment and Sense of Place." In *Place Attachment,* edited by Irwin Altman and Setha M. Low, 253–78. Boston: Springer.

Kalich, Angela, Lyn Heinemann, and Setareh Ghahari. 2016. "A Scoping Review of Immigrant Experience of Health Care Access Barriers in Canada." *Journal of Immigrant and Minority Health* 18 (3): 697–709. https://doi.org/10.1007/s10903-015-0237-6.

Kenny, Sue. 2002. "Tensions and Dilemmas in Community Development: New Discourses, New Trojans?" *Community Development Journal* 37 (4): 284–99. https://doi.org/10.1093/cdj/37.4.284.

Korpela, Kalevi. 1989. "Place Identity as a Product of Environmental Self-Regulation." *Journal of Environmental Psychology* 9 (3): 241–56. https://doi.org/10.1016S0272-4944(89)80038-6.

Lyon, Katherine. 2017. "'There's No Excuse for Slowing Down': Doing Gender, Race, and Class in the Third Age." PhD diss., University of British Columbia.

Manzo, Lynne C., and Douglas D. Perkins. 2006. "Finding Common Ground: The Importance of Place Attachment to Community Participation and Planning." *Journal of Planning Literature* 20 (4): 335–50. https://doi.org/10.1177/0885412205286160.

Metro Vancouver. 2019. "First Nations in and outside the Region." http://www.metrovancouver.org/services/first-nation-relations/first-nations/Pages/default.aspx.

Monroe, Kristen R. 2012. *Ethics in an Age of Terror and Genocide: Identity and Moral Choice.* Princeton, NJ: Princeton University Press.

Phan, Mai B., Rupa Banerjee, Lisa Deacon, and Hila Taraky. 2015. "Family Dynamics and the Integration of Professional Immigrants in Canada." *Journal of Ethnic and Migration Studies* 41 (13): 2061–80. https://doi.org/10.1080/1369183X.2015.1045461.

Portelli, Alessandro. 1991. *The Death of Luigi Trastulli and Other Stories: Form and Meaning in Oral History.* Albany: State University of New York Press.

Pretty, Grace H., Heather M. Chipuer, and Paul Bramston. 2003. "Sense of Place amongst Adolescents and Adults in Two Rural Australian Towns: The Discriminating Features of Place Attachment, Sense of Community and Place Dependence in Relation to Place Identity." *Journal of Environmental Psychology* 23 (3): 273–87. https://doi.org/10.1016/S0272-4944(02)00079-8.

Proshansky, Harold M. 1978. "The City and Self-Identity." *Environment and Behavior* 10 (2): 147–69. https://doi.org/10.1177/0013916578102002.

Proshansky, Harold M., Abbe K. Fabian, and Robert Kaminoff. 1983. "Place-Identity: Physical World Socialization of the Self." *Journal of Environmental Psychology* 3 (1): 57–83. https://doi.org/10.1016/S0272-4944(83)80021-8.

Razack, Sherene H. 2018. "When Place Becomes Race." In *Race and Racialization: Essential Readings*, edited by Tania Das Gupta, Carl E. James, Chris Andersen, Grace-Edward Galabuzi, and Roger C.A. Maaka, 113–29. Toronto: Canadian Scholars' Press.

Riaño-Alcalá, Pilar. 2013. *Remembering and Narrating Conflict: Resources for Doing Historical Memory Work.* Bogota/Vancouver: Centro Nacional de Memoria Histórica/University of British Columbia. https://blogs.ubc.ca/reconstructing historicalmemory/.

Riger, Stephanie, and Paul J. Lavrakas. 1981. "Community Ties: Patterns of Attachment and Social Interactions in Urban Neighborhoods." *American Journal of Community Psychology* 9 (1): 55–66. https://doi.org/10.1007/BF00896360.

Ryden, Kent C. 1993. *Mapping the Invisible landscape: Folklore, Writing, and the Sense of Place.* Iowa City: University of Iowa Press.

Shumaker, Sally A., and Ralph B. Taylor. 1983. "Toward a Clarification of People-Place Relationships: A Model of Attachment to Place." In *Environmental Psychology: Directions and Perspectives,* edited by Nickolaus R. Feimer and E. Scott Geller, 219–51. New York: Praeger.

Statistics Canada. 2017. "Census Profile, 2016 Census: Vancouver [Census Metropolitan Area], British Columbia and British Columbia [Province]." Updated June 18, 2019 https://www12.statcan.gc.ca/census-recensement/2016/dp-pd/prof/details/page.cfm?Lang=E&Geo1=CMACA&Code1=933&Geo2=PR&Code2=59&Data=Count&SearchText=vancouver&SearchType=Begins&SearchPR=01&B1=All&TABID=1.

Trujillo, Gloriana, and Kimberly D. Tanner. 2014. "Considering the Role of Affect in Learning: Monitoring Students' Self-Efficacy, Sense of Belonging, and Science Identity." *CBE – Life Sciences Education* 13 (1): 6–15. https://doi.org/10.1187/cbe.13-12-0241.

Tuan, Yi-Fu. 1974. *Topophilia.* Englewood Cliffs, NJ: Prentice Hall.

Tuck, Eve, and Marcia McKenzie. 2015. *Place in Research: Theory, Methodology, and Methods.* New York: Routledge.

Twigger-Ross, Clare L., and David L. Uzzell. 1996. "Place and Identity Processes." *Journal of Environmental Psychology* 16 (3): 205–20. https://doi.org/10.1006/jevp.1996.0017.

Vancouver Foundation. 2012. *Connections and Engagement: A Survey of Metro Vancouver.* Vancouver: Vancouver Foundation. https://www.vancouverfoundation.ca/about-us/publications/connections-and-engagement-reports/connections-engagement-report-2012.

–. 2017. *Connect & Engage: A Survey of Metro Vancouver / 2017.* Vancouver: Vancouver Foundation. https://www.vancouverfoundation.ca/about-us/publications/connections-and-engagement-reports/connect-engage-2017-report.

Vitek, William, and Wes Jackson. 1996. *Rooted in the Land: Essays on Community and Place.* New Haven, CT: Yale University Press.

Yan, Miu Chung, Sean Lauer, and Pilar Riaño-Alcalá. 2017. "Incorporating Individual Community Assets in Neighbourhood Houses: Beyond the Community-Building Tradition of Settlement Houses." *International Social Work* 60 (6): 1591–1605. https://doi.org/10.1177/0020872816633889.

6

From Immigrant to Citizen

Life Stories of Transformation

JENNY FRANCIS

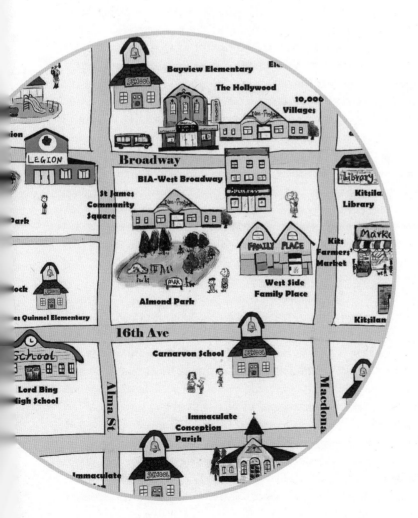

In this chapter, we share, in their own words, the stories of twelve people whose lives have been transformed through their connections with their local neighbourhood house. Some immigrated to Canada as young people or are members of the "1.5 generation" for whom the neighbourhood house provided a foundation enabling their development into active, contributing citizens. As immigrants, the people who shared their stories struggled to find employment, navigate new systems, make friends, and develop a sense of belonging. Social isolation, non-recognition of foreign experience and credentials, and low incomes initially left them feeling out of place, lonely, and "worthless." Immigrants who arrived as children faced the challenges of integrating into a new school system and making friends. The neighbourhood house provided local opportunities for newcomers of all ages to utilize their skills and talents and empowered them to develop social connections by sharing their stories and, in turn, inspiring others. The concept of empowerment provides the unifying theme in the stories that follow. Within that framework, I identify six motifs or steps that characterize the passage from displacement to the formation of a positive sense of place. All six themes may be identified in each of the stories as well as in previous chapters of this book; however, for each theme I provide two narratives that illustrate especially well particular steps along the path from dislocation to belonging.

Overcoming Isolation

The first step involves having one's immediate needs met, which reduces stress and provides space for curiosity to develop so that newcomers can focus beyond the bare necessities. However, a sense of isolation can be profound at this stage, and there is often little trust in others. Many immigrants mentioned *feeling "useless" and dependent* and said that being an immigrant was a burden they had to carry around. Living far from everything they knew, including friends and family, and often struggling to integrate into an unfamiliar labour market that tends not to recognize skills and experience gained elsewhere, can lead to an identity crisis as immigrants lose a sense of who they are and their place in the world. The following narratives elaborate this difficult process and reveal the role that neighbourhood houses can play in reducing isolation (also see Introduction).

Wen Ling: No Longer Alone

Wen Ling Chan is an art therapist who has volunteered in numerous programs at Kitsilano Neighbourhood House (Kits House). She arrived in Vancouver from Taiwan in the summer of 2010. She related:

> At first I was lost, not knowing where to go, what to do. I felt a sense of failure because I had two master's degrees, yet I couldn't secure a job. I didn't know where to turn to because I didn't have any connection at all. A lot of people told me: "Oh, you just need to secure a survival job," but I was hoping for a different kind of future.

Wen Ling heard about a program for immigrant women at Kits House. She recalled:

> I joined the group and from that point on, things started to get better because I felt less alone. At the time, I was a little depressed because if you imagine the only connection you have is going to the library or grocery store, it's very lonely. In that situation your self-identity turns out to be not what you assumed it was, and you need to rebuild from ground zero. When I was in Taiwan, I had everything. Then when I came here, I had totally nothing, so my self-confidence was quite low. Coming to Kits Neighbourhood House – I was really relieved!

Wen Ling elaborated on the impact Kits House has had in her life:

> We shared our experiences and we learned that it's not us; it's the system. So at that moment I thought: "Okay, I am not that bad after all: I still have the potential or ability to do something here in Vancouver." It made a great impact on me; it kept me trying and moving forward.

Illustrating one of the many ways in which neighbourhood houses support the capacity to aspire noted in Chapter 5, she continued: "Kits House is very supportive. For example, because I have a master's degree in art therapy, they suggested, 'Why don't you form an art therapy group?' I started to feel great – just having someone acknowledge your ability is amazing. As a result, I got back my self-confidence." Unfortunately, the women's support group lasted only three months; everyone was left wanting more. Wen Ling found a solution: "After the funding was cut we applied for a Neighbourhood Small Grant and I became the facilitator and ran two groups, each with around fourteen people."

Since then, Wen Ling has volunteered for several other programs, including Mother Goose, a parenting program, seniors' drop-in, and others. She also offers individual art therapy for children and participates in the English Circle. Additionally, she ran a program called Expressive Art for Immigrant Pre-teens, for which she was paid. She related:

> Through this work, I found the strength of volunteering; I need to keep in touch with the community to know what's going on in Vancouver. Whenever they have some kind of program, Kits House always sends an email. Also, based on a suggestion from Kits House, I have done a lot of volunteering at other places as well.

She added:

> However, in the other places, there's no sense of belonging. The attitude at Kits Neighbourhood House really made me feel like: "This is where I want to stay." There's a sense of connection, a sense of community. I know if there's anything going on I can just drop in and say: "Can you help me with this or that?" and they will definitely say yes.

Currently, Wen Ling is pursuing a third master's degree, this time in clinical counselling. She reflected: "I'm not sure what the future holds so I just keep challenging myself. I find that everything that I'm doing is connected. For example, women experiencing domestic violence are very isolated and don't know where to turn. Now I am trying to find resources for such women. I am doing what I love!"

As noted in Chapter 4, capacity-building at different scales is a key function of neighbourhood houses. Kits House sponsored Wen Ling's attendance at the Community Capacity Building program at Capilano University. She recollected:

> It was like a big family – it was great! The reality here in Vancouver is that it is very hard to make friends. The neighbourhood house provides a moment of safety; you just need to share your story with someone else who understands, and then the next step will be to get more involved with

locals. I learned new vocabulary too. Now I know what "bottom-up" means and I like that idea. Anyone can approach the staff and say: "You know, we could do this and I'm willing to do it." And the staff always say: "Okay, let's try it out." It's a collaborative relationship. One time Sandra invited a lot of people, especially newcomers or immigrant women who have a family here, to ask them: "What do you need?" That was so unique. It's not just saying: "You need to do this or that." Here, it's more equal.

She continued: "If I hadn't found Kits Neighbourhood House, I wouldn't understand how important community-building is for my future. I now see my future in non-profit because it is where people need services the most." Wen Ling gratefully acknowledged some of the staff at Kits House:

Patricia is my mentor; as an immigrant woman, when I look at her I think: "This is what I want to become." She's very successful, not in the sense of getting rich, but in terms of building strong connections among women and providing services and connection for all the people around her. That is what I want to do in the future. I feel like she's changing my life.

She continued:

Sandra also gives me a lot of opportunities, always saying: "Do you want to try that? What do you think about this?" She just keeps giving you opportunities to prove to yourself that you are worth it. Because people at the neighbourhood house believed in me, I began to think: "Maybe I am good at something." Their trust in me gives me the confidence to do so many things.

Finally, Wen Ling reflected on the importance of Kits House in the community: "Kits Neighbourhood House offers an opportunity for people to come out – this is so important! Having someone to talk to, someone to hear your story, can validate people's experiences and their feelings. It's more important than anything else. Neighbourhood houses offer a space for people to share their stories."

Theresa: Frog Hollow Is My Gas Station
Originally from Taiwan, Theresa Lin Zhao has volunteered for a number of programs at Frog Hollow Neighbourhood House (FHNH) and also leads a drop-in program for parents of young children. Theresa came to Canada in

2005 but it was only after her son was born in 2007 that she learned about Frog Hollow. She recalled:

> I went to FHNH for the first time when my son was three months old. I decided to bring him to FHNH because I felt isolated at home; I was very lonely because my husband had to go to work every day. I lived with my in-laws, who were very helpful, but sometimes gave me suggestions that I didn't really appreciate, so I felt very stressed. And with a little baby, that's not healthy, so I knew that I needed to go out. So I came to Frog Hollow.

Theresa continued:

> We started coming to the drop-in. I met other parents and my son found friends to play with and he was very happy here. At that time my son had a serious asthma problem and I needed information, but everybody I asked only suggested going to the family doctor, who doesn't help a lot. At FHNH I found out that the community nurse really helps a lot. They gave me lots of information and also told me that I have to care for myself, too. They told me how to give myself proper nutrition. And then they also taught me a lot about emotional well-being and about some programs for parents. That helped a lot because after I had a baby, I was not the person that I used to be. I changed a lot and it was very, very stressful. If there was no Frog Hollow here to help me, I don't know what I would have done.

Theresa described how her relationship with Frog Hollow developed through intergenerational endeavours (see Chapter 5):

> We came three days a week for drop-in and then a parenting program every Friday. So almost every day I was here at Frog Hollow. When my son was eight or nine months old, the staff asked me if I was interested in doing some volunteer work. I used to teach preschool in Taiwan, so they asked if I could do something similar to Mother Goose, but in Mandarin – and that's what I did. The other mothers had their babies with them, and my son was there beside me. When he went to preschool I started to do more vol-unteering. I came to FHNH because I needed help with parenting and then I began helping other parents. Most of the people who live in this neigh-bourhood speak Chinese. Some women just come here, get married, and have a baby right away and they don't speak English at all, or know about

the resources that are available to them. I shared my experience and I told new people what kind of programs we have at FHNH. I did that program for seven years. I had a very good time with the parents in that program. They also helped me a lot. For example, they helped me with the relationship between me and my in-laws because you realize that you are not alone facing this; many of them were experiencing the same thing. And then most of the parents don't speak or read English well so I help them to find resources. In fact, that also helped me a lot because now I know about so many things.

Theresa recalled some of the most significant events that have occurred during her seven years at Frog Hollow, beginning with the Compassion Project. She explained:

We do a lot of work bringing compassion to children and families. Through sharing those stories, I learned about responsibility and I discovered that there was something important that I had forgotten. As children we used to care about things; we used to have compassion for others, but when we grow up we often forget. The Compassion Project reminds you and brings out the compassionate feeling that you have for the community. Not only for your family but also for friends, animals, and the environment. I really appreciate that Frog Hollow did that – if there was no Compassion Project, then maybe I would just sit at home and read my Bible and think about compassion, without practising it. FHNH and the Compassion Project really give you an opportunity to practise and become a better person.

In another project, Theresa applied for a grant to create a program to bring teenagers to the Frog Hollow seniors' groups to sing and, at the same time, create connections among different generations. Theresa recalled: "Everybody loved it, especially the seniors. I also gained a lot from that experience because before I did this program, I'd had a problem talking to teenagers. I was afraid that they would say to me: 'Oh, I don't want to do that,' but they came regularly and really enjoyed it."

The accomplishment that Theresa is perhaps most proud of involves her successful organization of a mock election at Frog Hollow before the provincial election. Underlining the vital role neighbourhood houses play in promoting civic participation and institutional visibility (see Chapter 2), she described the experience:

I knew that many people didn't have information about voting, especially high school students. I also wanted to do it for the seniors. My mother and father-in-law from China had lived here more than ten years and were citizens, so they voted here. During one election period, I told my mother-in-law: "You should vote for someone who you feel can represent you in the Parliament." And she said: "Yes, there's one person like that." But when we went home, she told me: "I didn't vote for that person because she's not in the party that's in power." My mother-in-law had lived in a communist country for seventy years, so she felt like if the party loses, the country will lose. I told myself: "I have to do something about this."

She continued:

On that day, I invited some candidates. I had many immigrants come to practise voting. The seniors were very excited and happy. They had lots of discussion about who to vote for. We also registered them, because some of them didn't know that before you vote, you have to be registered. Fifty-eight new people registered – mostly seniors and high school students. It was a lot of work.

Theresa also attended programs and training opportunities. She elaborated:

I attended a very helpful program here at FHNH for immigrant women called Pathway to Leadership. I met so many different people and we learned about how to search for a job and attend an interview, how to start a small business. There are so many resources available for us to use. They teach a lot in the program and they also give you "Canadian experience." I went to so many programs and training sessions at Frog Hollow and learned a lot about health, emotional well-being, and about lots of different resources. Frog Hollow gives me a chance to learn. And FHNH gives you confidence.

Theresa explained that Frog Hollow also influenced her personal development:

Frog Hollow makes me a better person: to be more responsible, to have better time management, and to have more compassion. I have to come here because I need a break from home. I feel that Frog Hollow is like a gas station for me because when I come here, I have energy again to go out and face the world ... I made friends here too. I am so happy. Frog Hollow is like my kitchen – I mean I feel that comfortable here. Also, when they need me, they call me and I come down. I always want to do more for Frog Hollow.

Building Relationships and Friendships

As the stories of Wen Ling and Theresa show, once initial needs are met and new relationships have begun to flower, immigrants start to feel connected to the neighbourhood and to the community. Forming social connections and learning how to navigate unfamiliar social, political, and economic systems open up the space newcomers need to gain the confidence to follow their dreams, allowing them to develop their passion in a supported environment that builds on their existing strengths, skills, and knowledge. *Building relationships and friendships* that are reaffirmed everywhere in place – at grocery stores, in cafés, on the street, at school, and at the neighbourhood house – enables immigrants to feel they are part of something; they start to feel more at home because people they know greet them on the street. As the following stories shared by Najia and Ana demonstrate, it is during this second step that a nascent sense of place begins to emerge (see also Chapter 5).

Najia: This Is What Family Means

Najia Elacel is the community kitchen leader and liaison cultural outreach presenter at Collingwood Neighbourhood House. Eight years ago, she moved into a co-op near Collingwood. Her reflections emphasize the ways in which the neighbourhood house creates an inclusive homey environment that grounds participants in an understanding of the value of community (see Chapter 5): "Right away I got involved in many things. I don't have my family here, so my friends and the people that I am close to become family. For me, 'family' is when everybody gets together, enjoys the moment, and laughs. When I see that, it gives me warmth, and I think: 'This is what family means.'"

Najia described how she became connected with Collingwood:

When I moved into the co-op, I didn't have money and I didn't have a job, so it was a difficult time. One day a lady at the co-op brought me to Collingwood to a program for single mothers and low-income people with their children. I started coming every week, but I'm not the kind of person that eats and runs; I need to do something, so I began helping by washing dishes and cleaning the kitchen after the meal.

For the next three months, Najia attended the program with her kids. She was still looking for work, sending out resumés without success. One day, she decided to go to the neighbourhood house to see if there was anything she could help with. Her experiences perfectly illustrate the importance of non-purposive relationship formation and mutual learning (see Chapter 4). She walked into the kitchen at one o'clock and found a disaster. She related:

> The lady who was in charge of the program that day was yelling: "Oh my god! The lady who was supposed to cook the Christmas dinner called in sick and there's eighty people coming at six o'clock! What are we going to do?" I looked at her and said: "I can cook the dinner." I started opening the cupboards and drawers to see what I could use.

Najia continued:

> Somehow, by five o'clock when the woman came back, I was able to tell her: "The stuff is in the oven. This is here. This is what you need to do." I went to pick up my kids and by the time we returned, they had already served dinner. When I walked in the door with my twin boys, something amazing happened. The lady in charge of the program said: "Hey everyone, this is the lady who saved Christmas! This is the lady who cooked the dinner for you guys." Around eighty people with their kids stood up and clapped and said: "This is the most amazing food we have ever had." I was like: "Oh my god! Seriously?"

She added:

> When I came to Canada, I had problems from the first day I came. I went through abuse: physical abuse, mental abuse, everything. I had been told so many times that I was nothing, that I was worthless. At that moment those people [at the neighbourhood house] changed my life. Everybody stood up for me. I realized: "Oh my gosh, I'm not what that person told me I was. Now I'm back to me!" It took just that moment to give me "me" back. They gave me the courage to believe in myself. I was myself from that time, and I've never left that program.

For the next year, Najia volunteered whenever she could and eventually got a job elsewhere, but what she really wanted was to work at the neighbourhood house. She applied for a couple of positions but wasn't hired.

When Collingwood again needed to hire someone, the kitchen program co-ordinator discussed Najia's resumé with another coordinator. Najia related their conversation: "'I have a resumé from a lady who says she's volunteered here, but I'm not sure about her.' 'Is it the lady with twins? Hire her! She saved Christmas! She saved me!'" Najia concluded: "So, finally I got a job at the neighbourhood house! I was happy that they saw me as an asset instead of focusing on my resumé, which does not tell the whole story about a person. That was five years ago."

Reflecting the findings outlined in Chapter 4 that many neighbourhood house participants take part in more than one activity, Najia explained that she had worked with several different programs, including seniors and family programs. She related:

> When I started my program with the seniors, we had around twenty people; now I get about sixty people for lunch twice a week. They bring joy to my life because they help me see life from a different perspective; our seniors carry valuable wisdom within them. I always encourage my kids – they're twelve years old now – to come and help the seniors and talk, so they also feel that they are part of something and can contribute. The neighbourhood house Christmas party is also amazing – this year we had 176 people, including 120 seniors. It was the best!

Najia also described one of the changes she initiated at Collingwood:

> I took the seniors' program to the community. I had an idea: "Why don't we call it 'community lunch' instead of 'seniors' lunch'?" And we did it! We opened it up so that now children and other people are welcome to walk in. I don't really like separate groups – like seniors, children, moms – because they're all connected. If you look at a family, you see a grandmother and then you see a mother and then you see a child ... Through these changes, the kitchen became the place where everybody meets.

Najia recalled a proud moment that occurred with one volunteer:

> When he started with Collingwood at age sixteen, he wouldn't speak, but slowly we got to him. I try to connect with people by saying: "You need to connect with yourself." At the neighbourhood house, we connect and create possibilities for that to happen. One Christmas, he brought me a flower and a card, and I will never forget what he said: "Thank you so much for all

you've done for me. The things you do for people have opened my eyes to the things I would never have learnt anywhere else. I appreciate you so much, and I look up to you. You are my hero!" Oh my god, I was like: "Really? You look up to me?"

Reflecting on the value of neighbourhood houses, Najia related:

When I put my foot in here, I was welcomed and I was treated with respect. When you love what you do, it shows. When you see people working because they care, you will see it. All the directors are easygoing people who always encourage new ideas. A lot of people here put in a lot of time that they don't get paid for, but they never say anything. I'm one of them. You can't just say: "Sorry my time is up, I need to go home." That creates a barrier and prevents trust from developing. It's those relationships that keep people coming back to the neighbourhood house: they know that somebody here cares ... It's amazing when you make a difference in someone's life. That makes up for all the money in the world. It gives you power. When you put love first, the things you get back are priceless. When I go home, and I put my head on the pillow, I'm the happiest person on the planet.

Ana: This Is the Place Where I First Opened My Eyes

An internationally renowned journalist and filmmaker from Romania, Ana Mateescu runs the Aboriginal Family program at Collingwood Neighbourhood House. She has also worked at Little Mountain Neighbourhood House (LMNH), where she led an Expressive Art and Dialogue Circle and coordinated a number of other projects. Ana explained how she got her start at Little Mountain in 2012:

My first time at the neighbourhood house I observed a social enterprise project where people were sharing stories and creating small bird nests from beads and other art materials to sell to support their program. I was thrilled by the people's stories. I didn't want to go home. I wanted to listen more because I love stories and that place was so powerful – the stories the participants were telling, the things they were making, and the fact that they were from I think twenty countries. I'd brought my child and as we were leaving, she said: "Mommy, I want to come back here" ... The next time I went to the neighbourhood house I brought my camera and started recording people's stories. It's hard to express how "at home" I felt – I felt like

I could sleep at the neighbourhood house, it was just so comfortable there – even though it's small and crowded.

Ana had come to Canada three years earlier with her partner and five-year-old daughter. A new immigrant who didn't speak English, she worked at different jobs but also took time to explore Vancouver. She elaborated on the importance of stories:

People can be empowered by sharing their stories and listening to other people's stories. Through stories we come together because everybody's story overlaps and creates the connection between people; we all have the same stories. At LMNH I made three life-changing videos. In one session, a Mexican woman who owns a café said: "I hate Canada. I hate the fact that I lost everything. I don't know anybody, and everything is just going down, down, down." After hearing her story, I contacted another journalist and asked him to share this typical immigrant story. As a result, many people came to that coffee shop and their business is successful now. It's amazing how someone hearing your story can change your life.

She continued:

In another session, people took pictures in the neighbourhood of the things they love, hate, are scared of, feel comfortable with, or that call up strong memories or emotions, and so on. We put those stories and pictures up in the neighbourhood house. After that, so many opportunities opened up for me. For example, LMNH invited me to attend the community development course at Capilano University. I learned about the "asset-based model," which became my life model. I realized deeply that everybody has a gift, and that every contribution matters.

She concluded: "My story is part of the neighbourhood story because they all overlap to create the neighbourhood. I want to learn more about community development and ways to create more resources for people, especially for immigrants, and how I can better apply the tools I've learned." Her reflections point to the ways in which neighbourhood houses serve a critical brokerage function that not only creates a kind of neighbourhood commons (Chapter 5) but also leads to increased social capital through the utilization of social infrastructure (Chapter 4).

Ana shared how her connection with the neighbourhood house led her to a new career path. She stated:

My career here basically opened up as a result of my involvement with the neighbourhood house. I was hired last year to do videos for so many places because of the videos I made for the neighbourhood house ... I changed a lot because of my work with the neighbourhood house. Back home I was very career-driven. I had everything but I didn't feel complete; here, it's totally different. I feel so happy with what I am doing and I feel it has meaning. I feel in touch with people in a way that I couldn't be as a journalist; now I am part of the people, part of the life that I am looking at; I'm on the inside rather than looking in from the outside. I changed my life and the path of my job. The neighbourhood house was the place where I discovered where my career is going and, having established that, my career is guiding my personal life. At Little Mountain Neighbourhood House, just as when you are born, this was the first place where I opened my eyes.

Ana elaborated on the changes that have occurred in her personal life:

I discovered myself here. I had a hard time because of immigration and then my relationship ended so I am now raising a child by myself. But I don't feel overwhelmed by these things. I have people around me and I love them. I was also able to leave an unhealthy relationship as a result of the support I found at the neighbourhood house ... The neighbourhood house changed my life. I changed my values as a result of being part of the neighbourhood house. I don't judge people anymore. As a result, I like myself now more than before. Because of the neighbourhood house, I am totally different from how I was before. Now I feel very good when I wake up in the morning because I feel I have meaning.

New Ways to Contribute: Volunteering and Working Part-Time
As they began to feel accepted for who they are, Najia and Ana embraced the knowledge and relationships they were developing as a result of their connection with their local neighbourhood houses. The next step, which often develops alongside *volunteer work* or perhaps *part-time paid employment* undertaken at the neighbourhood house, is characterized by an emerging realization that one is able to contribute to the community and to the neighbourhood (see Chapter 2). This occurs precisely because of the mentorship, training, and volunteer and employment opportunities provided by

the neighbourhood house. Such experiential learning opportunities allow newcomers to became informed about Canadian culture and systems organically. They often involve outings around Vancouver, during which relationships deepen, and individuals also learn about local transportation networks and other services (see Chapter 4). As a result of these processes, earlier feelings of fear and suspicion are replaced by a growing sense of trust in Canadian institutions. The stories of Marcela and Tommy illustrate this next step in the journey.

Marcela: I Discovered Myself Here

Marcela Mancilla-Fuller has been the settlement services coordinator at Collingwood Neighbourhood House for eight years. She described her early interactions with the neighbourhood house:

> I really didn't know what a neighbourhood house was. I come from Mexico where we don't have this type of community organization. My first perception was that it was a daycare or preschool. Then, when I was on my mat leave, I opened a second-hand toy store nearby. At lunch time I'd come to one of the programs for moms and toddlers. I started to connect with people and understand a little bit about what the neighbourhood house did. However, I felt like the services were not for me. Nobody told me that – it's just what I thought for myself. I was afraid of accessing something that was for people who "really" needed it. I was afraid of saying who I was: I started to develop relationships with the other moms but I never shared my personal life.

She continued:

> After a year I closed my business and decided to stay home with my child. The reason I wasn't more involved with the neighbourhood house at that time was that I didn't want to take the place of anybody accessing services – until one day I realized some white women were here and I thought: "Wait a minute, if they are accessing these services, I don't have to feel guilty about it." So that was when I got more connected with the organization. When a job posting came out for settlement coordinator, I applied and was offered the job. Before I signed the contract, I told my boss that I was pregnant. She said: "I don't think there's any problem: we nurture families and we want our staff to represent what the community is about." I cried when she said that. In Mexico, if you're pregnant you'll never be hired. In fact, sometimes when women become pregnant, they are fired.

Marcela explained how she grew into the position, stressing the importance of place-based belonging and interdependence (see the Introduction):

> My baby was born six months after I started, and the neighbourhood house
> supported me so much through that process. My husband took parental
> leave. He looked after the two kids and he used to bring the baby here for
> me to nurse. I felt really stressed at that time because I felt like I was like not
> being serious about my job. Which place in the world allows you to have
> your baby with you twice a day and even provides a room for you to nurse?
> I could not understand why this place was allowing me to do that, but now
> I understand. It's because it is a house, and because you have to provide a
> space where people feel safe, whether you are an employee, a community
> member, a volunteer, or whoever. It was amazing! The beauty of the neigh-
> bourhood house is that it's for everyone to feel connected and included,
> and to develop a sense of belonging; it's not only for one community or
> group of people.

Despite the warm welcome she and her baby received, Marcela sought to
maintain a separation between her family and the neighbourhood house.
She explained: "In the beginning I was very clear with my husband: 'You
don't access any services here. No. That makes me feel uncomfortable. I
don't want you here. This is my job.' I told myself, 'I might be seen as un-
professional if I bring my family here.' That was a huge misconception!"
    Marcela described how her perception began to change when her daugh-
ter started school:

> My kids were born here but we spoke only Spanish at home. When my
> daughter started school, she was really afraid. Working here, I was able to
> connect with my daughter, which made her feel safe. At the same time, it
> was very hard for me in terms of feeling: "Oh my god, I'm not doing my
> job." In fact, it was helping me do my job better because I work with fam-
> ilies, including immigrant families, and people who are not able to express
> themselves in English.

Marcela explained how the relationships she developed at work also helped
her deal with challenges outside of work:

> My daughter was bullied in kindergarten. Fortunately, I was able to work
> with her to overcome that, rather than fighting with the community. That

was possible because I had those relationships where I work. I was able to talk to moms and teachers. I felt like I made a great impact with the school and that my daughter was part of that. Creating those connections was my way of growing, not only as a worker but also as a mom, and a way of giving my kids the opportunity to understand that living in a community is very important. Doing these things empowered me so much.

Underscoring the idea explored in Chapter 5 that neighbourhood houses provide much more than services, she added:

By providing employment opportunities to new immigrants, we are living our values in a very practical sense. When I came to Canada, I never thought I could have a job like this, but the leadership was very encouraging: "Believe in what you know already and build on it." It didn't matter whether you spoke or wrote the language perfectly. Welcoming that richness and diversity of being gives people the opportunity to discover themselves and the richness they have within. I discovered myself here ... It's about recognizing the contributions of the people that we serve and feeling the connection between us rather than seeing it as "We're helping you with a service." I feel really great when people feel like they have grown and can move on. I guess that's what I learnt from my mother. When my mother died, she told me: "I can go because you are grown."

As Marcela has grown, so has her department. She explained:

When I started here, I had four staff under my supervision; now I have fourteen. My relationship with them is very strong and I feel richly rewarded. I love my job – it motivates me. People care about me here. As soon as I arrive: "How are you?" If I don't come, I know that my team is going to call me to make sure that I'm fine.

Collingwood Neighbourhood House has also had a significant impact on Marcela's family (see the discussion of "chain effect" in Chapter 3). She elaborated:

The impact this place has had on my children is huge. For example, my daughter is ten years old and she comes here to volunteer. She has developed a high level of compassion. Volunteering gives her a sense of "I can do things and I can help." My son has also been affected. He said to me of the youth worker who taught him how to play basketball: "I want him to be my big brother." When I asked him why, he told me: "He makes me feel like I can do it, Mom." For my son, it was a moment of complete connection. My husband is volunteering in our ESL class. My nieces came to Canada out of abusive relationships. They also volunteer here. My sister now comes for the ESL classes and she volunteers in the kitchen.

Marcela spoke warmly of Collingwood's special nature, which creates a kind of neighbourhood commons (see Chapter 5):

It's like a house – everybody's welcome. Whatever you have, just bring it and share it! And the best conversations happen here in the kitchen just like they do at home. Home is where the heart is. It's a real home in the sense of sharing an atmosphere where you bring yourself ... [pause] As I was telling this story, I realized very deeply that my body is connected to this place. That's what happens and that's exactly what this house means – not only for participants, but also for those that work here.

She concluded: "That's my story. I never realized that my story had any kind of meaning. Now I feel like I have a story! And my story can create connections between people: my story, my staff's stories, my children's stories – they're all connected. We are all connected."

Tommy: A Toolbox for Life

Tommy Yip lives in Toronto, where he is studying to be an actuary. Until he moved to Toronto three years ago, Tommy had lived in the Cedar Cottage neighbourhood since his family immigrated to Canada from Hong Kong when he was six. Tommy shared how he first heard about Cedar Cottage Neighbourhood House (CCNH) at age fifteen, when a youth worker from CCNH went to Gladstone Secondary School to inform students about the Youth Leadership program, which provided a $100 honorarium. Tommy recalled: "Honestly, I was attracted by the cash rather than a deeper humanitarian motivation. At that time I wasn't involved in the community at all; I was really just getting along in high school. What was valuable to me was getting good grades and hanging out with friends." Tommy wryly summarized his initial experience: "I was this guy who didn't know anything, who only wanted a hundred bucks. He knew nothing about neighbourhood houses and didn't really care about community, but ended up getting involved in a community. He learned new terminology, such as 'social boundaries,' and different types of leadership styles. And he somehow got really interested."

Tommy described the first session of the Youth Leadership program and what happened afterward:

I walked into this big room and there were around twelve other people from my high school. I didn't know them because I wasn't really connected in my high school either. In that first session, I did not have the experience or confidence to speak up ... That's one example of how the neighbourhood house helped me grow up and learn to speak and socialize in various social settings ... I completed the program and at the end of it there was an opportunity to work in the Summer Fun program with kids. After a while I was moved into a family program with much younger kids. That program taught me to speak with people outside of my social circle. I was starting to extend my comfort zone.

Describing some of the things he learned, Tommy summarized:

I learned leadership skills. It was much more fun than I had expected. I learned a lot of skills to deal with different people and the importance of attitude and how you respond as a leader. That experience helped me learn to manage different audiences. I also learned how to work in a team and how I fit into a team. I was really learning about myself. My mentor from Summer Fun taught me how to resolve conflicts. The accumulation of skills like this made me grow up.

Tommy explained how his relationship with Cedar Cottage developed over time:

Shortly after the Youth Leadership training I was involved in a program called Get Out, which grants money to youth-initiated programs. I wanted to make a program for youth with disabilities: I would hire a guitar teacher and the youth would learn how to play guitar. I think I was attracted to the topic because I have to wear hearing aids to participate in everyday life. With the help of people from Cedar Cottage, I got the grant; the facilitator who ran the Youth Leadership program helped me put the application together ... It turned out there weren't many youth with disabilities who wanted to learn guitar, so I decided instead to create a program where youth with disabilities could interact with youth who did not have disabilities. In school, the two cohorts would not normally hang out together, so my program would be a site for them to get to know each other and break down social boundaries. For most of my school years I had seen that segregation, but as a kid you often don't realize that you can say you disagree with something. But through the Leadership program, I learned about the idea of being inclusive. Neighbourhood houses love diversity and that idea got into me. It got embedded into me to value diversity and inclusiveness.

Tommy described how his life began to change as a result of what he was learning at the neighbourhood house:

I started to participate and volunteer more in the community. I started to develop a wider social network because I hung out with people who were in the Youth Leadership program. I started to talk to them in school as well, rather than just outside of school. I started to have a life outside of caring about grades and I become less of a perfectionist. Also, in grade twelve I took the special ed class because I wanted to help other students with their homework. The neighbourhood house experience influenced that decision and helped me get to the point where I could talk freely enough to offer my skills to somebody else.

Meanwhile, Tommy continued to deepen his involvement with CCNH. He related how his experiences helped him move from a sense of individual agency to a strong belief in community and mutual learning (see Chapter 2):

In grade eleven they invited me to the Small Grants Committee to review grant applications. That was my first experience of a committee-based meeting environment. Through that process, I began to understand what I needed to improve on in order to take part in these committees. I wanted to learn how to create value in such a setting by understanding the different perspectives from which I could look at a problem, so I carefully took in what people said. I needed to build up a toolbox in order for me to speak up on different aspects of problems.

His experiences show how even as a young person he was able to understand, through his work at the neighbourhood house, the value of organizing multiple stakeholders at the local level, a key function of neighbourhood houses (Chapter 3):

After that, I did the Summer Fun program again. This time I was in charge of ten kids. I took them around the city with other youth leaders. It was a very good learning experience. Then in grade twelve I did a second version of the guitar program, again involving youth with and without disabilities, using drumming. I wanted to involve three associations: CCNH, [the Canadian Hard of Hearing Association], and the local community centre. It was really difficult because it was my first time doing something like that. Again, the main purpose of the program was to get youth to interact with each other and dissolve social boundaries. It was a huge lesson for me in terms of the various aspects of putting a program together and running it. I learned some very tangible skills.

While attending university, Tommy continued volunteering at CCNH. Two years after the drumming program, he decided to organize another youth program:

Citizens of Change targeted marginalized youth. I wanted to generalize the idea of diversity from disability/ability to larger categories of minority/majority. I also wanted to give youth something of substance where they could learn different things, discover their passion, and also acquire tangible skills. I wanted to do it because of the journey I, myself, had taken. During my journey with the neighbourhood house I acquired different skill sets that really empowered me to make a difference in my community. I wanted to help youth younger than me to have this experience as well.

Tommy recalled:

The youth who took part wanted to tackle the issue of homelessness, so we brought in people who worked in homeless shelters and they educated us. We wanted to take action, and the youth decided to fundraise for this cause, so we held a bottle drive. This was significant for me because it signifies my move from being a service user of the neighbourhood house to a service provider and mentor ... After the Citizens of Change program, the executive director invited me to the CCNH board. I was the youth voice on the communications committee. I felt very honoured. That committee really helped me learn about what a board does and what it looks like. Now I realize that all these things I did really helped me prepare for working in the professional world. I don't think I would be where I am now, without the neighbourhood house. The neighbourhood house developed my character.

Tommy's story shows clearly how experiential learning undertaken in a social infrastructure framework builds social capacity in neighbourhood house users (see Chapter 4). He concluded: "It was a very good investment in myself! It was also a really enjoyable journey. Without those experiences I wouldn't be able to do a lot of the things I am able to do today. In so many ways, CCNH made me a much bigger person than what I would have otherwise become."

From Outsider to Insider

The narratives of Marcela and Tommy point to the importance of trust in *developing a sense of personal well-being*. Our fourth theme revolves around confidence and a growing *desire to learn more and to contribute* more fully to both the neighbourhood house and the neighbourhood itself. Having identified what they would like to do, and realizing that they have the ability to do it, newcomers experience a new sense of identity that enables them to find their niche – their special place within the larger community. With their immediate needs met, and having gained valuable Canadian experience, the stress that immigrants experience in the earlier periods continues to decrease. Rather than feeling like *"useless" outsiders, they develop a sense of "insideness"* – in other words, as Agata and Satinder illustrate below, they (re)find their voice and sense of self-worth, and start to feel like they fit in.

Agata: Passed through Turbulent Waters, Now Smooth Sailing

Agata Feetham is the program director at Gordon Neighbourhood House (GNH). Her journey with the neighbourhood house movement began in 2000 when she volunteered for 100 hours at South Vancouver Neighbourhood House (SVNH) Homework Club program and earned $800 toward her tuition at the University of British Columbia.

While volunteering at SVNH, Agata saw a posting for a part-time child care worker for the Nobody's Perfect parenting program at GNH. She applied and was offered the position. While working for the Nobody's Perfect program, she also started working in GNH's out-of-school care program. For the next four years, she worked in out-of-school care during the school year and at summer camps in the summer. She recalled fondly:

> During that time, I became one of those people at the neighbourhood house that worked in every program and filled in everywhere possible. I literally worked in every program, including the front desk! The unique thing about that period was how much experience I gained from those

positions and how relevant they were to my education. Working with children and families, in a non-profit, with diverse and vulnerable populations, was the ideal situation, and laid the foundation for my career. I'm really proud of the fact that I have a psychology degree and a job that relates to it! Gordon House is the foundation of that.

After obtaining her bachelor of arts degree, Agata enrolled in a one-year counselling diploma program and worked at other neighbourhood houses, including running a leadership program at Burnaby Neighbourhood House and a Homework Club at Collingwood Neighbourhood House. Finally, in March 2005, three months after her graduation from university, her dream position (family and youth program coordinator) became available and neighbourhood house staff encouraged her to apply. As a young person in a new position, Agata deeply appreciated the open, accessible, and non-judgmental nature of the neighbourhood house staff noted in Chapter 3. Only twenty-four at the time, sensitive Agata recalled: "I was so nervous – I was literally sick in my husband's elevator going up to print my resumé!" She noted: "It was a huge learning curve for me and it took about six months before I stopped feeling sick at work." Although she lacked confidence in herself, the other neighbourhood house staff knew she could handle the job, and Agata has grown into the position over the years. She is particularly grateful for the support she received, noting: "Jessie and Linda have been here since the beginning for me and they're like family members." She added:

There were a lot of things I had never done before, so it was a big jump! I was so flattered when Linda said: "Agata can do that!" I'm thankful to her for having that confidence in me. I learned so much in that first year. Linda always told me: "Don't worry! We'll help you!" And they did! As a twenty-five-year old, I was really proud of myself.

She mused:

And now I've been here for ten years! I've always wanted to be here. I was hired as the family and youth program coordinator, then it changed to family and youth program manager, and now program director. With Paul, the new ED [executive director], I'm learning even more than I have in the past. I look forward to coming to work every day. I can't believe how lucky I am!

Agata described the subsequent four years until her daughter was born in 2009 as a plateau characterized by profound enjoyment of her job. Life was proceeding smoothly. She explained what happened next:

A lot of stuff happened in my personal life: I got married and had kids. As a new mom, it was a real challenge to balance child care and work full time. At GNH though, everything was going smoothly, and that stability helped me get through the challenges I was dealing with at home. GNH was always a safe place where I could be myself and get support. That helped a lot.

Eventually her home life settled down. As she described: "There was a balance and happiness at home, but meanwhile at GNH John, the ED, got sick; it was a more stable life at home, but turbulent times at Gordon House." After John left, Agata, Linda, and Julio shared responsibility for the ED position until a new person came on temporarily. Finally, Paul Taylor joined GNH as the new ED. Less than three months later, Agata went on her second twelve-month maternity leave: "It was amazing. I remained connected to Gordon House: I went out for lunch with Jessie and Linda and I came to the play groups. Finally, I emailed Paul to let him know that I preferred to come back to work part-time, if possible. He said, 'No problem! We'll make it work.'" When Agata returned to GNH in 2014, she became the program director in charge of family, children, youth, adult, seniors, and newcomer programs.

Agata explained that GNH is also an important part of her family, which has been pulled into the neighbourhood house through the chain effect (Chapter 3):

I brought my older daughter in for day camps and special events. And now I come with my younger daughter to the Mom and Tot drop-in. I know a lot of the moms and the caregivers who come to the group. It's like a big family. It's my second home and these people are my second family. I think that's such a blessing.

She described some of her most significant achievements, such as organizing the hugely popular GNH block party:

When I see a room full of people getting together and enjoying themselves, that brings me such joy. The best part of my job is seeing first-hand the difference we can make in people's lives. I think having immigrated to

Canada from Poland as a child enables me to come from a place of understanding in my work with immigrant families. There have been numerous examples over the years where there was a single mom or a family, or recent immigrants, who we were able to support. And they come back and say "Gordon House saved my life!"

Agata has also changed over the years: "I used to live in fear of the future. That gave me a lot of anxiety. But I've stopped hoping that nothing will ever go wrong: instead I pray for strength when things do go wrong." She is thankful every day for what she has:

I have my wonderful life at home, my family, wonderful friends. I have this amazing job. But I also have friends at my workplace, so it's a social life as well. There's so much going on, so much buzz. So we're all happy to be here. It's a good team and I'm proud to be just one part of it.

Reflecting further on her personal and professional development, Agata credited GNH with providing her with a career path. GNH also supported her financially in continuing her education with a certificate program on non-profit sector management at the Justice Institute of British Columbia, as well as regular attendance at conferences and workshops.

Agata has no intention of working elsewhere. She exclaimed: "I'm retiring from here! I love this place! There's no salary that can replace the family I have here, and the support and the love." Inspired by Paul, she may one day consider becoming an ED, "but," she emphasized, "I'm not at that level yet, so for now I just follow Paul and learn!"

Satinder: Finding Her Place under the Sun

Satinder Singh is the family program coordinator at Collingwood Neighbourhood House, where she has run Family Place for almost twenty-five years. Underlining the importance of non-purposeful learning (Chapter 4), she recalled how she first became involved with Collingwood:

The day is etched in my memory because when I and my family came to Canada ... we didn't know a single soul here. My husband and I wanted to look for work, but first we needed daycare for our two children, who were ten and six years old. We didn't know where to start. Fortunately, Collingwood Neighbourhood House was at that time doing a community research project to find out what the needs were in the community ... The next day I went to the CNH storefront on Kingsway. At some point during my conversation with the staff, one of them suggested that I help out in the Nobody's Perfect parenting program as a volunteer Punjabi facilitator. I am from India and I speak Punjabi. They even offered to send me for training first. That's how I started my journey with the neighbourhood house.

Satinder was among the first people to receive training as a Nobody's Perfect facilitator. After volunteering for about a month, she was offered part-time paid work at Collingwood and ran one of the first parenting groups in 1990. The program was small then, but, as the neighbourhood house grew with each passing year, Satinder worked a few more hours each week. She became a full-time staff member in 1998, which suited her perfectly because by then her kids were older and more independent. Working at Collingwood was not only Satinder's first job in Canada but also her first experience of paid employment. Despite completing post-secondary education in India, she had never worked outside the home.

Satinder recalled that her life was not always as comfortable as it is now:

The early years, the 1990s, were my period of learning and struggle. I was learning to drive. I'd never been to a bank. I had never worked outside of the house. In my family everything was exclusive because we came from a privileged stratum of society. The word "inclusive" was something I learned when I came to CNH. And then, seeing my husband struggling to establish himself in his career was hard. We had come from a country where we had lots of friends, and here at first there seemed to be no connection.

Since then, however, life has only gotten better:

By 2000, I had finished studying, and the family program was well established. On a personal front, we were back where we wanted to be financially. My husband is happy with his work and so am I. I am very proud of what I have done. Within Collingwood, I've created my own space in a new country. It is very cozy here. When people come here, they say: "This is Satinder's place."

Working at Collingwood helped Satinder deal with the challenges she faced as a new immigrant and eased her difficult transition from being a lonely newcomer to serving as a pillar of her community. For example, assisting in the English as an additional language classes at Collingwood gave her the opportunity to travel around the city. As a result of these place-making activities, the idea that Vancouver was her new home became more concrete in her mind. The neighbourhood house also supplied emotional support, and Satinder's gratitude for this support spurs her to do the same for others:

> When I see any immigrant woman walking through the doors, I have to support that person – because the neighbourhood house supported me and I want to give back to the community. And they always come back to me. Some way or the other, they say: "How you changed my life!" And I say: "It's not me; you had the desire to change. I was just there to show you the way." But it's a huge thing, because immigration is not easy. I'm glad that I could contribute to their success in a small way.

Despite no longer living in the Collingwood neighbourhood, Satinder still runs into people she first met during her early days at the neighbourhood house. She recalled: "In this community, a lot of the families used to really struggle, and I was part of that struggle with them. I feel like a queen when I walk down Kingsway, waving to half the families; the kids may have grown up, but they still remember me."

Satinder related how the warm, caring atmosphere of Collingwood Neighbourhood House draws people in: "Whoever comes in falls in with our philosophy of being welcoming, of being non-judgmental. When families come in, they feel it is their place. The neighbourhood house is a very special place. It has a heart." She also emphasized its importance for the neighbourhood: "If there wasn't Collingwood Neighbourhood House, there would be no cohesiveness in this community. It would be very fragmented because this is the place where people meet. I've lived in Coquitlam for fifteen years and I still don't know my neighbours. It's not a community like Collingwood because there is no neighbourhood house to connect them." The importance of these connections cannot be overstated. Underscoring the connecting and grounding functions of neighbourhood houses (see Chapters 3 and 5), Satinder explained: "When you know a lot of people, it makes you feel so connected, so grounded. When I came to Canada I felt very isolated. Now I feel I have a history. This is the place where people connect, but they continue their relationships outside of the neighbourhood house."

In addition to maintaining loving connections with current and past program participants, Satinder has also developed lifelong friendships with other staff members and volunteers:

Once people have gone through Collingwood Neighbourhood House, they often don't leave. We all grow up and learn together. Jenny at the front came in as a student, and I remember her studying for her exams. She's been with us for eighteen years. Many other staff members have also been around for that long. In Family Place, I've had only three staff in twenty-four years. This place is very blessed to have such people working for it. It is very inspirational, and I am so proud to work here.

When asked what keeps people at Collingwood, Satinder responded:

Turnover is so low because there's a lot of respect in this place. There's a lot of trust and respect of diversity. Everybody has such a passion for their work. People at Collingwood put a lot of heart into their work and it shows. The strong connections that we have among staff come through in our work and the people that come in to use our services become part of the magic.

As a result of her work at Collingwood, Satinder underwent a tremendous transformation in her personal as well as professional life. She developed a new capacity to aspire, not only for herself but also for her community, through active citizenship (see Chapter 3). Those changes were made possible because Collingwood offered her the chance to find out who she was and what her life's work would be. "The compassion," she stated, "I already had in me; I had the energy to connect with people. So I just needed to be in an environment like Collingwood Neighbourhood House to mould me." She recalled: "My husband thought that I would never be able to do anything outside of the house. When I had my first business card printed, I took it back home to India – I was so proud."

Satinder developed the skills she is most proud of at Collingwood. There, she explained: "I found that I can be a great leader and I'm also a very good team player. I've also developed strong problem-solving skills." Moving to the new Collingwood Neighbourhood House building offered space to expand existing programs. Satinder recalled that building up the program constituted another huge learning curve. In addition to knowledge about community development programming and management, she also learned practical skills, including taking minutes for the first time, and chairing meetings. She is rightly proud of what she has accomplished. Speaking about Family Place, she said: "I worked hard to establish all of this and I am very happy where I am. I forget I'm working for money. My work is something that I enjoy doing so much."

Working at Collingwood also provided Satinder with an individual identity. She asserted:

> I was always known back home by my husband's name, "P. Singh." I was "Mrs. P. Singh." I didn't have my own identity. So Collingwood gave me my identity ... Collingwood gave me my own space to grow as a person. I am what I am because of my work at the neighbourhood house. Here I've found my own place under the sun.

It Is Empowering to Empower Others

The stories shared by Satinder and Agata underline the processes through which being an immigrant eventually ceases to be felt as a burden and instead becomes a source of valuable experience and knowledge that can be leveraged to help others. Although the leitmotif of *empowerment* is interwoven throughout our six themes, it is perhaps in the fifth theme that its significance is most fully realized. Thus, the following two narratives point to the ways in which participation in community development empowers newcomers to "give back" (see also Chapter 2). It is *empowering to empower others*, and neighbourhood houses provide this opportunity. The theme of empowerment is particularly important given the larger context of racialized power in a white settler society with which our immigrant participants, all of whom are people of colour, must contend (see Chapter 5). During this step, formerly dependent or isolated immigrants actively create and define the place they live in; they are literally developing their communities by building on their individual achievements to promote community improvement. No longer simply a physical location, their neighbourhood becomes a *place with meaning: a home*. Below, the narratives of Lynn and Maheen reveal that, as community members, they feel part of a bigger story and their sense of place has expanded beyond the neighbourhood to embrace the wider community.

Lynn: Our Neighbourhood House Always Pulls Us Back

Lynn Leong has been the community kitchen coordinator at Burnaby Neighbourhood House for thirteen years. Her relationship with neighbourhood houses began when Dave Stevens visited her elementary school nearly forty years earlier. He presented a slideshow and described Camp Wallace. Lynn explained:

> We begged our parents for months to let us go. My parents ran a grocery store on Commercial Drive and they worked fourteen hours a day, seven

days a week, so we never went camping. It was a foreign idea to send your kids to camp when you've got grandma in the back of the store to look after them. It was a hard sell, but my brother, sister, one of our cousins, and I ended up going to camp together. We were thrilled. It was such a fun time.

Lynn continued her neighbourhood house journey by forging a connection at South Vancouver Neighbourhood House, working in the Hello World kids' program in summers. Getting the job at SVNH was a major milestone for her: "Getting a real job outside of my parents' store was really exciting! It built independence for me and introduced me to a whole new world."

Lynn attended the leadership program in grades eleven and twelve, and after graduation participated in the Adult Outdoor Club. Meanwhile, she worked at Camp Wallace and at Cedar Cottage Neighbourhood House. As a result of her experiences, and to her parents' chagrin, she decided to study recreation at university. While at university, she worked in the leadership program at Gordon Neighbourhood House and as the Summer Fun program coordinator for the City of White Rock before she and her husband headed overseas for several months.

On returning to Canada, Lynn began looking for work. It turned out that Antonia Beck, the Mount Pleasant Neighbourhood House (MPNH) program coordinator, was going on maternity leave, and Lynn filled the position while she was away. Lynn reflected: "It was cool to have a chance to work there because every neighbourhood house has a different feel and what they do is a little bit different. I thought, 'Hey, things are all lining up.'"

When Antonia returned, Lynn left MPNH. In subsequent years, she worked at the BC Centre for Ability in Vancouver and also gave birth to her first child. However, she maintained her connection with neighbourhood houses through annual attendance at Sasamat Camp. She described how her commitment to spending more time with her family led to a new connection with Burnaby Neighbourhood House:

One day at Sasamat Outdoor Centre I ran into Antonia and she told me: "We need somebody to help with the community kitchen." When I heard "community kitchen" – food plus people – I thought: "Wow, great!" because those are two areas that I love, and to be able to combine them and get paid to do it is pretty cool. That was twelve years ago!

Lynn's description of the reasons she loves coordinating the community kitchen underscores the value of social infrastructure as a connecting mechanism for the creation of social capacity and for the development of lasting friendships across multiple lines of difference (see also Chapter 4):

Even after twelve years, the work excites me. All the groups are different and we have so many interesting conversations and so many good laughs! It's the people that make it exciting – there are few jobs where you can have an open-ended conversation every week for three hours! Over food! The conversations are so rich and that's how the group members influence each other, so that's a beautiful, important piece. And it's intimate. We talk about everything! I have been quoted as saying: "The group is going well when we start talking about sex." Religion, family … nothing is off limits because people feel safe. We build trust by doing things together; people also feel empowered because they can share their ideas and put them into action. Just holding formal meetings doesn't bring people closer. The people who come to the community kitchen are struggling with many different issues: diabetes, anxiety, body issues, weight, fear, depression, isolation, immigration, family problems. People can help one another because they get to know the other participants and care about them: they're neighbours. It's a natural way of people getting together without forcing anything. Another important aspect is that we are communicating face to face: you cannot do community development via email; getting together is the key to growing good neighbours.

She continued:

Once I began this job, I never turned back. In so many ways, this job is a good fit for me. It's also a good fit for my family, because, although my kids are teens, they still need us after school. And we've got four aging parents, so there needs to be some flexibility to help them. There have been a few times when the kids have come to work with me and I don't know many workplaces where that would have been okay! There are a couple of staff members who bring their dogs to work. A cat lived at the neighbourhood house for a while and that's just the way it is. They give you what you need in order for you to come to work. I think that's why a lot of people stay at neighbourhood houses, because it's certainly not the wages!

Looking back over some of her fondest memories, Lynn reflected: "Our camp always pulls us back. It's a part of our life. Also, because you spend several days with people, you are able to have many good conversations – even with people I wouldn't normally have a conversation with. That was especially valuable during those teen years when you tend to talk to your six friends and that's about it." Lynn met her husband at camp and still has close friends from that time. She also acknowledged her long connections with co-workers:

> It happens that way with the neighbourhood house. For most of us, including participants, we expect that when we come to our neighbourhood house somebody will know us and give us a big hug, or at least a big smile, and say: "Hi Lynn!" Even after moving away for a while, when you come back, it's always: "Hey, welcome back!" It's very different than, say, the community centre where people don't know my name even though I'm there on a weekly basis.

Lynn's kids also enjoy a connection to the neighbourhood house movement:

> When my kids were babies, we went to Mother Goose at CNH. They've both gone to camp at Sasamat as day campers and res-camp campers. My husband also works at family camp on those weekends. As the boys have got older – they're now fourteen and seventeen – they help people carry their luggage to the cabins. They're so proud of that place, because from summer to summer you often see the same families, so they have that connection. My older son has gone on some of the canoe trips and now he's in the leadership program. My younger son has also spent part of many summers at Sasamat.

Lynn described how her connection to neighbourhood houses influenced her personal development:

> I was a very quiet kid, not talkative at all. But I had skills and a belief in the value of community development. I love that you can take an idea, have no money, and still do something. When you get a bunch of people together, there are sparks, and bigger things happen. Even when I worked for other places, the idea of community development that I first learned at the neighbourhood house remained part of me.

In fact, Lynn has applied the passion for community development that she learned at the neighbourhood house to her neighbourhood and also at her sons' school:

> Something happens when people work together, and good things get built in neighbourhoods because of that. I think that's my biggest learning from the neighbourhood house – along with being able to talk to anybody through the experience of being around all kinds of different people. Another learning piece relates to taking on more responsibility for guiding and supervising staff and volunteers, which has enabled me to pass on what I've learned to others.

Looking forward to the future, Lynn reflected: "As an older person who's not working, I'll need places to go, and things to do, and opportunities to connect with people. The neighbourhood house will be that place and connection. Even if I don't know anybody, I know there's always good stuff happening at the neighbourhood house!"

Maheen: Gave Her Heart, Found Her Voice

Maheen Khorram is the family programs manager at Burnaby Neighbourhood House. She and nine family members arrived in Canada in 1986 as government-sponsored refugees from Iran via Pakistan. They joined eight family members who were already in Vancouver, making up a close-knit group of eighteen family members. At that time, Maheen's daughter was two years old; her son was born nine months after the family settled in Canada. Once her daughter turned three, Maheen began looking for preschool classes and found herself at Mount Pleasant Neighbourhood House. The program director, Sharon Babu, who soon became her mentor and close friend, advised her: "Every so often, come to my office, and we will talk about how life is going and what you would like to do." Meanwhile, Maheen's daughter began attending preschool at MPNH.

One day, not long after Maheen's first visit to MPNH, Sharon asked her if she would like to showcase her Iranian culture to people in Vancouver. Maheen was shocked:

> I couldn't believe I was hearing right that people were interested in my culture. Sharon told me: "You cook Persian food, and you bring things from your culture to put on the table and you can talk about them. You can arrange things however you like; it's going to be your night." Sharon also said:

"Don't worry, we'll take care of the shopping, and bring volunteers in. I just want you to coordinate it." She mentioned that around a hundred people would attend! At first I was freaked out. But some of my Persian neighbours and my sister-in-law agreed to help me and the dinner went really well! Actually, I am a very organized person. And Sharon noticed that I have some skills.

Following the success of the dinner, Maheen put her name down to volunteer at the neighbourhood house on weekends or evenings. She elaborated: "I wanted to be part of this amazing thing that I found helpful and heartwarming." What began as a volunteer position became a lifelong career:

> Little by little, whenever I was ready, Sharon would offer little jobs. Two years after I started volunteering, I became part-time staff. Then about ten years later, full-time. Now I am so passionate about neighbourhood houses. I think the neighbourhood house really saved my sanity in many ways. Other agencies were also helpful, but the neighbourhood house is really special.

As a result of the challenges her family was experiencing, Maheen's connection with MPNH played an important part in her life by providing her with a feeling of moving forward and a sense of fulfillment. At one point, one of the group facilitation courses that she was taking involved a practicum component, and MPNH staff helped her work with an existing fitness course for seniors. As the program progressed, Maheen realized that Persian seniors in the neighbourhood, many of whom did not speak English (including her in-laws), could also benefit from the program. She recounted:

> I asked Sharon if I could use one of the rooms upstairs to run a program for Persian seniors. And she said: "Sure, I'll pay you to do it." Another amazing moment! I would have done it voluntarily! So that was my first job at the neighbourhood house, and I created it myself. By then I had some experience working with the neighbourhood house and I knew how things worked. The program was really successful and I had about twenty Persian seniors coming from all over Metro Vancouver.

Over time, Maheen worked an increasing number of hours at MPNH in different programs, including support groups for families, women, persons with disabilities, and seniors. She recollected working with seniors: "I loved that job. I travelled. I learned a lot about Vancouver, and I loved the seniors." One day, Maheen asked Sharon if she could register for the Nobody's Perfect parenting program. Sharon offered instead to send Maheen for training to become a facilitator, and Maheen ran two or three groups per year for many years. She reflected: "It was one of my favourite things to do. From facilitating, I became a better person and I learned so much from all the parents."

Meanwhile, Maheen's husband started a roofing company and soon became very successful. Maheen continued to take on part-time contracts with MPNH. She started the drop-in program and worked there for seventeen years. Having been given an opportunity to explore her passions and talents in a trusting atmosphere (see Chapter 3), Maheen finally found her niche. She asserted:

> I think my passion always was to work with families and young children. I really value parenting. I know it's a hard job. I also know the first five years of a child's life is very important. So, if I can do anything to make that first five years a little easier, then I will. Of course I am not perfect. I learn something every day that I work with families, and I try my best not to judge people. But I knew I had found the right place for me.

Maheen added proudly: "Nobody offers what neighbourhood houses offer. Many organizations are amazing, but they work with specific groups. The beauty of it is that we are here, and we are going to be here for a long time." To illustrate, Maheen related the following anecdotes:

> I went to the hospital when one of the moms who came to my drop-in program had given birth prematurely. Now her daughter is sixteen, and she's in our Foundation group. I was working at MPNH at that time, and when the family moved to Burnaby, they found me at the neighbourhood house here. I know many such families like that. People will even come to find me again after five or ten years. The neighbourhood house captures people because it has so much to offer. That's why I love my job.

Maheen's family members also became involved in the neighbourhood house. She remarked:

> I organized lots of community dinners and family nights and my family members always came along. Both of my kids went to preschool and

summer camp, attended leadership programs, and volunteered with summer programs. They kind of grew up in MPNH – they were always there. If
I didn't finish work on time, they would walk to the neighbourhood house
from school and we would go home together. It was our second home. My
mom also came to a lot of the Family Nights and Multicultural Nights. My
husband came if he had time. My sister-in-law volunteered. My nieces and
nephews got involved in the leadership program and they also volunteered.
The neighbourhood house was part of our family.

After a few years as a family worker, Maheen became a coordinator. Then
the executive director, David Adair, passed away. Maheen recalled: "Fortunately, Antonia hired me as Family Place coordinator at Burnaby Neighbourhood House and I've been here almost twenty years!" Both MPNH and BNH
played a central role in Maheen's personal growth and in helping her develop a sense of Vancouver as home:

> It was through my involvement with the neighbourhood house that I
> started becoming strong and able to stand up and have a voice and be able
> to look for things that I wanted. The first five or six years in a new country,
> you don't even know who you are. It's like being a singer without a voice.
> The neighbourhood house saved me because being a part of anything at the
> neighbourhood house gives you some sense of how the world works, how
> Canada works. You can't put a value on that.

Pointing to the ways in which neighbourhood houses further democratic,
community-based governance and place-based integration, which in turn
create a powerful sense of individual agency (see Chapter 3), she continued:

> The neighbourhood house helped me to be grounded here and to realize
> that Canada is a great country. It has a lot of challenges, but I feel like these
> are my challenges now. It's my country, so what am I going to do to make it
> better? I'm grateful to the neighbourhood house for giving me the oppor-
> tunity to be part of the solution. I feel fulfilled in so many ways every day.

Maheen explained how being involved in the neighbourhood house impacted her professional development:

> As my kids were growing up, the neighbourhood house allowed me to fig-
> ure out what I am capable of – it was the key to finding myself. They allowed

me to grow at my own pace. It was never: "Well, if you want a job, you have to work full time." Or: "You only can work from nine to five"; I could negotiate the time and do the tasks I was willing and capable of doing. I also received a lot of encouragement: "You'll be great, why don't you apply? Why don't you do it for three months to see how it works?" Ultimately, I learned, and I contributed too. The neighbourhood house allowed me to develop skills that I might not even have had the confidence to try.

Maheen now models the same behaviour with neighbourhood house program participants. She explained: "You find mentorship at the neighbourhood house, and you pass that on. Mentorship is part of everybody's job here. Neighbourhood houses were a huge part of my journey to become a better person."

Looking ahead to the future, Maheen anticipates volunteering at the neighbourhood house when she retires in eight years. She insisted:

I want to be involved with the neighbourhood house no matter where I live or how old I am. As a senior, I can read books to kids. I can attend seniors' programs, go on trips when I can no longer drive, become part of the social activities, cook soup together with the group in the kitchen, and bring my grandchild to the preschool and to the summer program.

She chuckled: "It looks like my grandchildren will be born in Japan and Los Angeles. If I end up going to LA, I'll probably start a drop-in program. If I go to Japan, I'll probably start a neighbourhood house there, even if I'm already retired. That's how much I believe in neighbourhood houses."

Coming Full Circle

Our final theme is titled "Coming full circle," as by this time immigrants have become integral parts of Canadian institutions – active and contributing members of their neighbourhood and the larger community. They help others who are new and alone by drawing isolated newcomers and community members into the web of shared meaning that characterizes a community and a cohesive neighbourhood. From being mentees, they have become mentors who actively and thoughtfully contribute to positive changes in their community through what Wei Wei, below, calls the "ripple effect."

Tatiana: It's a Circle

Tatiana Wong is a youth worker at Kiwassa Neighbourhood House (KwNH).

The daughter of Chinese immigrants, Tatiana has lived in East Vancouver all her life. She first became connected with Kiwassa when several Kiwassa youth workers visited Hastings Elementary School to promote their programs. Tatiana started volunteering in the Junior Leadership program and became a junior leader when she was twelve, recalling: "I worked my way up from volunteer, to getting my own group of ten kids and being a leader, and then to day camp manager when I was around twenty."

Tatiana described some of the programs she has led over the years, especially Eastside Teens and Eastside Power Mamas. Despite the value of the programs to the community, Tatiana's observations reveal the constant struggle for funding that characterizes the neoliberal context (see Chapters 1 and 4):

> I have a soft spot for Eastside Teens. I have known some of the youth in that program since they were five. Just thinking about it, I start to tear up because I think about the situations these kids have come from and the fact that some of them are now asking about university applications, and thinking about where life is taking them; they are coming to me to talk about these decisions. I don't tell them what to do, but work with them to figure out what they are thinking. We provide a safe space for a diverse group of youth to hang out and around sixty youth come to the drop-in twice a week. It's really, really cool. Eastside Power Mamas stemmed from Eastside Teens. We realized that there weren't any programs for teen moms to just hang out with each other and provide support. We do fun activities that are about the moms or their kids. Everyone's having a good time and that's when the connections get made and where the resources and information get shared. We've run it for about four years but funding is increasingly a struggle.

Since Tatiana was a student for much of the time she's worked at Kiwassa, she greatly appreciated Kiwassa's flexibility with respect to scheduling (see also Chapter 3): "They always found me the hours I was looking for." Tatiana also appreciated that Kiwassa has afforded her the opportunity to grow at her own pace:

> What stands out for me is the moments where I got to run programs on my own as opposed to helping someone run a program. Being able to take leadership and realize that I can deliver a program how I see fit is always a crucial moment. I love the feeling of: "Okay, this is working!" It gives you confidence to move forward.

Tatiana is grateful to Kiwassa for providing her with so many opportunities over the years. She reflected: "There's always this amazing community support, not just for participants but for the staff as well." She continued: "I've been very open about personal stuff and my schooling and they've just been incredibly supportive: giving me information and saying, 'Whenever you need to talk, we are here.' They always guide me to make my own decision. I'm extremely lucky to have them keeping an eye on me with my well-being in mind." Kiwassa has also provided Tatiana with numerous opportunities for professional development and training. She explained: "I've done so many seminars and lectures on topics such as mental health in schools, delivering curriculum, working with groups, how to talk to youth, building resiliency in youth, and so many more."

The supportive environment Tatiana finds at Kiwassa positively affects her work with youth. She reflected:

> The understanding that I get makes my work with youth better because I see leadership by example. It trickles down. It's really special if you have a talk with your supervisor – then you think: "Oh wow, they spent time with me to do this thing that is totally about me." That shows the passion they have for this line of work. There's no other reward than seeing change in your community, and being a part of it through our work is amazing. The management's very open-door and we're like that with our youth. So, it's a circle.

Tatiana described how her personal development has been shaped by Kiwassa:

> In high school I was very quiet and shy. I remember intently watching my leaders to see how they talked to people and then I'd take what I liked best from each leader and create my own style. So over the years it's been progressive growth. The thing with Kiwassa is that there is always somebody to help me grow ... Another thing I've learned through working at KwNH is how to mix friendship and work. What happened was that I worked with a friend at Kiwassa and, being young, I had no idea that there could be complications from that or how to deal with them. I didn't know how to problem-solve in a work setting. At one point a supervisor said: "We've got to talk about this." The conversation that ensued really helped me realize how I need to work with people as part of a team effort; that was a huge thing for me.

Tatiana discussed some of the values she brings to her work while also emphasizing the importance of proximity as an enabler of place-based integration and community development (see Chapter 3):

> I believe in consistency with youth. Many come from unstable environments and to know that I can be a consistent factor means a lot. It's the connections that you make, and stability is important. I see the youth I work with everywhere. I've lived here my entire life, so I see them in the program, outside the program, I've bumped into their families and talked to their grandparents, aunts, and uncles, and it's really cool. I know young people not only as participants, but within their families, at school, within their life here as community members and neighbours ... I'm always going to keep the values of community and integration because I've been lucky to see what they achieve on the front line. Not a lot of people can say that.

Looking forward to the (distant) future, Tatiana enthused: "As a senior, I want to be that crazy old lady that everyone wants to be around. I'm definitely joining the seniors' program. Kiwassa is full of seniors and they are so happy and so loud. I can't wait!"

Wei Wei: Ripple Effect

Wei Wei Siew is the family and adult team leader at South Vancouver Neighbourhood House and has been in the position for ten years. She was born in Malaysia, but when she was three her family moved to Tahsis, a tiny logging town on Vancouver Island. Then in high school she moved to Killarney in Vancouver and has lived there since. She related:

> Initially it was difficult to find my way and make friends at a new school. But then I found out about the neighbourhood house in grade eleven when a youth leader came to the school to give a presentation on a youth leadership training program. It looked so exciting! I got my friend to sign up with me, and that basically changed my life; it opened up a lot of doors for me, giving me the gateway to where I am now.

The leadership program exceeded Wei Wei's expectations and also led to paid employment. She explained:

It was fantastic. The leaders were great role models and they became my heroes. The program taught us how to be day camp leaders, about group dynamics and behavioural management, and how to self-care so that we could care for others. There were also games, songs, and campfires; growing up I hadn't done those things so it was great to experience them as a youth. After the training, I worked at SVNH for my very first job as a day camp leader when I was seventeen years old. The second year I came back and did it again. That got me connected to other neighbourhood houses and to Sasamat Camp as well. After that I worked at SVNH part-time as a Cultural Buddy coordinator. I loved it ... The leadership program was crucial because it got me on this road. I met new people and saw different ways of communicating and engaging that I wanted to emulate. That had a long-lasting effect on me.

Wei Wei's neighbourhood house journey continued after high school as she continued to participate in a variety of neighbourhood house activities (see Chapter 3). She explained:

After finishing high school, I went to Capilano University for the recreation program and then completed my degree. In the meantime, I worked seasonally doing day camps at MPNH and CCNH for a couple of years. And then Sasamat had some positions open so I went up there and did day camps, and also facilitated youth leadership and camping programs. At the same time, I was also a snowshoe guide and then did a practicum for GVRD [Greater Vancouver Regional District] as a park naturalist. This path was started by my taking part in the SVNH leadership program. Before that, I didn't know what "outdoor recreation" was, but afterward it became a passion. So the neighbourhood house basically brought me to who I am now; I am exactly what I am because of neighbourhood houses.

She continued:

Eventually I realized that it was all "meant to be" because I love working with the community and I love learning and growing and challenging myself and working with people. They say: "It takes a community to raise a child," and my story really illustrates that because it was the neighbourhood house community that made me who I am.

Wei Wei described some of the challenges she has overcome in her new position:

> This is the most growth I've experienced in a job. In groups, I am very task-oriented. I've had to learn that process is important too, that conversation is important, and that the relationship-building piece is important. I've also had to realize it's okay if I don't have all the answers. That was a huge lesson for me because I'd had the idea that I needed to be perfect. Realizing there's no such thing as perfect, and it's better to make mistakes and learn and grow from them, has been huge.

She emphasized: "Having the support from my boss to be able to make mistakes, stumble through, learn, and then go through it, has been critical. It's been a supportive environment. I think that people stay here so long because it feels like a family."

Finally, Wei Wei reflected on the broader impact of the neighbourhood house:

> I remember bumping into a youth. She asked: "Hi, do you remember me?" Then she turned to her colleague and told her: "The whole reason I am here now is because Wei Wei was my leader!" Sometimes I forget about the ripple effect that I have in my job – the personal impact I have on other people. We really impact the community. Just as my heroes had ripple effects on me, I have ripple effects on other people. So it's lovely to have that full circle of participating and now giving back and then providing capacity and training to other people and having them give back. It's just amazing because I gain capacity, pass it on, and then others are also able to pass it on. So it's that wonderful circle-of-life ripple effect.

Conclusion

These inspirational and heartwarming stories reveal the intense pain of "unbelonging" – of living in close proximity to many people yet feeling socially distant from them – which many immigrants experience. Social connection is the key to overcoming isolation and it is in this context that neighbourhood houses forge the linkages needed to create meaningful places out of anonymous urban space. Providing immigrants with accessible opportunities to share and hear similar stories not only reduces anxiety, ignorance, and isolation, but can also inspire folks to perceive the wonderful ways in which all stories overlap to create the community. As friendship and professional networks develop through the caring and supportive encouragement of the neighbourhood house, immigrants also experience profound personal growth, obtain employment, learn about Canadian culture, develop confidence, move from dependence to independence, acquire new ways of thinking about the world (e.g., inclusion, community development, bottom-up), and ultimately cultivate a desire to learn and contribute more. Thus, neighbourhood houses empower immigrants, who in turn empower others, and are themselves yet further empowered in a potent iterative process: a ripple effect.

A place is more than simply a location; it has a special meaning. Through the connections created around the neighbourhood house, neighbourhood residents become a community; when one feels part of a community, then the city becomes a place with meaning: home. Immigrants who once felt like useless outsiders are able to develop a feeling of "insideness" and of belonging because of the relationship between empowerment and sense of place, and the neighbourhood house is the link. The neighbourhood house movement is grounded in a belief in the power of collective action, which is also fundamental to sustaining a successful democracy in Canada. Collective action requires connection with others. Connection is empowering, and empowering others is also immensely empowering; these processes enable one to feel confident, like one belongs. And when one belongs to a place, one typically cares about it and tries to make it better. It is this unique contribution of belonging and empowerment that makes neighbourhood houses so vital in an otherwise increasingly discordant world.

7

Limitations and Potentials of Neighbourhood Houses in Community-Building

MIU CHUNG YAN and SEAN LAUER

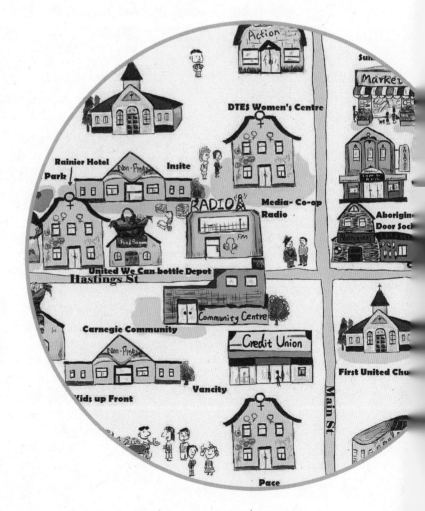

W e have examined the many roles and functions of neighbourhood houses (NHs) in political and personal change, community connectivity, and civic engagement. At least in our findings, NHs in Vancouver are successful in building and supporting local community by providing services that meet local people's needs, nurturing leadership among the residents, enhancing civic engagement and skills, particularly among newcomers and women, connecting local residents, and building an institutional bridge with greater service networks. However, NHs are not without limitations and challenges, many of which, such as budget limitations and precarious employment, are common to many community organizations due to the prevailing neoliberal public policies. In this concluding chapter, we first examine some limitations and challenges that NHs experience. Despite these limitations and challenges, we argue that, as demonstrated by our findings, NHs have great potential for community-building in our contemporary urban communities. We conclude with some policy implications. The discussion in this chapter is based on findings of the Clearinghouse Survey and key informant interviews with a group of former executive directors (EDs) or senior management of neighbourhood houses (see Appendix 1 for the Clearinghouse Survey).

Place-Based Paradox: Confined Public Recognition and Limited Resource

The success of neighbourhood houses can be attributed to their place-based nature; ironically, however, their major limitation and challenge is precisely caused by their place-based nature. As locally governed multi-service community organizations focusing mainly on a relatively small community, they run into a *place-based paradox*. While they have proven successful in nurturing and mobilizing local resources to serve the local community, their reputation is often confined in the community that they serve. Their place-based focus hinders them from being known in the greater society and limits their appeal for public resources, including private donations, outside the community (Yan and Sin 2011).

At least in Vancouver, most neighbourhood houses are smaller community organizations focusing mainly on the needs of a relatively small neighbourhood. Of the fifteen NHs, most (eleven) serve a neighbourhood equivalent to four to six census tracts, each of which has a population of 2,500 to 8,000 persons (Statistics Canada 2017). This place-based focus limits them in terms of program development, budget, and staff size. In Canada, government funding comes from different departments of the three levels of government – federal, provincial, and municipal. Federal and provincial funding tends to address social issues at a societal level, which favours large social service organizations that have a mandate beyond the scope of a local community. The place-based scope likely disadvantages NHs in the competition for large funding provided by federal and provincial governments.

Meanwhile, the prevalence of neoliberalism among governments further disadvantages community organizations, particularly small and place-based ones, in competing for funding (Evans and Shields 2005). Adopting a neoliberal regime, governments have cut down their financial commitment to social problems by shrinking public funding on social services. They also introduced a new public management model that embraces the principles of cost-efficiency, competition, and instrumental rationality (Yan, Cheung et al. 2017). Program-based funding models that tend toward short-term and non-renewable projects have become the dominant approach in distributing public resources (Fabricant and Fisher 2002). Instead of collaboration, competition is now the rule for securing government funding, particularly at the federal and provincial levels. Funding competition is hurtful to the partnership among community organizations (Hasenfeld and Garrow 2012), which, as demonstrated in Chapters 2 and 3, is critical to building trust among and breaking the silo in the service network (Evans and Shields 2010). As a community partner of Little Mountain Neighbourhood House shared when asked about the consequences of competition:

> It's made it difficult, yeah. And I think there has been some tensions over the years of seeing, they [NHs] see us as a competitor, you know, because we do have some overlap of services. And I would say it generally ... there's some tension in other ... not just community services, but as the funding in general becomes tighter and has put a bit of strain on some of those relationships generally between organizations that you know, like work together really well. It's that. Oh, you know, how [come] you got the funding for this and, or I'd better not share too much information 'coz they're gonna start [their] own program.

FIGURE 7.1

Funding sources for Metro Vancouver neighbourhood house programs

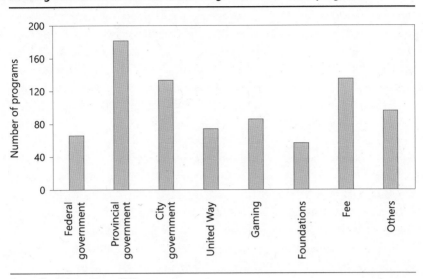

Source: Clearinghouse Survey, 2013.

In a Clearinghouse Survey conducted in fiscal year 2013, we took a snapshot of the budget and human resources of neighbourhood houses. Three had a budget of less than $200,000, seven had budgets of around $1–2 million, and five had budgets of over $3 million. As Figure 2.1 in Chapter 2 shows, they have tried to secure funding from various sources, mainly through open competition. Yet, competition has also become very technical. The competitive funding comes with a complicated application process that requires substantial preparation of information and documentation. Very often, a professional grant writer is needed to tackle the technically demanding application process. As small, place-based community organizations, NHs have trouble competing with large non-place-based organizations, particularly under the neoliberal welfare regime. For small community organizations such as NHs, this is an almost impossible task – not to mention that on average, each NH annually has already written numerous proposals for small-scale funding to support its programs.

Findings of the Clearinghouse Survey also indicated that neighbourhood houses have relied heavily on government funding, and the nature of funding is mostly short-term and non-renewable (for details, please see Chapter 2). The new public management model is also notorious for its tight control and monitoring, as seen, for example, by the imposition of a tedious and time-consuming reporting system (Yan, Cheung et al. 2017). Their place-based nature also limits the fundraising capacity of NHs, which mostly target their fundraising at local residents, who are often economically deprived themselves. As a result, the overreliance of NHs on government funding, which is rather precarious in term of stability and duration, has weakened their traditional community-building and advocacy capacity (see also Chapter 2; Evans and Shields 2005; Fabricant and Fisher 2002; Yan, Lauer, and Sin 2009).

Neighbourhood Houses: A Movement – or Not?

Individually, neighbourhood houses easily fall victim to the place-based paradox, i.e., well known locally but invisible in the larger society. Together, however, they may be able to build a movement that can appeal to the greater society. Settlement houses in the United States first set up an umbrella organization, the National Federation of Settlements, in 1911 (Trolander 1987). Then in 1920, the British Association of Residential Settlements was established (Matthews and Kimmis 2001). Internationally, the international association of settlements was formed in Paris in 1926 and reconstituted into the International Federation of Settlements and Neighborhood Centers (IFS) in 1949 when a group of community associations and centres joined the federation. Since its formation, IFS has led the International Settlement Movement. It gained a consultative status in the United Nations with UNICEF in 1966 (Johnson 1995) and currently with the Economic and Social Council (IFS, n.d.).

In Canada, there is no evidence to indicate that the early settlement houses and later the neighbourhood houses have ever developed a strong national network to form a larger movement. In Vancouver, the formation of the Neighbourhood Services Association (the predecessor of the current Association of Neighbourhood Houses of British Columbia [ANH]) in 1966 was instrumental in the creation of six neighbourhood houses (Cedar Cottage, Kitsilano, South Vancouver, Mount Pleasant, Frog Hollow, and Little Mountain) in the 1960s and '70s (for details, please refer to Chapter 1). Five of these NHs stayed with the association. Together with Gordon and Alexandra Neighbourhood Houses, ANH today comprises seven neighbourhood houses and one outdoor camp. Its leadership in the development of neighbourhood houses cannot be underestimated.

However, the relationship between ANH and other independent neighbourhood houses is not always smooth. For instance, Little Mountain NH petitioned to join the association, but after one year as a member decided to leave and operate independently. Downtown Eastside NH was initiated by ANH and affiliated with Gordon NH for two years in the beginning, but eventually decided to go its own way. Collingwood, North Shore, and Burnaby Neighbourhood Houses and Oak Avenue Neighbourhood Hub have always been independent for various reasons. As a bigger organization with a centralized administrative system, ANH is relatively resourceful. For instance, as a former executive director of one of the association's member houses noted, it is large enough to have a pension plan and regular wage increase for all its staff, which puts pressure on smaller independent NHs to follow suit. Meanwhile, the competitive funding situation also generates tensions between ANH and independent NHs. As a former ED of an independent NH explained: "I think there's still a huge amount of tension between houses within ANH and outside of ANH. I think there's a huge environment that needs to somehow get broken down. And this isn't just about the competitive environment that the government created; it's about the competitive environment that the NHs created." To her, this environment was created by the leadership of ANH and other NHs who did not see the value of collaboration, and is exacerbated by the neoliberal program funding regime. A former ED of another independent NH explained why collaboration among NHs was eroded: "Let's say, as a result ... the dynamics of funding, dollars. And that has, which is very much government. You know, you going to convert funding to the RFP [request for proposal] process, I think it was quite of the damage [to] the whole sector."

The place-based nature of neighbourhood houses has made individual houses vulnerable in terms of budget and resources. As reflected in Chapter 3, all NHs in Vancouver have tried to tackle this vulnerable situation by extensively tapping into resources from other community organizations and public institutions. Several former EDs of independent NHs who were active in the sector in the 1990s and 2000s did not see any NH movement in Vancouver. They did agree that they worked more closely with other NHs instead of other community organizations. As another former ED of an independent NH said: "We were all relatively small. And at that time, similarity was significant. And size being one of them. So there was much more similarity in terms of operation, content." But collaboration among NHs is ad hoc and issue-based and also depends on the personal relationships of individual EDs. Lacking a cohesive movement that can draw public attention, the success of individual NHs is still very much invisible to the greater society and is an asset hidden to the public.

De-professionalization or Returning to Community

The budget has no doubt had significant implications for the size and job security of staff. In the 2012 fiscal year, the number of staff members of neighbourhood houses, which reflects their capacity, was generally small. One-third (five) houses had 30 or fewer staff, another third (five) had 31–60 staff, a quarter had 61–90 staff, and only two had 150 or more staff. Less than half of the staff were full-time, and 35 percent of them had less than three years of service at NHs. Close to two decades ago, similar observations on how neoliberal program funding impacted community service organizations, particularly settlement houses, had already been well noted in New York City by Michael Fabricant and Robert Fisher (2002). In a nutshell, they found that the program funding model has led to unstable job security, high workload, low morale, unsustainable aging infrastructure, and disconnection with residents and community partners. Our respondents, including NH staff, volunteers, and community partners, shared similar stories with us. A community partner of Downtown Eastside NH noted: "People [NH staff] are trying to do more and more with less and less. I think there are vicious cycles that start to occur. People are not getting the same quality of service, not because staff aren't great, but they're seeing too many people." Indeed, high turnover is a challenge for NHs in attempting to fulfill their function. As a service user of Kitsilano NH observed: "And I think that's what happens sometimes when you have change of staff all the time is that good ideas come up and somebody might just be in the process of doing that, then it falls through the cracks again when they leave, so the ideas that people suggest for programs get lost."

The turnover of staff has direct impacts on programming – on services to the local residents. Meanwhile, to be competitive, community service organizations, including neighbourhood houses, are expected to cut costs, including wages. This jeopardizes the stability of staffing. As another community partner of Little Mountain NH pointed out: "I worry about things like fair wages for staff, because we all depend on these exceptional people. They need to be properly compensated so they'll stay."

Low wages have contributed to the de-professionalization of staff at neighbourhood houses and many other community service organizations. Chapters 5 and 6 examined how NHs have successfully nurtured and incorporated local residents, many of whom are young people or new immigrants, into their infrastructure to serve the community. However, while many of them are recruited from local residents and service users who are sensitive and respond well to local needs, most are not formally trained in

TABLE 7.1

Educational level of neighbourhood house staff

Highest level attained	Number	%
High school diploma	104	14.9
College diploma	319	45.7
Undergraduate degree	192	27.5
Postgraduate degree	83	11.9

Source: Clearinghouse Survey, 2013.

TABLE 7.2

Professional qualifications of neighbourhood house staff

Professional qualification	Number	%
Early childhood education	189*	22.8
Children and youth services	111	16.5
Social service–related	144	21.5
Social work	35	5.2
Health disciplines	17	2.5
Counselling	28	4.2
Business-related	54	5.4
Others	93	13.9

* Respondents could check more than one option.
Source: Clearinghouse Survey, 2013.

social services. Indeed most NH staff have only a college diploma or high school education (see Table 7.1).

In terms of professional qualifications (see Table 7.2), early childhood education, social service–related (e.g., gerontology, social worker), and children and youth services are the three most common qualifications among the staff, which can be mostly earned at the community college level. Intriguingly, only a very small percentage of staff held a social work qualification. Indeed, social work, the root of which was inherited from the settlement movement, had once been a leading professional qualification of staff, particularly at the senior staff level, working in the settlement house movement in North America (Trolander 1987). As Judith Ann Trolander (1987) notes, the domination of social work–trained staff once "professionalized" the neighbourhood houses. To her, this professionalization was a major force that weakened the community-building function and mandate of settlement house in the United States, due to its preference for solving individuals' problems rather than taking a community intervention approach.

Similar professionalization was also observed in neighbourhood houses in Vancouver. As discussed in Chapter 1, unlike the early settlement houses, such as Toynbee Hall and Hull House, NHs in Canada generally and in Vancouver specifically have always relied on paid staff instead of volunteer "settlers," since the very early days. ANH founder Elmer Helm recalls what it was like when he started his career in neighbourhood houses in the late 1950s: "When we were in the NHs those days, you looked for people with a master's degree in social work for replacing, even executive director ... and they always look for a person with a master's degree. That was one of the requirements I had in terms of looking."

Indeed, as early as the 1940s, social work educators and neighbourhood houses worked closely in Vancouver. George Whiten (1975), executive director of the former Alexandra NH, who left an audio record, indicated a close relationship between the University of British Columbia School of Social Work and neighbourhood house development in Vancouver. Helm remembers that until the 1970s, Gordon and Alexandra NHs were major placement sites for social work students. As reflected in Table 7.2, however today, social work is no longer a required qualification for NH staff. When we conducted the Clearinghouse Survey, in 2013 out of the fifteen NHs in Vancouver, two were headed by EDs with social work training. Similar de-professionalization processes have occurred among neighbourhood centres in San Francisco (Yan and Sin 2010).

There are many possible reasons why social work has faded from neighbourhood houses or the settlement house movement. As Trolander (1987) suggests, other than the change in socio-political contexts that weakened the settlement house movement, the individualized therapeutic approach adopted by the social work profession in the 1980s also generated tension between the social control orientation of social work and the neighbourhood house tradition of social reform. This tension weakened the involvement of social work in settlement houses in the United States. Indeed, as Harry Specht and Mark Courtney (1994) have long noted, in the United States, social work's pursuit of professionalization has shifted the profession toward *therapeutization* and caused it to gradually drift away from its mission in social reform. A similar observation was made by Helm, who suggested that the diminishing emphasis on social group work, a major service approach in NHs, in social work education alienated social work graduates from NHs.

The state's ideological shift to neoliberalism is another reasonable explanation. As discussed in Chapter 1, the BC government and the City of

TABLE 7.3

Neighbourhood house staff as local residents and service users

Neighbourhood house staff		Number	%
Former/existing service user	Never	273	37.2
	Active user	311	42.4
	Former user	150	20.4
Currently living in the neighbourhood?	Current residents	321	43.1
	Former residents	93	12.5
	Others	331	44.4

Source: Clearinghouse Survey, 2013.

Vancouver were instrumental in facilitating the establishment of neighbourhood houses. However, when a right-wing provincial government came to power, funding shrank and became competitive. Paula Carr, a former Collingwood NH executive director, recalled: "When I first started [1988], it was a bigger pot or appeared like a bigger pot of money because there was less players, right, and less demands at that time, right. But, there was always the question of re-cutting the pie." As discussed above, the competitive funding environment also drove down the wages of NH staff, which may have pushed their qualifications down.

De-professionalization of staff may engender doubt about service quality, but it may have had an unexpected positive consequence for neighbourhood houses, at least in Vancouver. As Trolander (1987) argues, professionalization alienated settlement houses from the community they serve and weakened its grassroots democratic approach. Professional workers often lived outside the community and tended to adopt an expert approach in meeting the needs of local residents. From what we have learned about NHs in Vancouver, most of the staff, although without a professional qualification, were drawn from local residents and service users (Table 7.3).

Being local residents and service users, these staff performed a function similar to that of the early settlers in the settlement house movement – namely, to learn from and serve the neighbours by living together with them in the neighbourhood. Neighbourhood houses in Vancouver have successfully nurtured and incorporated local residents as board members, staff, and volunteers (for details, please see Yan, Lauer, and Riaño-Alcalá 2017 and Chapters 4 and 5). They are highly effective in connecting NHs with the needs and concerns of local residents, as well as mobilizing local resources to address these needs and concerns. However, Baines found that, under the neoliberal funding regime, the staff of many community organizations also feel trapped in precarious and underpaid positions (Baines et al. 2014; Baines and Kgaphola 2019).

Building Welcoming Community: Neighbourhood Houses in Contemporary Urban Neighbourhoods

In view of these limitations and challenges, we may ask whether neighbourhood houses should still be an important part of any urban strategy for building a welcoming community. Our answer is in the affirmative. We began our book with this question, and the chapters that followed explored how these unique community-based organizations contribute to their communities. We will conclude by assessing this question in the context of the six empirical chapters of this book.

The question of whether neighbourhood houses are a key part of the social infrastructure of a welcoming community has not been asked often, but two authors have previously considered the need to "bring back" or "revitalize" the settlement house tradition of which NHs are a part (Husock 1993; Yan 2004). Howard Husock (1993) argues that there is a need to bring back the unique model of the settlement house, including its broad community development mission and its interest in bringing people from diverse backgrounds and experiences together. Miu Chung Yan (2004) echoes much of Husock's suggestions, but with a heightened sense of urgency given his recognition of the changing nature of community. Yan sees the fragmentation that follows from globalization and the increased movement of people through international migration as a threat to community. Today, attention has been focused on new patterns of migration to cities known collectively as super-diversity (Vertovec 2007, 2019). These patterns include new combinations of gender and age, immigrant statuses, and greater varieties of ethnicities, including diversities within ethnicities, to name a few. Steven Vertovec (2019) points out, these new patterns bring within them new patterns of divisions, and these in turn pose challenges for community-building.

Can these challenges be overcome by revitalizing the traditional model of the settlement house? There is a paradox in putting formal organizations at the centre of the discussion of building vital communities. It is typically the move toward formal organizations and away from informal face-to-face interactions that raises concerns about the pressures of modernity and the decline of community (Wirth 1938). With the inevitability of complex, modern social worlds, however, perhaps it is formal organizations that need to address the challenges to communal life. Of course, not just any formal organization will accomplish this goal, but at the local level, the place-based model may play that role. As Nicole Marwell and Michael McQuarrie (2013) have pointed out, we need to consider the unique aspects of particular organizational forms in order to fully appreciate the contributions of organizations to community processes. Organizations are a collection of interests, actors, and practices, and their particularities distinguish organizational forms and their outcomes. What we have seen in the empirical chapters of this book are examples of how the unique characteristics of neighbourhood houses have facilitated making meaningful connections and face-to-face interactions rather than contributing to their decline. Organizations are also adaptive and striving for survival in changing contexts, and we can also see those pressures on the operation of the NHs.

Perhaps the best evidence that neighbourhood houses are important for building welcoming communities comes from the documentation of connections and engagement in the neighbourhood that follows from participants' experiences at the NH. These themes are addressed directly by Sean Lauer in Chapter 4 and Pilar Riaño-Alcalá and Erika Ono in Chapter 5. While both chapters address the question of building community, each approaches the question in a different way. Lauer provides a structural framework and empirical evidence of the association between participation at the NH and key outcomes such as friendship, getting together with neighbours, and developing social capacity. Friendships, the quintessential informal relationship, form at the NH, and informal get-togethers with neighbours show that these informal connections spill over to the neighbourhood. Lauer develops the argument that NHs are a unique form of social infrastructure that is uniquely suited to producing these types of outcomes. NHs are unique in offering a varied structure of programming, attracting diverse participants, and operating with a community development ethos. These characteristics are core to the NH model and contribute to these community-building outcomes.

Lauer's use of survey data emphasizes the structural impact of programming, while Riaño-Alcalá and Ono provide richer detail of participant experiences. From their analysis, a picture emerges of meaningful connections and engagement that take place at the neighbourhood house. Their use of in-depth oral histories of long-standing participants at NHs allows for a holistic account of participation. They show how NHs move beyond program-specific participation to meaningful engagement with the NH. The experiences these participants share make particularly clear the importance of face-to-face connections that take place at the NH. These in-person connections are integrating in that they provide opportunities to cross salient differences, and because they are by nature place-based. Using a phrase proposed by one of their respondents, Riaño-Alcalá and Ono describe the NH as a "common place" – a space where people connect across differences of income and class around inclusiveness, civic-mindedness, and capacity-building. Making connections, for instance, is more than individuals coming into contact; it also succeeds when an institutional context creates a safe space and recognizes the value of those connections (see also Chapter 3). In this way, a connection can lead to a feeling of belonging in a larger social context. Riaño-Alcalá and Ono show that in the most dramatic cases the relationships developed at the NH become like family and a second home.

Riaño-Alcalá and Ono highlight the importance of the institutional context of the neighbourhood house. It is not just that NHs provide opportunities for meaningful face-to-face interactions to occur, but also that the driving ideas and practices of NHs create a context that supports this community-building. They describe, for instance, the feelings of safety created at the NH, and how this impacts identification and belonging among participants. Lauer similarly considers the ideas and practices surrounding community development an essential characteristic of the NH model. The practice of staff members facilitating participants in one program or activity to join other activities at the NH is one that is supported through the leadership of the NHs. These observations reinforce the argument of Marwell and McQuarrie (2013, 133) that we must consider the organizational dynamics of community organizations and how particular organizational practices create and reinforce forms of social integration. Documenting this community development approach at the NHs is one of the key findings of Oliver Schmidtke's interviews (Chapter 2) with NH executive directors. These EDs emphasize that NHs are mission-driven, are about community and relationships, adapt to changing neighbourhoods, and foster a web of connection in the community. These governing ideas guide practices at the NHs and contribute to a context that supports community-building.

The social and autobiographical insideness that Riaño-Alcalá and Ono find is also an institutional element of neighbourhood houses. This can also be found in the twelve narratives that make up Chapter 6. These narratives capture the many ways in which participants are embedded in the NH through their participation and the participation of family and friends, and over the course of their lives. These narratives describe the unique pathway of some participants who go on to become working staff members at the

NH, but also capture much more. These voices from the NH illuminate the impact of the NH's presence in the neighbourhood and in the lives of its members, and do so in their own words.

There is an additional physical insideness that follows from the local history of neighbourhood houses. As we saw in Chapter 1, the formal organization of NHs enabled them to secure more-or-less permanent locations and develop the physical structures where their work takes place. This has enabled them to maintain a stable presence in neighbourhoods, often for decades. This stability enables them to hold a long-term or even lifetime place in the lives of participants. This persistence through the life course of individual participants and their ability to remain important fixtures in the neighbourhoods in which they operate contribute to institutional stability and allow for physical insideness. Within the city of Vancouver, most NHs have been operating for over forty years. This means that adults who were participants can visit the neighbourhood where they grew up and still see the physical presence of the NH operating as it did when they were young. The children of many of these adults might participate at the house, forming an intergenerational relationship. It is common for multiple members of a family and household to participate in programs and activities at the NH, sometimes separately, sometimes together.

The long-term presence of neighbourhood houses in their communities contributes to their ability to integrate local residents. This also provides long-term institutional accessibility in these neighbourhoods. In Chapter 3, Yan shows that institutional accessibility is provided in large part by the NH's physical presence in the community. This geographic proximity makes participation easier for those living nearby, thereby eliminating one barrier to accessing the services provided. But institutional accessibility is more than just geographic closeness. The NH also provides psychological proximity through the identification with the staff and other users of NHs who live lives similar or close to those who need to access services. Finally, NHs also play an essential brokerage role in the neighbourhood by connecting participants with activities and programs that are provided outside the neighbourhood. In this way, the NH brings these more geographically and psychologically distant services closer to the local residents of the neighbourhoods they serve.

This book has shown that the neighbourhood house model makes important contributions to building community and has done so consistently over time. When we return to the question of "bringing back" or "revitalizing" NHs that Husock and Yan have previously asked, it seems that this is probably not the right question for us to ask in the context of Metro Vancouver. Instead, the more appropriate question seems to be how to maintain the presence and support the growth of NHs to address the unique challenges and threats to contemporary community life. The answer surely lies in supporting a neighbourhood house model that includes a grassroots, community development perspective and is supported by local government. Although this answer is clear, we have found that the persistence of NHs over time has occurred in a contradictory context that includes long-term stability along with a persistent fragility.

Neighbourhood House and Government Partnership: A Fundamental Challenge

As we saw in the history of the settlement house movement and neighbourhood houses in Metro Vancouver in Chapter 1, NHs have developed in two ways. Many NHs started after grassroots mobilization in a neighbourhood, while others started after local municipalities or other experienced individuals identified neighbourhoods that would benefit from the presence of the NH model. While the approaches may seem contradictory, it seems clear that the history of the movement will always see these two approaches interacting in a symbiotic fashion. As Schmidtke shows, an essential part of the NH model is the integration of local residents into the day-to-day operations and leadership of the houses, but equally essential is the support of municipal governments.

There is a lot of evidence that local governments recognize and support the work of neighbourhood houses in Metro Vancouver. The BC government made a commitment to support NHs from 2008 to 2014, recognizing their contribution to building welcoming communities. At that time, provincial governments were responsible for delivering settlement services for newcomers to Canada. As part of that responsibility, the BC government initiated a Building Welcoming and Inclusive Neighbourhoods (BWIN) project and funded all NHs in Metro Vancouver, as a consortium, for three years (2008–11) as the core agencies tasked with building welcoming communities. In the press release announcing the new program, the Attorney General and Minister Responsible for Multiculturalism said: "Neighbourhood houses encourage residents from diverse backgrounds and cultures to interact by giving them a place to meet and participate in social programs and services and helping newcomers integrate into neighbourhood life," and "By implementing this pilot project with neighbourhood houses, we are funding tools and strategies that encourage inclusion and build on BC's cultural diversity." The success of the initiative in the first year led to its extension for another three years, until 2014. Although settlement services were returned to the control of the federal government in 2014 and the BWIN project came to an end, its initiation and success support the conclusion that NHs are an important part of welcoming communities.

This recognition of the contributions of neighbourhood houses by policy makers is further supported by Schmidtke's interviews with members of municipal government in Chapter 2. Interviews with social planners and other members of the municipal government show that the City of Vancouver recognizes the unique contributions of the NH model to building vital neighbourhoods. First, they recognize the broader community-building mission of the model, rather than a more narrow problems-and-programs approach. This includes a recognition that NHs offer unique opportunities for making connections that span the community. Schmidtke also points out that the city recognizes the role of NHs as important conduits to local communities. This includes the ability of NHs to form multi-stakeholder partnerships and their ability to provide the city with access to local residents for community consultation and engagement in planning processes. In recognition of this contribution, the City of Vancouver has been a long-standing supporter of NHs through non-program-specific funding and the leasing of property for NHs' operations. Schmidtke points out that this successful partnership in Vancouver rests on shared values and a shared approach to addressing social problems. While this strength is promising, it also suggests the fragility of this partnership. This is particularly clear when looking outside of the city of Vancouver, where the shared sense of values and approach to social problems is not always at the forefront of NH and municipal relationships in suburban municipalities such as Surrey and Burnaby.

This factor is also clear when we look at the history of neighbourhood houses in Metro Vancouver. As documented in Chapter 1, NHs in Metro Vancouver have persisted over time, and new NHs continue to open in the metropolitan area. This persistence and growth have occurred despite the challenges outlined at the beginning of this chapter. NHs have endured the limitations of funding and the place-based paradox of not having large-scale public awareness. The opening of new NHs has slowed in recent decades, however, and this is particularly clear in those suburban areas where population growth may suggest that NHs are most needed. The question is whether these fast-growing suburban municipalities will recognize the

contributions of NHs as the City of Vancouver has done. This pattern captures the contradiction of persistence and fragility that challenges the NH
movement.

This is one of the fundamental questions remaining for neighbourhood
houses in Metro Vancouver and around the world. The NH model appears
to be a successful approach to building healthy communities. Perhaps it
is even an essential part of building welcoming communities. Here in
Metro Vancouver, the North Shore NH, Burnaby NH, Oak Avenue NH, and
Alexandra NH have been established outside the city of Vancouver and
continue to exist, but they have succeeded despite the fact that some have
received only minimal support from the local municipal government. They
have had to spend considerable effort demonstrating the success of the
model to policy makers and generating political support for their work. In
municipalities across Canada and around the world, similar struggles are
likely taking place where neighbourhood houses attempt to walk this
persistence/fragility line.

Conclusion

What we have documented in this book are some rigorously collected and
analyzed pieces of evidence of what neighbourhood houses in Metro Vancouver, as place-based community organizations, have done to serve and
build local communities. We hope that their stories will be useful testimonies that can validate the experience and inspire the vision of policy makers,
local residents, community practitioners, and researchers who believe in
the importance of a strong local community in the globally diverse era. As
resilient and vibrant place-based community organizations, neighbourhood
houses in Metro Vancouver have vividly continued the success of the settlement house movement in serving and building strong local communities
over its 120-year history.

References

Baines, Donna, Ian Cunningham, John Campey, and John Shields. 2014. "Not
    Profiting from Precarity: The Work of Nonprofit Service Delivery and the
    Creation of Precariousness." *Just Labour: A Canadian Journal of Work and
    Society* 22: 74–93.
Baines, Donna, and Innocentia Kgaphola. 2019. "Precarious Care: International
    Comparisons of Nonprofit Social Service Work." *Women's Studies International
    Forum* 74: 210–17.

Evans, B. Mitchell, and John Shields. 2005. *The Third Sector: Neo-Liberal Restructuring, Governance, and the Remaking of State-Civil Society Relationships*. Toronto: CERIS.

–. 2010. "The Third Sector and the Provision of Public Good: Partnerships, Contracting, and the Neo-Liberal State." In *The Handbook of Canadian Public Administration*, edited by Christopher Dunn, 305–18. Toronto: Oxford University Press.

Fabricant, Michael B., and Robert Fisher. 2002. *Settlement Houses under Siege: The Struggle to Sustain Community Organization in New York City*. New York: Columbia University Press.

Hasenfeld, Yeheskel, and Eve E. Garrow. 2012. "Nonprofit Human-Service Organizations, Social Rights, and Advocacy in a Neoliberal Welfare State." *Social Service Review* 86 (2): 295–322.

Husock, Howard. 1993. "Bring Back the Settlement House: Settlements See Poor People as Citizens, Not Clients." *Public Welfare* 51 (4): 16–25.

International Federation of Settlements and Neighborhood Centers. n.d. "IFS Is an NGO in Active Consultative Status with the United Nations ECOSOC." https://www.ifsnetwork.org/ifs/about/united-nations/.

Johnson, Christian. 1995. "Strength in Community: Historical Development of Settlements Internationally." In *Settlements, Social Change and Community Action: Good Neighbours*, edited by Ruth Gilchrist and Tony Jeffs, 69–91. London: Jessica Kingsley.

Marwell, Nicole P., and Michael McQuarrie. 2013. "People, Place, and System: Organizations and the Renewal of Urban Social Theory." *Annals of the American Academy of Political and Social Science* 647 (1): 126–43.

Matthews, John, and James Kimmis. 2001. "Development of the English Settlement Movement." In *Settlement, Social Change and Community Action: Good Neighbours*, edited by Ruth Gilchrist and Tony Jeffs, 54–68. London: Jessica Kingsley.

Specht, Harry, and Mark E. Courtney. 1994. *Unfaithful Angels: How Social Work Has Abandoned Its Mission*. 1st ed. New York: Free Press.

Statistics Canada. 2017. "Census Profile, 2016 Census: Vancouver, City [Census Subdivision], British Columbia and Greater Vancouver, Regional District [Census Division], British Columbia." https://www12.statcan.gc.ca/census-recensement/2016/dp-pd/prof/details/page.cfm?Lang=E&Geo1=CSD&Code1=5915022&Geo2=CD&Code2=5915&Data=Count&SearchText=Vancouver&SearchType=Begins&SearchPR=01&B1=Journey%20to%20work&TABID=1.

Trolander, Judith Ann. 1987. *Professionalism and Social Change: From the Settlement House Movement to Neighborhood Centers, 1886 to the Present*. New York: Columbia University Press.

Vertovec, Steven. 2007. "Super-Diversity and Its Implications." *Ethnic and Racial Studies* 30 (6): 1024–54.

–. 2019. "Talking around Super-Diversity." *Ethnic and Racial Studies* 42 (1): 125–39.

Whiten, George. 1975. *History of Alexandra Neighbourhood House*. Vancouver: UBC.

Wirth, Louis. 1938. "Urbanism as a Way of Life." *American Journal of Sociology* 44 (1): 1–24.

Yan, Miu Chung. 2004. "Bridging the Fragmented Community: Revitalizing Settlement Houses in the Global Era." *Journal of Community Practice* 12 (1/2): 51–69.

Yan, Miu Chung, Chun-Sing Johnson Cheung, Ming-Sum Tsui, and Chi Keung Chu. 2017. "Examining the Neoliberal Discourse of Accountability: The Case of Hong Kong's Social Service Sector." *International Social Work* 60 (4): 976–89.

Yan, Miu Chung, and Rick Sin. 2011. "The Resilience of the Settlement House Tradition in Community Development: A Study of Neighborhood Centers in San Francisco." *Community Development* 42 (1): 106–24.

Yan, Miu Chung, Sean Lauer, and Pilar Riaño-Alcalá. 2017. "Incorporating Individual Community Assets in Neighbourhood Houses: Beyond the Community-Building Tradition of Settlement Houses." *International Social Work* 60 (6): 1591–1605. https://doi.org/10.1177/0020872816633889.

Yan, Miu Chung, Sean Lauer, and Rick Sin. 2009. "Issues in Community (Re)building: The Tasks of Settlement Houses in Two Cities." *Social Development Issues* 31 (1): 39–54.

Appendix 1

Technical Notes

The design of this study followed a community-based and multi-method approach. The staff of local neighbourhood houses were actively engaged and influential in every step of this research process (Israel et al. 1998). The idea for and focus of the research developed through conversations between academics and the staff of local neighbourhood houses. From the beginning, a project team was organized that included academic partners and an advisory committee that included four neighbourhood house leaders representing nine different neighbourhood houses. This group embraced collaboration: academic and neighbourhood house partners collaboratively developed research questions, strategies, and approaches to collecting data, and strategies to disseminate findings. We met regularly over a five-year period to discuss the progress and direction of the research. It is a collaboration that continues now with the publication of this volume.

The fifteen neighbourhood houses in Metro Vancouver have a long history and are vibrantly employing multiple means to fulfill their complex role in service delivery and community-building for their communities. To understand the many dimensions of their complex role and to triangulate the perspectives of different stakeholders, we employed a mixed-method approach not only to study official records and archival information related to their operations but also to capture the personal experiences and perspectives of different stakeholders who have close contact with neighbourhood houses.

TABLE A.1
Data collection activities

Data collection activity	Participants	No. of participants
Community resource mapping workshops	Board members, senior management, front-line workers, veteran volunteers	15 NHs, 72 people
Network mapping interviews (individual interview)	Board members, EDs, senior staff and front-line workers, veteran volunteers	15 NHs, 61 people
Clearinghouse Survey (collecting information on human and financial resources of NHs)	EDs and designated staff	15 NHs
Community partners focus groups	Staff from other community organizations or government officials	10 groups, >40 people
Service users focus groups	NH service users recommended by NHs and with recognizable contribution to NHs	10 groups, >40 people
BWIN study (focus groups + interviews)	EDs and staff who coordinated the BWIN projects of different NHs	14 NHs, 28 people
Government-NHs relationship (interviews)	EDs and government officials who work closely with NHs	17 people
Latin American community work and NHs (interviews)	NH staff who have a Latin American background	9 people
Archival study of NH history	Textual materials of different NHs	10 NHs
Oral history (life stories)	Board members, staff, and veteran volunteers who were once service users of NHs	45 people
Key informant interview	Current and former EDs or senior management	13 people
Service users survey	Service users of NH programs	14 NHs, 675 people

Notes: NH = neighbourhood house; ED = executive director, BWIN = Building Welcoming and Inclusive Neighbourhoods project

Table A.1 summarizes all the activities as well as the participants and number of participants for each activity. All together, over a thousand individuals took part in the study. The data collected from each activity were preliminarily analyzed separately by using appropriate analytical methods drawing from quantitative and qualitative research traditions. After the preliminary analysis was completed, the research team and the advisory committee held a full-day retreat to conduct a comprehensive analysis of all of the preliminary findings to verify the findings and to identify the interrelatedness of findings from different activities. Results of the discussion form the basis of this book.

Reference

Israel, Barbara A., Amy J. Schulz, Edith A. Parker, and Adam B. Becker. 1998. "Review of Community-Based Research: Assessing Partnership Approaches to Improve Public Health." *Annual Review of Public Health* 19 (1): 173–202.

Appendix 2

Neighbourhood Houses in Metro Vancouver

TABLE A.2

Neighbourhood houses in Metro Vancouver

Name	Abbreviation	Year of establishment
Association of Neighbourhood Houses	ANH	1891
Alexandra Neighbourhood House	ANH	1938–75 (in Kitsilano)
North Shore Neighbourhood House	NSNH	1939
Gordon Neighbourhood House	GNH	1942
Cedar Cottage Neighbourhood House	CCNH	1963
Kiwassa Neighbourhood House	KNH	1967
Kitsilano Neighbourhood House	KNH	1974
South Vancouver Neighbourhood House	SVNH	1976
Mount Pleasant Neighbourhood House	MPNH	1976
Frog Hollow Neighbourhood House	FHNH	1977
Little Mountain Neighbourhood House	LMNH	1978
Collingwood Neighbourhood House	CNH	1985
Burnaby Neighbourhood House	BNH	1996
Oak Avenue Neighbourhood Hub	OANH	2004
Alexandra Neighbourhood House	ANH	2009 (in South Surrey)
Downtown Eastside Neighbourhood House	DTESNH	2009
Marpole Neighbourhood House	MNH	2013, 2019

Contributors

Jenny Francis is a social/cultural geographer teaching at Langara College.

Sean Lauer is an associate professor in the University of British Columbia Department of Sociology. He was a co-investigator of the neighbourhood house study.

Erika Ono is a doctoral candidate at the University of British Columbia School of Social Work.

Pilar Riaño-Alcalá is a professor at the University of British Columbia School of Social Work. She was a co-investigator of the neighbourhood house study.

Oliver Schmidtke is a professor in the University of Victoria Department of Political Science and the director of the Centre for Global Studies. He was a co-investigator of the neighbourhood house study.

Eleanor Stebner is a social historian and professor emerita at Simon Fraser University.

Miu Chung Yan is a professor and the former director of the University of British Columbia School of Social Work. He was the principal investigator of the neighbourhood house study.

Index